American Global Pre-eminence

American Global Pre-eminence

The Development and Erosion of Systemic Leadership

WILLIAM R. THOMPSON

OXFORD

UNIVERSITY PRESS

OXFORD
UNIVERSITY PRESS

Oxford University Press is a department of the University of Oxford. It furthers
the University's objective of excellence in research, scholarship, and education
by publishing worldwide. Oxford is a registered trade mark of Oxford University
Press in the UK and certain other countries.

Published in the United States of America by Oxford University Press
198 Madison Avenue, New York, NY 10016, United States of America.

Library of Congress Control Number: 2022901326
ISBN 978-0-19-753467-0 (pbk.)
ISBN 978-0-19-753466-3 (hbk.)

DOI: 10.1093/oso/9780197534663.001.0001

1 3 5 7 9 8 6 4 2

Paperback printed by LSC Communications, United States of America
Hardback printed by Bridgeport National Bindery, Inc., United States of America

Contents

1

The Rise and Slow Retreat of American Systemic Leadership

One of the most glaring facts of the post-1945 world has been the United States' hard-to-miss predominance in world politics. Just how it is that one state tends to be singled out for potential systemic leadership is not as well understood as it should be. Nor is its presently diminished status and foundation for acting. The following commentary is most interesting in this respect:

> In 1948, George Kennan, State Department Director of policy planning, noted that the United States then possessed "about 50% of the world's wealth, but only 6.3% of its population. . . ." The challenge facing U.S. policymakers, he believed, was "to devise a pattern of relationships which will permit us to maintain this position of disparity." The overarching aim of American statecraft, in other words, was to sustain the uniquely favorable situation to which the United States had ascended by the end of World War II.
>
> With less than 5 percent of the population, the United States still controls 25 percent of global net worth. Here is the ultimate emblem of American success. . . . Wealth confers choice. It provides latitude to act or to refrain from acting. (Bacevich, 2016: 358)

Statecraft is certainly part of the process, but it is not the whole of it. The material foundation for systemic leadership is also part of the process, but it too does not suffice. The two must work hand in glove. A resource foundation makes some things possible that might not otherwise be conceivable. A disproportionate share of resources also implies some obligation to act, if only to preserve the disproportionality à la Kennan's advice. What needs to be appreciated is that moving from a 50 percent to a 25 percent resource position means that the potential for successful leadership is both much more constrained than in the past and more dependent on coalition building than ever before. Wealth may confer choice, but the choice is not to act or refraining from acting. It is more a matter of how best to act given changing circumstances. Not acting at all on some issues such as climate change, migration pressures, or spiraling conflict is not really an option. But if the sources of wealth or the diminished share of wealth are

American Global Pre-eminence. William R. Thompson, Oxford University Press. © Oxford University Press 2022.
DOI: 10.1093/oso/9780197534663.003.0001

misunderstood, acting is likely to be misguided and the strategic outcome will be suboptimal.

Yet contrast Bacevich's insistence that the United States still possesses a disproportionate resource base that provides latitude for action with observed US behavior in the global coronavirus crisis of 2020. A *New York Times* reporter (Erlanger, 2020) interviewed a German international security analyst, Claudia Major, who summarized well what US behavior should have been and was not quite:

> "[T]his crisis is confirmation of a structural change in U.S. political leadership," she said. "There is no U.S. global leadership and no U.S. model," Ms. Major added. "Success would be that you manage the problem at home, [the world] rally allies around you, [you] lead the alliance, supply global public goods and organize the global response, as with Ebola. Instead American institutions "don't seem to be able to cope at home," she said, and there is "a Trump response to act alone."

Acting alone is a charitable description of the US federal response (see Jewell and Jewell, 2020). It was totally unprepared despite a number of explicit warnings from the previous administration, its own intelligence agencies, and even agents reporting from China and the World Health Organization. Flights from China into the United States were restricted severely but less attention was given to travelers coming in from Europe, which had its own virus problems.[1] A centralized group for dealing with pandemics had been created in the Obama regime after its experience with an Ebola scare. The Trump administration had dissolved it in the name of cutting costs, in addition to reducing the budgets of the Centers for Disease Control and Prevention.[2] A federal reserve for medical supplies had been allowed to languish without maintenance of the respirators on hand. State governors were encouraged to fend for themselves in obtaining medical supplies only to have the market price for supplies bid up by competition among the states and the federal government. Commodities obtained by state agencies were in some cases seized by the federal government and then reallocated according to political criteria, with Republican governors faring

---

[1] The East Coast, especially the New York, version of COVID-19 represented a different and more deadly mutation of the parasite than the West Coast version.

[2] A subsequent Trump administration group put together under the lead of Jared Kushner was tasked with creating a centralized coordination of virus testing in the first quarter of 2020. A plan was developed but abandoned thanks to a trifecta of thinking that the virus would go away on its own accord, the President's concern that increased testing meant a higher count of COVID-19 infections, and the partisan belief that since the virus was initially focused on dense, blue states, it made more political sense to blame Democratic governors for their incompetence, One of the problems with this approach, of course, was that testing problems, among other leadership lapses, contributed to the subsequent surge in cases in Southern red states such as Florida and Texas.

better than Democratic governors. Clever governors learned how to conduct their own foreign acquisitions in secret to evade federal seizure. Valuable weeks were lost with no coordination or direction from the federal government. The outcome was that more viral spread occurred than would have been the case if more prompt central leadership had been demonstrated.[3] The reasons seemed to be that the US president hoped that the problem would go away with no action and especially any action that would temporarily harm the economy and subsequent electoral chances. Consequently, the United States led the world in number of infectious cases and deaths from the virus. To top it off, the United States was offered aid from China in the form of masks and other equipment, a former canine breeder was appointed to run the Federal Emergency Management Agency taskforce on the coronavirus, and the chief executive of the United States publicly recommended the ingestion of disinfectant as a remedy for the virus, in addition to other remedies for which no supporting evidence exists. Perhaps the only way to top all of these policymaking transgressions, once the virus spread seemed to be contained in the spring of 2020, President Trump encouraged a premature rush to curtail lockdowns without masks and other precautions in order to restart the economy as quickly as possible. Instead it was the spread of the virus that was restarted, with a number of new states becoming hot spots and many more people were to die from COVID-19 than might otherwise have been the case.

The list of scandalous incompetence could go on.[4] The point is that the US response to the global crisis was entirely absent on the global (let alone the federal) level—unless one counts blaming the Chinese, other foreigners, and the World Health Organization for bringing about the crisis in the first place. Its domestic policy plan was equally poor.[5] No model to emulate, no public goods, no coordination, as Ms. Majors noted. Instead, the US government was caught trying to surreptitiously purchase a German pharmaceutical firm with a potential vaccine for the virus, underlining its every nation for itself approach. At a later point, virtually the entire world's supply of remdesivir, a drug that can help

---

[3] One estimate based on modeling is that some 61 percent of the lives lost through late May could have been averted if social distancing had begun 1 week earlier. If it had begun 2 weeks earlier, 83 percent of the lives lost at that point might have been saved. See Glanz and Robertson (2020) and Pei, Kandula, and Shama (2020).

[4] In all likelihood, an evaluation of the federal governmental response to the unemployment associated with the virus lockdown will provide considerably more evidence of ineffectuality and corruption of the stated intentions with too little aid going to low- and middle-income workers too slowly and a great deal of assistance going to corporations and wealthy individuals that did not need it in the first place. The same evaluation is likely also to find that federal governmental relief ended too early in 2020.

[5] There is of course plenty of blame to apply in different directions. See, for instance, Shear et al. (2020). Nor is there a long list of places around the globe that did things well. Nonetheless, there were places that did do things about as well as could be expected, holding out hope (and models) for the development and diffusion of better planning in the future for the next pandemic.

reduce recovery time, was purchased for American use, albeit for a limited period of time (Boseley, 2020).

Whatever systemic leadership might be, this was not it. To be sure, some of the blame can be affixed to the idiosyncrasies of the Trump administration, as opposed to the US systemic leadership trajectory. But the advent of the Trump administration was neither random nor coincidental. It is part and parcel of the relative decline of the United States. While the Trump administration no doubt accelerated US relative decline, it is also very much a symptom of positional decay. How this works is something that needs to be elaborated in this book (see especially chapter 6).

At the same time, the intention of this analysis is not to provide another anti-Trump rant. While there was plenty to rant about, the point to be strongly emphasized is that the Trump administration, from a long-term perspective, was simply another sign of relative decline. It would have been possible to write much of this book before the 2016 election. Relative decline has been in progress for decades. It may very well be possible to write much the same book at the end of the Biden administration. What individual presidential administrations do or do not do, by this point, is unlikely to alter significantly the US trajectory in the short term. That is not the same thing as saying US relative decline is inevitable and that the US decline trajectory is in an out-of-control, downward spiral. On the contrary, US relative decline seems to be subject to something akin to a flooring phenomenon, which is to say that is unlikely to experience a great deal more relative decline beyond a 15–25 percent share in the resources that matter most. That share can be improved upon. But it is most unlikely to ever double or triple.

For instance, the Trump administration was followed by Biden administration that improved greatly on managing the COVID-19 crisis through a more attention to scientific advice and a more aggressive vaccine policy, albeit not without major glitches in terms of its contradictory advice on masking and its reluctance to override local resistance to vaccinations. In foreign policy, the Biden administration finally ended the long commitment to a losing Afghan war. The actual withdrawal of US and allied personnel did not go smoothly and the optics were made unusually poor by pictures of planes attempting to take off with desperate Afghan citizens clinging to parts of the planes.[6] Nonetheless, the withdrawal

---

[6]. Much of the awkwardness or downright clumsiness of the pullout seems to have been highly likely. The US decision to leave Afghanistan almost no matter what the Taliban opposition did strongly framed the negotiation process largely completed in the Trump administration. A more orderly withdrawal process was made less likely by a number of factors, including leaving the Afghan government out of the negotiation process, the difficulties encountered in maintaining technological support for Afghan forces once contractors left, the request of the Afghan government that the US withdrawal not be seen as occurring too openly (thereby accelerating the loss of support for the Afghan regime), and the widespread surrender of Afghan positions that took place far more rapidly

from the Afghan quagmire should be beneficial for focusing on the Chinese challenge. If some proportion of the legislation on infrastructure, innovation encouragement, climate change, and expanded welfare provisions makes it through the serious congressional obstacles, US domestic policies are likely to be seen as proactively addressing relative decline phenomena even if that is not how they are spun explicitly. Many of these proposed policies are steps in the right direction, but they will not and cannot turn around US relative decline completely. At best, they can improve US competitiveness and standards of living.[7] That is, they can keep the United States in the game but they cannot recreate the kind of lead attained in the 1950s and 1960s.

Attempting to get a better fix on what systemic leadership is and is not is a large part of what this book is about. That means looking at how the opportunity has emerged both historically and in the specific US context. It means relying more on theory about international relations as opposed to casual impressions of how things are faring, expressions of faith about US exceptionalism, or pessimism/optimism about US chances. It means charting the rise and slow decline of the US version of systemic leadership. It also means peering into the future about the prospects for continued systemic leadership, US or otherwise, and its implications for world politics.

American Systemic Leadership in World Politics: Reflections on Its Waxing and Waning

Whether the United States has exceptional characteristics or not, its rise can be explained in terms applicable to all other states that have risen to the apex of the global hierarchy. If it is exceptional, it is more about the scale of capabilities that it has wielded than it is about any of its alleged special characteristics. Its relative decline from the high position that it attained is also explicable in terms of established processes. What is most different about the United States is that it rose higher than any other state had and, partly therefore, its relative decline is likely to be slower than its predecessors. Moreover, and unlike its predecessors, there is a likely to be a relatively high floor for US relative decline. The Netherlands and the United Kingdom have become pleasant places for tourists to visit but are not exactly elite powers in the world system anymore. Tourists will come to the United States as well, but the United States will continue to be an elite power

than anticipated. Nonetheless, to have stayed in Afghanistan indefinitely would hardly have been a move that worked to slow relative decline.

[7] See Norrlof (2018) for an extended argument about how domestic redistribution can contribute to sustaining support for hegemonic policies.

for some time to come. Thus, while the United States has experienced relative decline, its position still puts it ahead of rivals, albeit not as far ahead of some rivals as once was the case. Whether one or more of those rivals will one day close the gap is difficult to predict. More likely, however, is that the traditional historical process of one state attaining and maintaining a political-economic position so far ahead of its allies and rivals for several decades is unlikely to persist. Technology and energy are at the heart of this process, as they have been for centuries, and while innovation will continue, the gains will be less easy to monopolize for very long. If this prediction holds, power gradually will become less concentrated in the twenty-first century—regardless of the gains made by competing rivals.

But do we really need another book on US decline?[8] The answer is yes because the issue is important to an accurate reading of the US foreign policy position and the state of global politics now and in the immediate future. If there are problems with previous positions, there is some incentive to keep trying to get it right. One of the byproducts of attaining that accurate reading, arguably, is an improvement on interpreting international relations in general. How we read the United States' position in world politics is telling about how we go about discerning what makes international relations tick. The book is structured into three parts (introductory material, rise discussion, and decline discussion) and ten chapters.

One of the central arguments is that most, if not all, observers of US relative decline (the loss of an edge over other states) have not quite captured the phenomenon accurately. One reason is the variable lack of a historical approach. Most observers tend to start and end with contemporary frames of reference. The perspective taken in this study is focused on a millennium-long interpretation of the evolution of world politics and, more specifically, the role of

---

[8] See, among many others, Kennedy (1987), Nau (1990), Tammen et al. (2000), Bacevich (2008), Brooks and Wohlforth (2008, 2015), Hachigian and Sutphen (2008), Khanna (2008), Mahbubani (2008), Thompson (2008), Zakaria (2008, 2011), Barnett (2009), Gelb (2009), Jacques (2009), Joffe (2009), Layne (2009, 2012), Edelman (2010); Fallows (2010), Mandelbaum (2010), Norrlof (2010), Beckley (2011/2012), Berman (2011), Friedman and Mandelbaum (2011), Hubbard and Navarro (2011), Kupchan (2011), MacDonald and Parent (2011), Mitchell and Grygiel (2011), Prestowitz (2011), Nye (2011), Wallerstein (2011), Walt (2011), Atkinson and Ezell (2012), Brzezinski (2012), Clark and Hogue (2012), Gross (2012), Kagan (2012), Keohane (2012), Lieber (2012), Luce (2012), Lundestad (2012), Wohlforth (2012), Itzkowitz Shifrinson and Beckley (2012/2013), U.S. National Intelligence Council (2012), Brooks, Ikenberry, and Wohlforth (2013), Brown (2013), Packer (2013), Starrs (2013), Acharya (2014), Joffe (2014), Posen (2014), Schweller (2014), Reich and Lebow (2014), Alden and Strauss (2016), Cowen (2016), Gordon (2016), McCoy (2017), Beckley (2018), Bulmer-Thomas (2018), Campbell (2018), Englehardt (2018), Farrow (2018), Layne (2018), Schake (2018), Walt (2018), Wyne (2018), Behm (2019), Douhart (2019), Massie and Paquin (2019), Parker, Morin, and Horowitz (2019), Axe (2020), Kroenig (2020), Lind and Press (2020), Sharman (2020), and Wright (2020).

leading states and economies in this saga. Admittedly, such an approach probably qualifies as an extreme version of a historical approach, but it is unique, it is defendable, and it leads to a different perspective on contemporary and future processes.

In this book the millennium perspective is kept low key after making some use of it at the outset.[9] It informs the argument but the burden of support for the long-term perspective is advanced elsewhere. In this analysis, the explicit historical element is largely focused on the emergence of US political-economic power in the nineteenth and twentieth centuries. Too often, even this historical background is missing altogether from other analyses. But the thesis here is that only by first establishing long-term dynamics can we capture what is unfolding in the contemporary era.

One of the assumptions of this book is that there are flaws in the positions taken by all or most of the contenders in this debate. Borrowing from the Goldilocks fable, declinists tend to be "too hot" and anti-declinists "too cold." Readers are free to reverse which side is deemed too hot or too cold. Both sides, nonetheless, have some good points. What we need is an intermediate position—a Goldilocks "just right" resolution of the porridge dilemma that can evade the arguments that are too "hot" or too "cold."[10]

Table 1.1 lists ten interpretation issues on which the two camps disagree:

1. How powerful is systemic leadership at any point in time, and how do we know?
2. How much structural erosion has occurred?
3. Is it the relative share of power maintained by the system leader that is important, or is it more simply merely a matter of which state is ahead (no matter how much ahead it is)?
4. Since observers intermittently describe the US position as declining, why should we pay any more attention this time?
5. Which processes are more powerful: structure or agency?
6. Is the US trajectory similar to, or distinctive from, earlier leader trajectories?
7. Was the US position in 1945 typical or anomalous?
8. What should we make of the positional improvements made by rivals (and allies)?

---

[9] There are other venues for stronger doses of the millennium-long perspective. See, for instance, Modelski and Thompson (1996) and Thompson and Zakhirova (2019).

[10] In Western folklore, Goldilocks visits a house inhabited by three bears. Discovering their breakfast bowls of porridge, she rejects two as either too hot or too cold and selects the one that is just right for her tastes.

Table 1.1 Differences between Declinist and Anti-Declinist Positions

	Declinist	Anti-Declinist
1	Leadership in world politics gives the leader a very strong position to attain its preferences	Leadership in world politics gives the leader a moderately strong position to attain its preferences
2	Emphasize maximal structural erosion; Emphasize changing relative share over time; Economic and military lead weakening rapidly	Emphasize minimal structural erosion; Emphasize current leading position; Economic and military lead still strong
3	Relative shares of capabilities matter to leadership possibilities	Remaining the largest economy and military matter to leadership possibilities
4	This time it is real	Declinism is cyclical; decline is not
5	Structure ultimately wins out over agency; Without a commanding relative share of capabilities leadership is less likely and less likely to be successful	Agency can triumph over structural change; Leadership is most dependent on political will and creative diplomacy
6	US decline similar to past leaders' trajectories	US trajectory is unique and exceptional; what past leaders?
7	US peak position in 1945 typical	US peak position in 1945 anomalous
8	Play up the rise of the rest	Play down the rise of the rest
9	Persistence thesis part of conservative/ optimistic/wishful thinking agenda	Decline thesis part of leftist/pessimist/ wishful thinking agenda
10	World order is contingent on power concentration	World order may persist despite the movement away from power concentration

9. Do declinists and anti-declinists have personal preferences that influence their interpretations?

10. Is it possible for a world order to outlive the power concentration that made it possible in the first place?

The two camps tend to take polarized positions on these questions. Yet the issues do not always lend themselves to a black-and-white conclusion. Some definite gray creeps in. Elucidating the gray in between the polarized endpoints of the decline continuum is also part of what this book is about.

More specifically, system leaders usually operate even when they are at their peak in less than full-blown hegemonic circumstances, if by the term "hegemony" we confer a strong element of dominance. They may be predominant in terms of their military and economic capabilities but rarely dominate. Structural erosion in terms of power deconcentration has taken place even though the pace of positional weakening appears to be slower than declinists estimate. Declinism arguments have been cyclical, but not necessarily because earlier estimations were off base. Nonetheless, a state that possess a vast lead over all its rivals is in a stronger position than one that just barely is ahead of them. Relative decline has been persistent since 1945—that is the way positional dynamics have tended to play out in great power history. Agency can certainly buck the structural trend (or make things worse) but, ultimately, structural change is likely to win out.

There have been earlier instances of systemic leadership, and the rise and relative decline of the United States has not been dissimilar to the rise and fall of earlier leaders of the modern era (most prominently, nineteenth century Britain, and the Netherlands in the seventeenth century). The US peak position was much stronger than earlier leaders and that factor, in part, has helped slow the pace of relative decline. In that respect, the US peak position was never anomalous—merely distinctively greater than its predecessors. Leaders decline in part (but not only) because their edge is worn down by the positional gains made by other states. It has been easy, however, to exaggerate the gains made by rivals and allies. It is equally easy to forecast greater or more rapid rival gains than may be the case. And, yes, a number of declinists and anti-declinists do tend to prefer the outcomes about which they argue. Some declinists look forward to the loss of US concentrated power, while some anti-declinists favor the persistence of US concentrated power. But this factor matters less than what our data suggest. In this case, the data suggest that the US position has genuinely declined in relative terms but retains a moderately strong position that it is likely to hang on to for several decades to come. But that moderately strong position is less strong than anti-declinists would like and appears to be moving toward, and perhaps beyond, a "first among equals" situation in which US leadership will be more frequently contested than it has in the past.

Given the diminished and diminishing concentration of power, it seems unrealistic to expect the persistence of a strong world order. The degree of world order is more likely, perhaps subject to a lag, to reflect the degree of concentration of power unless people come up with an entirely novel approach to the construction of order. Yet order decay does not mean an abrupt order collapse. Rather, it translates into a gradual retreat and at a faster pace in some places and in some issue areas than in others.

It is one thing to make these assertions. It is another to back them up and show as well how they develop and interact. That is where the other nine chapters come in. It is their task to elaborate the position taken in the past several paragraphs. The next chapter provides some theoretical architecture and vocabulary for evaluating rise and decline in world politics. The eight chapters that follow it can be broken down into considerations of rise, decline, and the future.

Chapter 2: Systemic Leadership, Rise and Decline

System leaders have emerged largely based on possessing the world's lead economy for a finite period. Because of concentrated technological innovation, energy, and global power projection capabilities, system leaders play preponderant roles in managing problems associated with the functioning of the world political economy. They base their leadership on the advantages bestowed by the creation of the most innovative economy (the lead economy). They set examples for others to emulate. They encourage (verbally and materially) others to behave in ways that might correspond to collective interests. They also use coercion on occasion. Scholars disagree about which states have earned this label.[11] The farther back in time one travels, the more difficult it becomes to compare the emerging predominance of various candidates. Therefore, few would dispute the United States' contemporary claim to the distinction—although whether the claim holds true to this day is a different matter. Many would accept Britain's nineteenth-century claim to systemic leadership. After that, choices become increasingly more controversial. However, the Netherlands in the seventeenth century has considerable support among those who have examined the question.

---

[11] Part of the disagreement is due to the reluctance to disentangle global and regional systems. Global systems (over which system leaders preside) involve trans-regional transactions and activities, or, essentially, the world political economy. At the same time, Western Europe became for a time the most important region in the system. But not all great powers are capable of maneuvering in multiple regions and, thus, one needs to differentiate between regional and global power structures. Analysts often mix global elite states with regional elites. In the late eighteenth and early twentieth centuries, for instance, some great powers did not help matters by being both, as in the case of Britain, Russia, or France. Austria-Hungary was exclusively a regional elite power. Germany and Italy were primarily European regional elite powers that sought to participate in the global system. Italy stayed close to home in northern Africa while Germany's non-European forays became more ambitious toward the end of the nineteenth century. Japan and the United States, initially, were elite powers in other, non-European regions. Thus, one analytical choice that is often made without a great deal of explicit consideration is between conceptualizing a single international system with one set of elites versus an international system with multiple regions in which elites have various standings. In the latter conceptualization, the main distinction is between elite powers that show up in multiple regions, as opposed to those that are significant in only one.

There is a reason why only three states have relatively strong support for the systemic leadership label. These three states have some distinctions that no other states can claim. The unique nature of their claims can be demonstrated quickly by looking at the most liberal slate of candidates. Leadership long-cycle analyses are based on a narrative about modern economic growth. The main technological problem of the last millennium has been to break free of agrarian constraints based on the limitations of human/animal muscle and a focus on relying on solar radiation for plant growing. Song China made the first attempt in the tenth through twelfth centuries to industrialize but ultimately failed. Information on many of its innovations was passed on to Europe and appear to have played an important role in stimulating later European industrialization. Three of the principal intermediaries for conveying Asian ideas to the West were the states (Genoa, Venice, and Portugal) that successively dominated East-West trade by first organizing new routes from the European end and also monopolizing the distribution of Asian commodities in Europe for periods of time. Their commercial successes were also predicated on harnessing and improving maritime technology beyond the competencies of European and Asian rivals.

The situation in Europe began to change in the seventeenth century with the Netherlands' rise to technological leadership in a variety of industries, based in part on an energy foundation of peat and the deployment of thousands of windmills.[12] The Dutch were soon eclipsed by its neighbors and, in particular, the British development of coal-based industries and industrialization. Britain, in turn, was eclipsed by the rise of the United States, which led the way in innovating petroleum-based industries in the twentieth century.

Leads do not last forever. They are constructed gradually and often erode gradually as well. The rate of erosion, however, may vary and the slower the rate of erosion, the more difficult it is to discern relative decline. This tendency helps explain the disagreements about the position of the United States. Not only was its concentration of leads more strongly established than those of its predecessors, its relative decline, partially as a consequence, has also been slow. Nonetheless, other states and their economies have been catching up to the US position. Fluctuations in the US share of technological innovation is the main criterion of the foundation for systemic leadership. The United States has maintained its lead, but other states have narrowed the gap. European economies, in general and in aggregate, are closest, followed by Japan, which has been falling back in the competition. China is moving up but still has some way to go. Thus, based

---

[12] Peat could be viewed as an inferior form of coal (or compressed vegetation). The point is how much heat the fuel can generate for manufacturing purposes. Peat is superior to wood and coal is superior to peat.

on this indicator, the US technological lead is slowly declining relative to what others have been able to achieve in narrowing the gap.

Rise Considerations

Chapter 3: The Rise of the US Economy

In contrast to the much-argued British case, the United States' economic growth story, curiously, has received far less attention—perhaps, in part, because there are fewer US economic historians left to give it attention. Americans also tend to take their phenomenal economic success for granted—thereby discouraging the need to explain it. There are, however, a number of popular treatments of the US ascendancy, often praising some dimension of exceptionalism and told largely through serial anecdotes—as opposed to serious academic debate with theory and evidence. Alternatively, the extraordinary wealth of the US resource base and its rapid growth in the late nineteenth and early twentieth centuries also lends itself quite readily to these exceptionalist beliefs and explanations. Yet while US economic growth did exceed anything experienced before on the planet, that alone should not encourage us to think that its trajectory is unlike earlier cases of technological leadership. Instead, what we need to do is to draw attention to how the US case was both similar and different from its predecessors.

Following in part an argument advanced by the economists Wright and Nelson (1992) in the 1990s, the US case is viewed as a two-stage process. The first stage involved acquiring dominance in mass production industries that were certainly contingent on technological innovation but also an unusually helpful resource endowment and an equally distinctive domestic market. The large domestic market made increases in the scale of production possible. The nature of the resource endowment ensured that raw materials were inexpensive. The combination of innovation, cheap raw materials including energy, and a very large domestic market pushed the United States into an economic process leadership position by World War I. But the second stage of the, world technological leadership, did not come until after World War II because it was based on science, and it took longer for the United States to acquire the lead in scientific research. In other words, the nature of technological innovation had evolved toward more reliance on university and corporate laboratory experimentation and findings as opposed to primarily the construction of more powerful and efficient power-driven machinery for manufacture and transportation purposes. Of course, at the outset, none of these factors was evident in the US case. The resource endowment, market size, and technology all had to be acquired and developed. While the resource endowment was always there, it was not until the mid-nineteenth century that mineral exploration truly intensified. Thus, while the size and variety of the endowment may be a matter of geophysical luck, it still had to be discovered and exploited by agents responding to increasing demand. By the latter decades of the nineteenth century, it was increasingly recognized that the United States led the world in mineral resource reserves.

Equally important, however, is the understanding that the US economy emulated and improved on the British model by first adapting its coal reserves to steam engines and then went on to develop petroleum and electricity as additional sources of industrial fuel. Its considerable lead on other states, thus, was a combination of resource endowment and technological creativity that altered the way modern economies function radically. Since that time, other economies have been able to apply the technological advances in their own production infrastructures. In addition to technological diffusion, the US resource advantage has diminished, with clear economic problems emerging with the increased reliance on imported petroleum. Fracking might seem to give the US economy a second wind, but that impression is likely to prove illusory. The volume of petroleum and gas produced may not be as great as forecasted but, more important, fracking production flies in the face of the need to decarbonize energy sources in response to the threat of global warming.

Size, location, and resource endowment are often noted as causal factors in this move upward in status. After 1945, though, there was little doubt that the US economy was the world's most advanced center of high technology and manufacturing production. It also emerged in 1945 as the leading political-military actor and the head of a coalition of the most economically advanced states in the world system. Interwoven in the customary story are World Wars I and II—major wars in the late 1910s and early 1940s (from a US perspective). The US entered the first world war late and had less impact than might otherwise have been the case. It is often thought that, at war's end, the United States retreated from the world stage. It entered the second one late as well but had more impact and, thanks in part to the exhaustion of everyone else, emerged in 1945 as king of the planetary hill. In contrast to what happened after World War I, the United States, after World War II, assumed its pre-eminent role in world politics.

The two world wars that most people designate as occurring in 1914–1918 (or 1917–1918 for the United States) and 1939–1945 (or 1941–1945) were not separate wars but early and late phases of an extended period of systemic crisis. War's effects on development are crucial to US history but not as a monovariate shock or series of shocks alone. Wars, rather, are nested prominently within a complex of other drivers of change.

The ascent of the United States happened because certain things fell into place that made global primacy highly probable. "Highly probable" is not a synonym for inevitable, however, as nothing is inevitable. But given what did transpire, if the

United States had evaded global primacy by 1945, it would have been a very interesting trick. Human agency was certainly involved. People must make choices and execute them for things to happen. Moreover, some of the choices that were made proved to be more important than some others. But these choices are not the main story. It is the systemic context in which they are made that is most critical.

Finally, the "certain things" that came together had done so before. What happened to the United States in the late nineteenth and early twentieth centuries certainly had distinctive and unique elements, but it was not the first time global primacy had been achieved in this manner. There are two main clusters of ideas used in advancing the ascent version advanced here. The larger of the two clusters concerns an argument referred to as the "Twin Peaks" model. This model refers to spurts of economic growth separated by a period of intensive conflict. In the US era, World Wars I and II were preceded by accelerated economic growth in the late nineteenth century and followed by another spurt of growth in the mid-twentieth century. This part of the application should not be considered particularly controversial. More interesting and controversial is the extent to which these developments were dependent on one another. In other words, the first growth spurt did not simply precede two world wars. The first growth spurt contributed to the outbreak of two world wars, which, in turn, led to a second economic growth spike—along with a host of other phenomena. World War II alone did not elevate the United States to systemic leadership, but the systemic leadership mantle would not have passed to the United States in the absence of this global war. Global war, in conjunction with the processes at work as described in chapter 3, is most responsible for the US ascent in 1945.

Chapter 4: Structure, Agency, and Grand Strategy

Grand strategy change analyses exhibit problems in balancing the interaction among ideas, external structures and developments, and domestic politics. An alternative theory is constructed that combines the correspondence between external problems and capability, shocks, political entrepreneurship, domestic politics, and reinforcement. The essence of the theory is that strategic shifts are more probable and likely to persist to the extent that more of these components involve significant changes. The 1920–1945 system leader puzzle—why the United States abstained from ascending to the system leader position in 1920 but not in 1945—is used as an illustration of the theory's explanatory utility. The emphasis on grand strategy is needed to complement the more material emphases of chapter 3. Yet the question at hand remains similar to one of the issues raised in chapter 3: what had happened by 1945 to push the United States toward embracing systemic leadership in global politics?

Decline Considerations

Chapter 5: The Relative Decline of the United States

This chapter is designed to address the question of US decline by focusing on the most pertinent data on military and economic capabilities. The military data examine strategic capabilities that have been developed to operate in the global commons and thus encompass naval, air, and space arenas. But there is also the question of whether China, the main challenger, really needs a competitive global profile to back up its claim to East Asian hegemony. Global and regional capabilities are not the same. While China has a long way to go to be competitive at the global level, its regional military capability has improved considerably. The economic data evade some of the problems of the typical gross domestic product–based indexes by looking at the identity of the top 100 multinational industrial corporations at selected points in time over the last hundred years and the concentration of energy consumption in an increasingly carbon fuel–based, world economy. The global military data tend to support the interpretations of anti-declinists while the economic data support the interpretations of declinists. Reconciling these perspectives empirically and theoretically gives us a better-grounded view of the extent of US relative decline that emphasizes technological change and energy transitions. In brief, it is hard to deny that net relative decline has taken place. The real questions are associated with what we should make of it. An anti-declinist position that little or no decline has occurred simply cannot be maintained. At the same time, a declinist position that the US relative position is in a rapidly descending, negative spiral is not the case either. The United States seems destined to decline to a floor that remains impressive vis-à-vis the relative positions of allies and rivals.

Chapter 6: The Dysfunctionality of Domestic Politics

Relative decline of the external variety is one thing. It is also addressable, though not if domestic politics is so dysfunctional that little can be accomplished. That US domestic politics is dysfunctional is not exactly a controversial position. Explaining how it has evolved to the present state of affairs is subject to disagreement. The argument developed in this chapter focuses on changes in and the interaction of three general processes: political-economic, political, and race/demographic. Long-term economic fluctuations are at work. American politics functioned better before the early 1970s. Since then, the US economy has been in an extended downturn that, among other things, has encouraged evolutionary changes in the Republican and Democratic parties and their combat within federal and state institutions and within the context of urban-rural differences. Compounding the political and political-economic problems are changes in racial and demographic characteristics of American society. A white majority perceives its predominance slipping with predicable responses in attitudinal and generational cleavages that feed back into the political arena.

These problems are unlikely to go away anytime soon. The most obvious implications are that that there will be less attention given to the roots of relative decline and persistent efforts to stem further shifts in relative power. The only conceivable antidotes are to outwait the shift away from a white majority and/ or to hope for unified government. When different parties control only some of the governmental apparatus, the dysfunctionality is likely to be worse. It may be that further shifts in the white majority will improve the chances of unified government. But the pace of the racial/demographic changes is slow. Sufficient change may take a generation or two at least. In the interim, the chances for unified government will always be iffy from election to election thanks in part to gerrymandering, voting suppression practices, and electoral/institutional features that hark back to constitutional compromises made hundreds of years before. One of the hallmarks of a democracy is that politicians must believe that they have a chance to return to power in a future election. One of the ironies of democracy is that if both US parties continue alternating wins, the dysfunctional interactions of parties that have become more polarized in terms of who they represent are likely to persist. Presumably, the dysfunction also precludes a possible US technological renaissance that could lead to a second round of Pax Americana.

Chapter 7: The Unipolar Mirage

One of the reasons the world may seem confusing to onlookers, especially in the United States, is that it was not very long ago that a very large number of people were convinced that the United States had won the Cold War, ideological history was dead, and a new era of US predominance in a unipolar world had emerged. Then came 9/11, long wars in Afghanistan and Iraq, and an almost return to world depression on a scale not seen since the 1930s. How can these disparate impressions be reconciled? Is/was US triumphalism warranted, or was it a matter of misreading the structure of world politics? In this chapter, the argument is that US triumphalism was not justified, and the world did not really turn unipolar overnight with the collapse of the Soviet Union. A mirage is an optical illusion that is not real. What happened after the end of the Cold War, more accurately, was a temporary deviation from a longer sequence of protracted relative decline by the system's lead economy—the United States. Starting from a very high level of power concentration, the United States has a long way to go to fall out of first place in the global hierarchy. Yet that does not mitigate the gradually weakening foundation for power and influence with which the United States operates. Some of that relative decline is natural and inevitable; some of it is traceable to poor US decision-making that privileges short-term over long-term considerations.

Part of the misinterpretation of systemic structure can be traced to the way in which we study polarity or distributions of power. Our collective approach is characterized by six problems that lead to debatable conclusions about how world politics works. After a discussion of the problem set, some solutions are advanced, and a new operationalization of global power is developed. The new metric is used to both characterize polar distributions since 1816. In the end analysis, power concentration comes and goes. Polarity is less powerful a variable than often thought, and other variables, such as the presence of challengers, are just as and perhaps more important.

Future Considerations

Chapter 8: The End of Systemic Leadership as We Know It?

Discussions of the relative decline of the United States and its possible supplantment by China have become common with observers usually arguing for or against hegemonic transition. Less discussed is the possibility that the systemic leadership cycle may have run its course. Several factors are put forward that may spell the end for one state acquiring a disproportionate share of political, economic, and military power as in the past. The factors encompass lead economies, technological innovation and diffusion, energy transition (or its absence), and global war. If the interpretation is accurate, we are in for a long period of limited systemic leadership in which the United States maintains a weak lead on other actors and can only operate as something approximating a genuine "first among equals." While this development could create space for the emergence of alternative political leadership formats, it seems more likely to increase competition and conflict than anything else.

Chapter 9: The Second Sino-American Rivalry

Whether or not a new system leader is just around the corner, what should we expect in the interim in the interactions between the incumbent leader and its presumed challenger? Curiously, there is at least as much interest among Asian specialists about whether the Asian region is ripe for rivalry as there is about the nature of the second Sino-American rivalry. Yet it can be demonstrated empirically that the Asian region is not moving toward increasing interstate rivalry. Such a demonstration implies that we should focus more on one very prominent rivalry than on the region's general propensity to antagonistic interactions. Even so, there is no consensus on how these types of rivalry might be expected to interact with one another. Eight models/theories are reviewed: Thucydides Trap, Power Transition, System Leader Retrenchment, Risk Assessments to Rising Challengers, Time Horizon Assessments of Rising Challengers, Rising Challenger Assessments of Incumbents Based on Strategic Value and Military Position, Rising Power Status Immobility, and Geostructural Realism.

There are a range of problems associated with these arguments. One, the Thucydides Trap, is configured around a poor research design. Several seem premature in the sense that the second Sino-American rivalry has yet to reach the point where some of the model's expectations are focused. For example, it is too soon to tell how or when Chinese elites may feel status mobility is thwarted by resistance from status quo–oriented powers. Others are focused on processes that seem to tell us too little to be all that useful. The power transition model, for example, is useful in sketching the parameters of power transitions, but it assumes that the transition will move toward completion. What do we do if a successful transition appears to be either unlikely or far in the future?

One of the eight models, however, does have apparent utility. Geostructural realism develops a comparison of bipolar confrontations in Western Europe and East Asia and takes advantage of differences in geography to predict very different types of confrontations. The applicability of the model, nonetheless, may not persist if key parameters change over time. One thing that will be sure to hold is that the antagonists will not be content to accept the constraints of the confrontation circumstances. Alternatively, it is not clear whether the antagonists will be able to alter the constraints no matter how hard they try to do so.

Chapter 10: The Future of World Order

"The suit that no longer fits" is an apt phrase describing the current world order coined by a Chinese observer. The current world order was designed to deal with postwar global problems as perceived in the early to mid-1940s by a coalition of states led by the United States. US relative power today is not as overwhelming as it was in 1945. Adjustments have been made in how the world order works. International organizations designed to do one thing have altered their assigned mission. Rising states have been given more influence in organizational decision-making. But these changes may not suffice to appease new demands from newly emerging elite states or to address problems that were less apparent in the 1940s. Moreover, one of the rising states is moving toward a political-economic foundation that could at least compete vigorously with the incumbent system leader. In the past, that has led to global war. Yet the probability of global war seems low given the high costs associated with such destructive behavior.

Given the ongoing relative decline of the United States and the low probability of global war, what might we expect to happen in the world order? The choices reduce primarily to two possibilities. One is that the present world order will persist and continue to decay in sync with the relative decline of its founding patron. The other is that a new world order will be put together by either China, should it supplant the United States at the global center, or some type of coalition of interested actors. The latter seems unlikely in the absence of the appropriate preconditions for changing world orders. It may be that the historically based conditions will prove to no longer be valid but, failing that, it seems most likely that the former option will prevail. World order will gradually diminish in geographical and substantive scope, albeit unevenly. Other partial orders may emerge in different parts of the world to take its place.

2

System Leadership, Rise, and Relative Decline

This chapter focuses on the interpretative tools needed to assess the relative decline of system leaders. Assumptions should be expressed explicitly. Why the fluctuating concentration of power is so important to the story must be spelled out. Similarly, it is critical to specify what kind of power is at stake. What lead economies, global reach, and global wars are and how they and their interactions anchor the interpretation constitute another set of arguments that need elaboration at the outset as well. Once these ingredients are clarified, we can move on to the rise and relative decline of the ongoing US case of systemic leadership discussed in subsequent chapters.

Assumptions

Assumptions are critical in international relations. One reason we disagree about what is happening and what has happened is that we have vastly different assumptions about how things work. Some analysts assume that nothing changes that is significant in international relations. Others assume that everything has changed since some critical juncture—1815, 1945, 1989–1991, 9/11—take your pick. If nothing of significance has changed, history does not really matter. It is merely a collection of anecdotes about who did what to whom earlier. If everything has changed, history does not really matter either because what is past no longer pertains. It has no relevance in a new world.

Neither of these extremes is very attractive. History does matter in international relations. Deciphering how it has mattered and continues to do so requires the construction of an explicit historical script. How have things evolved? What facets of evolutionary changes are most critical? Which actors and processes are most significant in comprehending what has happened?

Another curious facet of international relations analysis is the compartmentalization of activities that are labeled "political-military," as opposed to those that are viewed as "political-economic." With compartmentalization, analysts in one sphere proceed as if they can ignore what happens in the other sphere. There is some convenience in this practice. Getting up to speed in one sphere is hard

American Global Pre-eminence. William R. Thompson, Oxford University Press. © Oxford University Press 2022.
DOI: 10.1093/oso/9780197534663.003.0002

enough without also attempting to do the same in the other sphere. This tendency works much the same as in the question of how much history matters. Developing "sufficient" proficiency in the past is another hurdle that some analysts prefer to avoid. The problem is not that analysts in international relations are lazy and seek to cut corners. The real problem is whether one believes that history, political-military, and political-economic activities are interdependent and therefore difficult to keep separate.

Much of international relations theory is avowedly ahistorical, and too many political scientists seem to think that this is a good thing. Leadership long-cycle arguments take the exact opposite tack. There are no universal laws to uncover. Space and time matter. That does not mean that we are forced to deal only with current events as current events. Rather, how processes work needs to be qualified by where and when, and then we need to try to figure out the why of the where and when. Realists enshrine the balance of power process as the central focus of their perspective on international politics. A balance of power process, for instance, did function in Western Europe at least between 1494 and 1945 (Levy and Thompson, 2005). It was less evident before 1494, just as successful balance of power operations outside of Western Europe do not appear to be all that common.[1] Whether the European balancing was successful depends on how you evaluate it. It did not stop wars from happening, required warfare to make it work, and was only intermittently prominent in response to people such as the Habsburg Philip II, France's Louis XIV and Napoleon, and Germany's Kaiser Wilhelm II and Hitler. Even so, balancing was never axiomatic as a process; it was a type of behavior that some states engaged in some of the time. Whether it is a prominent process in today's world is open to debate.

Evolutionary arguments in the leadership long-cycle mode are about variation and selection processes—and not about social Darwinian survival of the fittest. Decision makers and other actors pursue a variety of strategies to achieve their ends. Some work better than others and are more likely to survive. Yet most things change and so, too, do the relative values of strategies. What worked in the past will not necessarily continue to work indefinitely into the future. As goals and/or capabilities change, or as environments change, some actor strategies are likely to change as well. Thus, all actors do not always seek to maximize power, optimize security, or seek out cooperative arrangements. Even if they did, changes in systemic environments would ensure that any strategy would not work equally well in all circumstances. Thus, we should not assume that state attributes such as democracy and autocracy have the same effect throughout

---

[1] Following Dehio's (1962) lead, perhaps balance of power processes work best when there is a strong mix of land and sea powers and less well when there is no mix or only a weak mixture?

time. More likely is that the effects of regime type, whatever they might be, are more likely to grow stronger or weaker over time (see, for instance, Cederman, 2001).[2] Similarly, we should not expect behaviors such as war initiations to be constant in their frequency. More likely, again, is that the war strategy is apt to fluctuate in numbers as incentives to go to war change. New behaviors emerge; for instance, global warfare only began at best some 500 years ago. Old behaviors die out (global warfare in the contemporary era?). Environments change as do actors. Explaining change, therefore, becomes the central problematique of leadership long-cycle theorizing.

As noted, international relations theory tends to be compartmentalized. Specialists in security questions attempt to explain conflict patterns. Specialists in international political economy (IPE) attempt to explain the intersection of politics and economics in questions of organization, policy, and distribution. Other specialists focus on international law and international organization. Leadership long-cycle theory, in contrast, is most focused on changes in systemic context. The basic premise is that things tend to work differently when resources and capabilities are highly concentrated than when they are less highly concentrated. Security, IPE, law, and organization all are likely to respond to these changes in various ways. Leadership long-cycle theory is about the whole of world politics—not just one or more of the ways in which we like to compartmentalize it.

Yet historical, evolutionary, and holistic emphases are not quite the same thing as concrete contributions to our knowledge base. Whatever else it might be, the leadership long-cycle research program is very much about concrete theory and its empirical testing. Frameworks are fine and good, but they fall short of doing the job of social science if they do not lead to testable hypotheses. If we do not test our hypotheses in some fashion, on what basis are we to evaluate our theoretical claims?

The Concentration of Power Premise

The main theoretical-empirical stipulation is that world politics has been characterized by long cycles of concentration and deconcentration for the last 1,000 years. Capability concentration has oscillated, as opposed to being constant or random, and a distinctive set of actors have succeeded one another in providing a leadership sequence. The claim is that China, building on a half-millennium of progress by earlier Chinese dynasties, initiated in the tenth century CE

---

[2] At the same time, it is possible to explain selective tendencies toward more pacific behavior without relying on regime type. See, for instance, Rasler and Thompson (2005b).

a relatively continuous process centered on technological innovation and efforts to break free from an agrarian reliance on solar energy. These concentrations are finite in time. By the thirteenth century, China was overrun by the Mongols. Chinese innovations diffused to the West via Genoese and Venetian monopolies on East-West trade in the Middle Ages. In the late fifteenth century, Portugal developed a new maritime route to the Indian Ocean. The Netherlands followed up with more routes and the first breakthrough in adapting fossil fuels (peat). The Dutch, in turn, were followed by a British maritime lead in the eighteenth century, which they managed to repeat with the breakthrough to coal-driven steam engines in the nineteenth century. The United States followed in this tradition in the late nineteenth and twentieth centuries with more and improved engines, electricity, and petroleum.

Thus, none of the leading states in this process exhibits identical profiles. They are a mixed bag of commercial powers (predicated initially on wind-driven sailing fleets), technological centers, and pioneers in new sources of energy— as demonstrated in table 2.1. The scope of the systems that they led varied and evolved over time. The degree to which they could concentrate power in their respective eras varied as well. So, too, did their ability to impact the world around them. Yet the most powerful were the ones that could muster leads in all three columns in table 2.1 and, in particular, the extent of their power revolved around the potency of the technology-energy interaction (Thompson and Zakhirova, 2019). Petroleum and electricity trumped coal, which had trumped peat. Nonetheless, they represent a lineage because they can be viewed as a sort of an odd historical relay race. No concrete baton was passed as in a real relay race, but

Table 2.1 Attributes of Successive System Leaders

	Commerce	Technological lead	Energy lead
Song China	No	Yes	No
Genoa	Yes	No	No
Venice	Yes (Europe)	Yes (Europe)	No
Portugal	Yes (East-West trade)	Yes (maritime)	No
Netherlands	Yes (Europe and East-West trade)	Yes (Europe)	Partially (peat/wind)
Britain I	Yes (Europe and Atlantic trade)	No	No
Britain II	Yes	Yes	Yes (coal)
United States	Yes	Yes	Yes (petroleum)

something figurative was passed along and each successor was very much aware of its immediate predecessor, if not the entire chain.

Table 2.1 clarifies the leadership pattern that characterized the past millennia. Each state had some claim to a commercial lead in at least some territory—with the scope of the trade gradually expanding to encompass the entire globe. Each state had some claim to technological prowess that differentiated it from its rivals of the time. Minimally, their technological leads were concentrated in the naval sphere—building new types of ships, developing navigational skills, and pioneering new trade routes. Increasingly, though, other technological innovations contributed to their ability to develop desired manufactures for trading purposes, especially ones that depended on intensive heat processes for their construction. The intensive heat processes, in turn, were based on harnessing the interaction between new technology and new sources of energy—successively, peat/wind, coal, and petroleum. Consequently, the Netherlands, the second British lead, and the US lead stand out in table 2.1. Only these three states were able to combine leads in all three areas—commerce, technology, and energy.[3]

These leads, it must be stressed, are not predicated on hegemony, empire, wealth, gross domestic product, or population size. The leads are focused on the possession of a lead economy for a finite period. At the core, it is a matter of becoming the world's center for technological innovation and developing appropriate ways to harness energy to fuel the new technologies—whether it be wind, fossil fuel, or alternatives-driven. Disproportionate wealth does ensue, not merely as a matter of peripheral exploitation, but as a function of monopolizing, for a period, trade and production. Ultimately, innovation centrality and lead economies move elsewhere. So, too, do trade and production head starts.

Systemic leadership emerges from these centers of technological/energy innovation out of self-interest, not altruism. Markets, trade routes, and sources of energy need some form of governance and protection for the lead economy to sell its wares profitably. The scale of its production demands access to external markets. Yet problem management or governance is constrained or minimal. Policing trade routes and maintaining access to distant energy sources have constituted the standard focus with order maintenance a third concern. System leaders have been reluctant to take the lead in championing global welfare—although it was British systemic leadership that first began to suppress slavery once they had lost control of American plantations. Eliminating restrictions on trade and the free flow of energy if located at some distance from its main

---

[3] Song China is a partial exception in the sense that it led its region and the rest of the world in technological innovation without fully utilizing its coal deposits for matters other than home heating and iron work. If it had been able to hold on to Kaifeng longer, that might have changed. Its commercial peak came several hundred years later. So it had many of the appropriate components, but they came out of order or were never completed (Thompson and Zakhirova, 2019).

places of consumption are much higher on the priority ladder. Leading global war coalitions in crisis circumstances is another high priority.

Many professional observers might accept the US claim to systemic leadership in the post-1945 era. Many of these analysts would also accept a significant leadership role for Britain in the nineteenth century. Rather few scholars seem comfortable with the eighteenth-century British claim that is undeniably weaker. A few more might acknowledge a significant Dutch role in the seventeenth century. Of the five, the sixteenth-century Portuguese claim seems the most outlandish to most people. The idea that Genoa and Venice might have played some role in the evolution of this leadership role seems equally odd. The notion that Song China might have started something new, however amorphously, tends to sound like a far stretch of the imagination. Yet some of the reaction is due to the fact that most analysts are simply not equally familiar with these actors and/or what they did in their periods of prominence. Unfortunately, that is not something that can be addressed in a book on the rise and decline of the United States.[4] Suffice it to say that this lineage has evolved. Song China was an East Asian actor. Genoa, Venice, and, to some extent, Portugal were transitional actors in moving the center of action to Western Europe. The Dutch, British, and American interdependencies and movement as a singular complex initiating industrial revolutions are greater than is usually acknowledged (see Scott, 2019 on what he calls the Anglo-Dutch-American archipelago). In sequence, they have formed an uneven lineage but one that has literally changed the world. Accordingly, they should be at the center of our attention. They are hardly the only actors that matter but, arguably, none have mattered more.

Lead Economies

Radical technological innovation clusters in time and space. One economy, the lead economy, monopolizes major economic innovation for a finite period. as delineated in table 2.2. Commercial predominance and technological centrality follow. Non-solar energy sources are cultivated to take advantage of the new technologies. The nature of the economic processes encourages a global orientation and the development of global reach capabilities. The threat of regional hegemonic aspirations provides further encouragement in the form of responding to the prospect of coercive territorial expansion in the home region. Victory at the head of a coalition in global warfare provides an opportunity to set rules for global transactions or a world order. The diffusion/

---

[4] See Modelski and Thompson (1996), Thompson (1999, 2001), and Thompson and Zakhirova (2019) for greater attention to historical details.

Table 2.2 Leading Sector Timing and Indicators, Fifteenth to Twenty-first Centuries

Lead economy	Leading sector indicators	Start-up phase	High growth phase
Portugal	Guinea gold	1430–1460	1460–1494
	Indian pepper	1494–1516	1516–1540
Netherlands	Baltic and Atlantic trade	1540–1560	1560–1580
	Eastern trade	1580–1609	1609–1640
Britain I	Amerasian trade (especially sugar)	1640–1660	1660–1688
	Amerasian trade	1688–1713	1713–1740
Britain II	Cotton, iron	1740–1763	1763–1792
	Railroads, steam	1792–1815	1815–1850
United States	Steel, chemicals, electronics	1850–1873	1873–1914
	Motor vehicles, aviation, electronics	1914–1945	1945–1973

normalization of new technology and the decay in the system leader's relative share of economic and military resources set up a repeat of the sequence of innovation-war-innovation-decay.

For pioneers, the initial source of new best practice technologies reaps major profits and lead in economic development. They need sea power to protect the affluent home base and the sea routes via which its products are distributed around the world from potential predators. For the early leaders, major advances in ship construction were critical to the packages of innovations being introduced to the world economy. More generally, though, the gains from pioneering new commercial networks and industrial production financed the leading arsenals of global reach capabilities developed by system leaders. Those same gains later led to each system leader becoming a, if not the, principal source of credit for the world economy in the past two centuries (Obstfeld and Taylor, 2004: 52–53).

At the heart of leadership long-cycle theorizing is a model of long-term economic growth (Modelski and Thompson, 1996; Rennstich, 2008; Thompson and Zakhirova, 2019). There is no denying the importance of population size, resource endowment wealth, mass and elite consumption, savings, and other standard foci of economic growth models. But these are primarily short-term considerations. Over the long haul, development is driven by radical technological revolutions that occur roughly every half-century or so. These are the long waves of economic growth that are also referred to as Kondratieffs or k-waves. By focusing on the leading sectors that are at the heart of these technological breakthroughs, it is also possible to measure them, thereby providing important empirical support for the claims that these phenomena exist. It has also been possible to demonstrate that their main carriers, the leading sectors, stimulate the economic growth of the system leader's national economy and the world economy.

Another theoretical-empirical contribution involves an ongoing effort to map IPE relationships in conjunction with the core systemic leadership processes of leading sector growth, leading sector concentration, and global reach concentration. We have demonstrated that the system leader's leading sector growth is a driver of the system leader's national economic growth and the world economy's growth, subject to various feedback processes. System leader, leading sector growth links to leading sector concentration which, in turn, is related to system leader military mobilization and global reach capability concentration. The foundations for systemic leadership (leading sector growth, leading sector share concentration, and global reach capability concentration), in turn, are linked to world trade openness. World trade openness appears to drive protectionism, rather than the other way around.

But, of course, systemic leadership did not spring forth as an international novelty in 1945. Regardless of how one envisions systemic leadership functioning, it had antecedents in the long nineteenth-century Pax Britannica. More maximally, it can be traced back a millennium to Song Dynasty China. Eleventh- and twelfth-century China was not the world's first lead economy, but it can claim to have been the first modern lead economy thanks to innovations in paper currency, early forms of industrialization, and widespread commercial activity. Prior to these developments, earlier leading economies were primarily agrarian in nature. Modern economic growth has not been independent of agrarian growth, but to become more self- sustaining, economic growth had to be weaned away from dependence on food cultivation alone. Innovations associated with industrialization and maritime commerce have been the two principal economic modernization conduits, and both of these were concentrated for a time in Song Dynasty China.

The emergence of modern lead economies did not immediately generate the phenomenon that we now recognize as global systemic leadership. Initially, the attempt to regulate inter-regional trade was carried out on a more circumscribed and usually regional scale. Although the Chinese economy was stagnating in terms of innovation by the time the Ming voyages around Southeast Asia and into the Indian Ocean were launched in the early fifteenth century, some of the motivation for these voyages involved ordering the Sino-centric world economy. Chinese economic innovations diffused to the West via the spice routes on land and sea. Initially, the primary beneficiaries were Genoa and Venice, which sought to monopolize Eastern products entering the Mediterranean through the Black

Sea, Persian Gulf, and Red Sea conduits with a number of maritime innovations (including, in the case of Venice, factory-produced warships) that gave them an edge in the European regional economy.

Portugal and the Netherlands were the next beneficiaries of East-West trade incentives. Portugal developed maritime innovations that enabled it to out-flank the Venetian-Mamluk and later Ottoman monopolies in the eastern Mediterranean by sailing around Africa into the Indian Ocean. There it estab-lished a predatory regime in the western Indian Ocean to tax a trade that it could not dominate otherwise. The Dutch next outflanked the eroding Portuguese regime by sailing directly across the Indian Ocean to the sources of Asian spices. Unlike the Portuguese, the Dutch reinforced their maritime-centric lead economy status with land-based innovations in harnessing windmills and peat, but peat could not generate the type of heat needed for iron production. After an initial phase as the successor to the Dutch maritime lead in the eighteenth century, the British learned how to exploit coal and steam in developing their industrial revolution. The lead economy that emerged underwrote British regu-latory efforts in controlling piracy and slavery and attempting to lower tariffs in the nineteenth century.

These antecedents to US systemic leadership are linked to a very specific in-terpretation of systemic leadership. Just as lead economies gradually became stronger, so too did efforts at systemic leadership. The long and gradual evolution toward contemporary manifestations of systemic leadership began in eleventh-century China and took a thousand years to emerge in more recognizable form. Leads in technological innovations in commerce and industry created states that were more interested in governing long-distance trade than in engaging in local territorial expansion. Consequently, their armies took second priority to navies that were increasingly blue water services as the scope of long-distance trade expanded.

The foundations of systemic leadership, thus, are leads in technological in-novation that bestow temporary monopolies in the transportation and produc-tion of selected and highly profitable commercial and industrial sectors and the naval forces to protect inter-regional transactions. As one moves toward the pre-sent era, global wars increasingly figure as periods of systemic leadership crys-tallization. That is, system leaders-to-be first develop lead economies and then engage in wars fought over at least in part who will be the next global system leader. The lead economy's edge over other economies is accentuated while other contenders exhaust their resource bases. Not coincidentally, the lead economy's edge in global coercive reach is also substantially expanded in global warfare while the weaponry of rivals is either captured or destroyed. Add coalition lead-ership during wartime, and the new system leader emerges in the postwar era even farther ahead of its competition than before the war.[5] The concentration of power is not driven exclusively by market dynamics. It needs a few nudges here and there to get to the top of the global hierarchy.

Global Power Projection

Systemic leadership is very much about the ability to project power over long distances. States that are satisfied with the defense of their home borders or that have the capability to project power solely within their immediate neighborhood do not make good candidates for carrying out global military operations. The ability to project power around the globe is different from the ability to send tanks across the border or to launch fighter planes against incoming bombing raids. Operating in the global commons requires different ambitions, vehicles, and the wealth to pay for it.

One of the many areas in which international relations scholars disagree is how best to capture the concept of military capability. The most popular approach is to create omnibus indices combining a bit of everything but often encompassing population, economy, and military size. The problem is that these indices are strongly biased toward bulk and against qualitative advantages. Large populations can be most useful but less so if they are undereducated and impoverished. Large economies are impressive but not necessarily very competitive. Large militaries can seem intimidating until they must fight and find themselves unable to get to the combat zone and/or prove to be under-gunned or poorly led when they do manage to arrive. Bulk emphases are particularly bad at capturing the ability to project power at long distance. The largest states and empires throughout history have not always been very good at operating beyond their immediate borders. Therefore we need to differentiate between more local and more global capabilities.

An alternative approach is to develop indices that are more discrete in terms of what type of capability is focused upon and where that capability might be employable. Leadership long-cycle analyses, for instance, always have stressed naval power as critical to understanding the distribution of capabilities at the global level. Trucks, tanks, and large infantry divisions have obvious utility in relatively local theaters, which we might designate generally as regional zones of operation. If a state cannot move those trucks, tanks, and divisions beyond the region, it is

---

[5] This argument is advanced in more detail in Thompson (1988, 2000), Modelski and Thompson (1988, 1996), Rasler and Thompson (1994), Reuveny and Thompson (2004b), and Rapkin and Thompson (2013).

restricted to regional theaters. To operate at the global level, one needs different types of capability. Certain kinds of ships, planes, and missiles have been developed to operate at the global level or over extra-regional distances. Thus, to best capture the distribution of military power at the global level, we need information on the types of capabilities that apply to global maneuvering. Naval power is a good start because oceans have offered the primary medium for projecting capabilities over long distance for most of history. Still, the twentieth century witnessed the increased utilization of air and space capabilities. An index that combined naval, air, and space capabilities should provide a superior counting mechanism than one that only focused on any one of the three mediums. Table 2.3 lists the components used in the development of a global power projection index. Essentially, it supplements the naval components found in the leadership long cycle index (Modelski and Thompson, 1988; Lee and Thompson, 2018) with air and space measures capturing information on the possession of strategic bombers, land-based ICBMs, and military satellites. The power projection index represents an averaging of the mix of fifteen components as appropriate for any given year.[6]

Given the technological changes experienced by navies over the last half-millennium, it was impossible to find any single and consistent indicator capable of spanning that entire period. Instead, a more complex schedule or set of indicators was constructed that changed in keeping with real-world changes. Beginning with armed sailing ships owned by the state, through ships of the line with an escalating minimal number of guns, to the mix of battleships, heavy aircraft carriers, and nuclear attack and ballistic missile submarines of more recent years, it proved possible to operationalize the distribution of sea power over a fairly long period. The empirical outcome (Modelski and Thompson, 1988) supports the hypothesized sequence and timing of leadership between 1494 and the current period. That is, we find five intervals of concentration in power projection capabilities for global reach. Since those initial tests, we have expanded the global reach index to encompass air and space capabilities as seems appropriate for post-1914 developments.

An overview of the distribution of more recent global power projection capabilities is provided by table 2.4 and more selectively in figure 2.1. Several observations can be made about the general shape of change at the global level shown by these data. In 1900, Britain led and thereafter even improved its relative share of power projection capabilities through World War I. But World War I was the last gasp of British pre-eminence at sea and in the air. The United States took first place in these capabilities in World War II and has maintained that position ever since. The Soviet Union made steady progress in its relative projection

---

[6] Further details on the components may be found in Lee and Thompson (2018).

Table 2.3 Indicators for Power Projection

Indicator	Time period
Sea Power	
Number of armed ships	
Number of ships of the line	1816–1860
Naval spending	1816–1938
Number of first-line battleships	1861–1879
Number of pre-dreadnoughts	1880–1909
Number of dreadnoughts	1910–1945
Number of heavy aircraft carriers	1946–present
Number of nuclear attack submarines	1954–present
Number of nuclear SLBM submarines (weighted by SLBM, CMP, and EMT)	1960–present
Air and Space Power	
Number of long-range strategic bombers (weighted by bomb load)	1916–present
Number of ICBMs (weighted by CMP and EMT)	1960–present
Number of military satellites	1959–present

Table 2.4 Power Projection Capability Shares in the Twentieth and Twenty-first Centuries

Year	USA	UK	USSR/RUS	FRN	GER	ITA	JPN	CHN
1900	.142	.366	.097	.167	.106	.075	.046	
1910	.201	.432	.037	.050	.218	.036	.025	
1920	.283	.582	.012	.035	0	.062	.027	
1930	.285	.303	.082	.109	.012	.098	.111	
1940	.159	.218	.118	.071	.246	.107	.081	
1950	.829	.156	0	.015				0
1960	.822	.031	.014	.007				0
1970	.624	.085	.278	.013				0
1980	.567	.037	.368	.026				.001
1990	.622	.013	.338	.025				.003
2000	.685	.026	.246	.037				.007
2010	.623	.030	.285	.030				.032
2018	.577	.021	.275	.035				.091

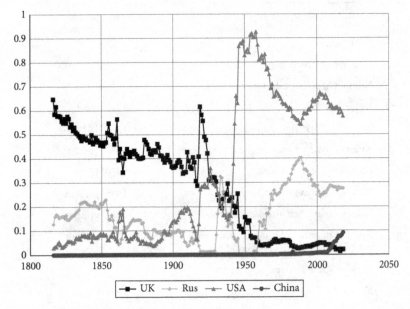

Figure 2.1 Power Projection Shares, 1816–2018

position in the 1960s through the 1980s, at the expense of the US relative position. Just how bipolar one views the US-USSR Cold War division may hinge on what thresholds are used and/or which capabilities are considered most critical. If one requires something like a 50:50 split, the Cold War era was only moving toward bipolarity without ever achieving it. If one requires both bipolar powers to possess at least 25 percent of the capabilities and no other power to possess anything close, the Cold War era only became bipolar around 1970. This same date is often used as a marker for the attainment of something resembling nuclear capability equality, which might offer a third metric. Thus, no matter which approach one uses, the new data suggest that we may not have categorized polarity in the Cold War era all that accurately.[7]

However, if the 25 percent threshold is employed, global power projection capabilities did move toward and into unipolarity after the end of the Cold War, but only barely. Of course, these data focusing on the possession of ships and planes do not capture the inability of Russia to be able to pay for deploying its surviving capability. In that respect, the shares in table 2.4 underestimate the movement

---

[7] See chapter 7 for a schedule for identifying polarity types. Unipolarity requires one state to hold 50 percent or more of the pertinent capabilities (and no other state holds 50 percent); bipolarity involves two states with each possessing 25 percent shares of the total capabilities (and no other state controlling as much as 25 percent); multipolarity has three or more states, each controlling at least 5 percent (and none of the prerequisites for unipolarity and bipolarity holding).

into a short-lived unipolar phase after 1990. Yet the same data underscore how far China must go to develop extra-regional capability. It has caught up with and surpassed France and Britain but seems unlikely to pass the positions of Russia or the United States in the near future.

Energy Consumption and Global Reach

In this context mixing economic and military resources, a new, three-indicator index can be proposed to distinguish changes in systemic-level power distributions. It relies on energy consumption to substitute for more conventional economic indicators in part because it does not require extensive manipulation to create a series back to 1816. The data are already available and do not have to be converted into a common currency or adjusted for parity purchasing equivalence or inflation. But, beside their convenience, energy consumption captures the very heart of modern economic development. The first two industrial revolutions, usually dated from the later eighteenth and nineteenth centuries, respectively, ushered in revolutionary new technology for production and transportation purposes that were fueled by coal, petroleum, and electricity. Up to a point, those economies that adapted best to these new expectations became increasingly heavy consumers of the new sources of energy that now powered their economic growth.[8]

Energy consumption, therefore, is a good (but not perfect) indicator of modern economic and technological development—that is, from the nineteenth century and thereafter. Yet it has its bulk and qualitative dimensions just like GDP. The first two proposed indicators, thus, are energy consumption and energy consumption per capita.[9] Total energy consumption tells us how powerful the overall economy is, assuming that the energy is consumed in an efficient manner. Energy consumption per capita tells us how complex the energy package is. Moreover, one of the more attractive features of an energy consumption focus is that it captures perhaps the main way in which the world changed as it began to modernize after the first industrial revolution's transformations in new technology and energy sources.[10]

---

[8] Advanced industrial economies eventually level off in their energy consumption.

[9] The indices are computed based on energy and population data found in the Correlates of War's national capability dataset utilized to construct the CINC index (Singer, Bremer, and Stuckey, 1972).

[10] Buzan and Lawson (2015) contend that international relations scholarship has not fully recognized the significance of changes introduced in the nineteenth century. In terms of the energy shifts associated with the two industrial revolutions (coal, petroleum, electricity), I would certainly agree.

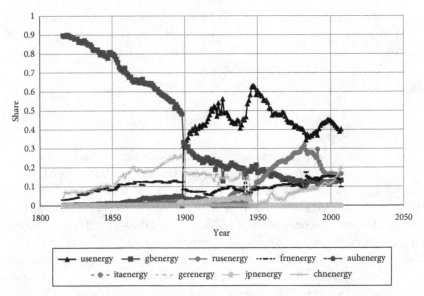

Figure 2.2 Energy Consumption Shares (Combined Total and Per Capita Shares)

Figure 2.2 depicts the fluctuations in relative energy consumption for the past two centuries.[11] Total consumption and per capita shares are combined in one index. Britain's energy lead as the first economy to commit to coal and steam engines was phenomenal, and its lead was clearly maintained through the nineteenth century if Correlates of War (COW) major power rules are observed for entry into the elite pool. The figure shows an abrupt transition at the turn of the century, with the inclusion of the United States as newly minted great power. The United States went on to peak in the late 1940s before beginning its own relative decline in position. The decline was interrupted by the collapse of the USSR in 1991 but, interestingly, the "bounce" in the US position did not rise above the 0.5 threshold. There will be more to say about that in chapter 7. As China rises, the United States has resumed its positional decline trajectory.

The third indicator focuses on the power projection capabilities already discussed. The final operationalization decision involves which states to include in the pool. If the modern world were not so concentrated in power capabilities, this decision would be more significant than it is now. Given high capability concentration, it does not make too much difference whether one adds or subtracts comparatively weak states. As a matter of operational conservatism, the power capability data are pooled using the COW rules for great power status. This decision

---

[11] It seems more straightforward to rely directly on the percentages at the expense of the polarity categories. This approach has always been the hallmark of leadership long-cycle analyses. See, as well, Mansfield (1993).

means that Britain, France, and Russia are included for the entire period. Austria-Hungary drops out in 1918. Prussia-Germany drops out in 1945. Italy enters in 1860 and leaves in 1943. Japan and the United States enter the system in 1895 and 1899, respectively, with Japan bowing out in 1945. China begins its great power status in 1950. The COW approach also brings Germany and Japan back into the elite subsystem in 1990, but that seems an easy change to ignore. Using this interpretation of elite powers does not imply any endorsement of the wisdom or accuracy of the great power operational specifications. Utilizing what is the industry standard simply eliminates one possible source of perceived bias.

A maximal list of elite actors is adopted on the presumption that their relative shares will help sort them out. That is, marginal power projectors will show up in the figure toward the bottom of the scale, as in the cases of Austria-Hungary or China. What comes through most clearly in figure 2.4's crowded array is Britain's long slide, the United States' abrupt ascent and relative decline that is less linear than Britain's, and the Soviet Union's abortive challenge in the mid-to-late twentieth century.

What remains is to integrate the three series (shares of total energy consumption, energy consumption per capita, and power projection) into one index. There are different ways of going about computing this combination. All three indicators capture power potential—the power to produce or to do damage at distance. If that potential is highly concentrated in one state economic-military inventory, it may not really matter all that much how one combines the three indicators. Yet the two spheres—economic and military—are very different. Imagine a state with high energy scores but limited military capabilities. Contemporary Germany and Japan come quickly to mind. They are important actors but highly dependent on others to do their fighting for them. Reverse the combination—low energy scores but advanced military capabilities. Such states are also handicapped in the extent to which they can engage in world politics, but they can punch above their weight from time to time. Contemporary Russia is a good illustration of this phenomenon. For this reason, one could argue that power projection capabilities deserve more weight in the aggregated index than do the energy indices—of which there are already two. Thus, the two energy indices are given equal weight, while the power projection shares are doubled in terms of their input so that the resulting index is based half on the two energy shares and half on the power projection shares.

Figure 2.3 shows the outcome for an 1816–2007 depiction of the two leaders' share. Britain emerged from the Napoleonic Wars at its high point and declined continuously for the next 130 years. The only departure from this trend line was the brief and restricted revival of Britain's relative fortunes in the interwar years due to the defeat of some of its rivals in World War I. The US ascent was quick and towering after World War II. But it also began to lose relative share position quickly and continuously as well, with two exceptions. The US relative share of power capabilities rebounded after the end of the Cold War thanks to the temporary sidelining of Russian capabilities (and the slow emergence of Chinese capabilities).

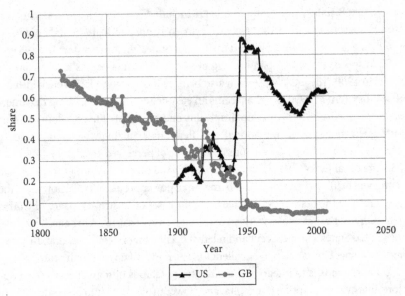

Figure 2.3 British and U.S. Relative Power Capability Shares

The other exception is that the US relative decline started at a very high point, which gives it some leeway in allowing others to catch up. For instance, if one starts at a 50 percent peak and relative decline takes away, say, a quarter of one's leading position, the lead state is down to a 37.5 percent share. If one starts at an 80 percent peak, however, and relative decline takes away a quarter of the lead, the lead state is still at an impressive 60 percent position. Other things being equal, we should expect that the higher one's starting point, the slower the progress of relative decline.

Global Wars

Global politics is distinguished from regional politics in the leadership long-cycle perspective. Regional politics has often revolved around coercive attempts to consolidate dominance (e.g., in Western Europe, the dramatic efforts of Philip II, Louis XIV, Napoleon, and Hitler). Regional hegemony is often sought and attained by force relying on army capabilities to defeat the opposition to these schemes.[12] Global politics focuses instead on problems that need to be solved to facilitate the movement of commodities over long distances and especially

---

[12] Outside of post-Roman Western Europe, regional hegemons have tended to be successful.

inter-regionally. It is in this realm of protecting the world economy's status quo that the winners of global wars, the world powers, are predominant, most clearly in the aftermath of a hard-fought global war.

Global wars figure prominently in long cycle arguments (Modelski, 1987; Thompson, 1988; Rasler and Thompson, 1989, 1994, 2001, 2005b; Alexseev, 1997).[13] In the past 500 years, intermittent systemic crises have led to global wars—bouts of intensive warfare fought increasingly throughout the planet in which most or all of the most powerful states participate. An added quirk to this process is that between 1494 and 1945, one region developed political-military centrality thanks in part to its escalatory, intra-regional competition for predominance and the byproduct of advantages in military organization and lethality. On repeated occasions, one state in the region sought (or was perceived to be seeking) regional hegemony. This European state (Spain, France, Germany), for its time, tended to have the largest regional population, a strong agrarian economy, and the largest army. The principal strategic approach to regional hegemony consisted of military conquest and control of adjacent territories. Ultimately, its ambitions and actions threatened states engaged in different strategies—namely, eschewing territorial conquest at home and focusing on penetrating markets abroad. Global wars thus end up constituting "showdown" wars between two different types of powerful states, their vastly different strategies, and their hastily constructed coalitions of allies.

Intermittent attempts at regional hegemony presented survival problems for weaker states located within the European region. Such efforts also constituted a threat to the global political order. If one state controlled Western Europe, it would also control European ports, maritime resources, and considerable commercial-industrial potential. Territorial expansion in Western Europe also meant absorbing the old lead economy (in order—Venice, Portugal, the Netherlands, Britain) and its resources. A European regional hegemon, as a consequence, would be a more potent contender for power at the global, inter-continental layer. Not only was an aspiring regional hegemon a direct threat to the old system leader, it usually constituted a proximate threat to new and upcoming centers of technological prowess as well. By at least the end of the nineteenth century, the aspiring regional hegemon (in Europe) was also a leading candidate to usurp the central technological innovation position. Thus, global crises have tended to fuse with European regional crises.[14] The outcome has been global warfare in 1494–1517, 1580–1609, 1688–1713, 1792–1815, and 1914–1945 (as outlined in table 2.5).

---

[13] Major power rivalries have also been linked to macro structural change (Thompson, 1999; Colaresi, 2001).

[14] By the 1930s, Asian regional hegemony had also fused with European and global crises.

Table 2.5 Global Wars

Global war	Timing	Issues
Italian/Indian Ocean Wars	1490s–1510s	Franco-Spanish contest over Italian states; Portuguese breaking of Venetian/Mamluk eastern trade monopoly
Dutch Independence War	1580s–1600s	Opposition to Phillip II's expansion; Dutch breaking of Spanish/Portuguese eastern trade monopoly
Louis XVI Wars	1680s–1710s	Opposition to Louis XIV expansion; French attempt to break Dutch trading monopoly in Europe and elsewhere
French Revolutionary/ Napoleonic Wars	1790s–1810s	Opposition to French expansion; French attempt to resist British industrial lead and systemic leadership
World Wars I and II	1910s–1940s	Opposition to German expansion; German attempt to succeed Britain as system leader

Global wars have seen a simple yet consistent lineup of opposing actors. On one side, there is an aspiring regional hegemon and its allies that choose to or are forced to bandwagon. Typically, these allies are not among the strongest actors in their home region. They also may turn out to be more a liability than an asset. On the other side are the maritime/global actors that include the old leader and, if applicable, the most likely successor. They are joined by at least one powerful land power that is a principal rival with the aspiring regional hegemon. The maritime/global actors provide naval capability, maritime blockades of resources entering the main war theaters, commercial-industrial supplies to their allies, and coordination of a planetary-wide struggle. Their land allies typically provide the bulk of the armies to oppose the aspiring regional hegemon in the home region.

This interpretation (Thompson, 1992; Rasler and Thompson, 1994, 2001) co-opts a Dehioan premise (Dehio, 1962) that aspiring regional hegemons in Europe were thwarted by counterweights that were able to win by introducing extra-regional resources into the balancing contest. One authoritarian counterweight supplied land power from the east. The other entered from a western position based on its sea power and commercial mediation focused on Europe-Asia-America. Operating simultaneously, the two counterweights were able to defeat a sequence of hegemonic attempts by forcing states attempting to take over the region to fight on two fronts and usually without much access to extra-regional resources.

A 1494 French bid for Italy was stopped primarily by Spain. France and the Ottoman Empire combined to block a sixteenth-century Habsburg hegemonic effort. A true Western counterweight emerged later in the sixteenth century in the form of Dutch-English resistance to Philip II and Spanish ambitions. The same Western counterweight was mobilized to help defeat Louis XIV in the late seventeenth and early eighteenth centuries. By the end of the eighteenth century, Britain alone served as the Western counterweight to the regional threat posed by the French Revolutionary and Napoleonic Wars. Against the German challenges of World War I and II, Britain and the United States co-operated in the West while the earlier Austrian role in the East had been taken over by Russia.

What Dehio contributed was an appreciation for the pattern of regional-global structural change. At the regional level, peaks in concentrated land power alternated with troughs in regional concentration. New regional aspirants tended to emerge during the regional trough periods. It was during these same low regional concentration periods that Western counterweight strength was greatest. Thus, the principal dynamic was one of alternating relative strength. The leading land power in the region tended to be strong when the Western sea power was relatively weak and vice versa.

Moreover, the two states pursued dramatically different agendas. The leading land power utilized absolute royal powers and large armies/bureaucracies to co-ercively expand its territorial control in the home region. The leading sea power sought to evade territorial control by specializing in monopolizing markets at home and abroad. Yet success for the leading land power implied a direct and indirect threat to the leading sea power. Regional hegemony either led to the oc-cupation of the reigning or former sea power and/or created a very strong base for a subsequent challenge for extra-regional colonies and markets. Western sea powers, therefore, never lacked structural incentives to coordinate the suppres-sion of regional hegemonic aspirations.

Western sea power, specializing in maritime containment of regional he-gemony, could limit the expansion of a regional hegemon beyond the confines of the region but it would not suffice to defeat the hegemon on land. Someone else needed to supply substantial land power for that purpose. A coalition com-bining the requisite naval and army capabilities could then squeeze the aspiring hegemon into overextending itself fighting on eastern and western fronts at the same time and, ultimately, unsuccessfully.

The typical outcome of these intensive global bloodlettings is that most of the actors who participate are exhausted, at least temporarily. In partic-ular, the aspiring regional hegemon is defeated, and limitations may be placed on its subsequent involvement in international affairs. Whether or not that happens, considerable time is necessary to rebuild its shattered economic and military capabilities. Many of the winners of global wars have become exhausted by the effort as well. The land powers on the winning side carry the brunt of the land campaigns. The old system leader is apt to be financially exhausted if it has not developed a strategy for retaining pioneering technological innovation. It is the new global system leader that profits from the intensive bloodletting. Its competition has been beaten down. Its own military and economic resources and infrastructure have been expanded. It has played a leadership role in coordinating the coalition responding to the aspiring regional hegemon. As a consequence, it is primed to exert more global leadership in the immediate postwar era.

Note that no claim is made that global wars occurred prior to 1494. This is a phenomenon that emerged toward the end of the fifteenth century. As an increasingly lethal exercise, it may have ended in 1945. Since then, major powers have prepared for another global war but there has been increasing suspicion that one will not come about as long as accidental onsets can be contained. The anticipated costs of a third world war seem too great to ever justify resorting to such a primitive way for deciding the structure of regional and global hierarchies.

Why exactly the probability of global warfare has diminished is not subject to consensus within the leadership long-cycle program. Some favor democratization or the democratic peace as a major driver of pacification (Modelski and Gardner, 1991, 2002). Another view is expressed in Rasler and Thompson (2005a) in which Rosecrance's (1986) trading state theory is reinterpreted in leadership long-cycle clothing. Rosecrance's argument is basically a scissors motion between the rising costs of warfare and the increasing attractiveness of economic development and trade. The long-cycle variation is that the escalation of global wars is most responsible for the rising costs of warfare, at least among the major powers (Levy and Thompson, 2011). Systemic leadership and intermittently expanding technological frontiers are also most responsible for contemporary interests in development and trade. Add in 500 or more years of near-exhaustion of the pool of wannabe regional hegemons in Western Europe, and one has an alternative explanation for selective decreases in conflict among the more affluent states in the system.[15] Trends toward selective pacification, however, hardly mean an end to conflict.

---

[15] The democratic peace has been found to characterize relations between economically developed democracies but not among less economically developed democracies. See Hegre (2003) and Mousseau, Hegre, and Oneal (2003).

The Twin Peaks Model: Combining Technological Surges and Global War

The argument underlying the Twin Peaks model subsumes theories of long-term economic growth and the evolution of world politics. Long-term economic growth is viewed as depending greatly on intermittent spurts of radical techno-logical innovation that fundamentally alter the technological frontier and the way the most advanced economies function. The innovations tend to be monop-olized by one pioneering economy at a time. This pioneering lead economy undergoes the transformations associated with a package of innovations and re-lated implications for energy sources. It then reaps the material profits of leading the way to new commercial and industrial best practices.

Possession of the world's lead economy implies several collateral develop-ments. The lead economy becomes the system's primary source of investment capital geared to the surpluses generated by the highly profitable innovations. As a matter of self-interest, the lead economy also becomes the principal protector of a global economic system geared initially to long-distance trade and increas-ingly technologically sophisticated industrial output. In turn, this role generates a need for the development of global reach superior to that possessed by all other actors. Given the distribution of land and water on Earth and the lower trans-action costs associated with contemporary maritime exchange, global reach capabilities have tended to concentrate on naval power over much of the last millennium. The system's lead economy, therefore, must develop a relative mo-nopoly in blue water naval capabilities to provide the military armature for its system protection activities.

Economic and technological sophistication does not guarantee predominant influence in the global layer of long-distance exchange and industrial production. World politics remains primitive in the sense that political and policy leadership continues to be a prize that must be won by force.[16] Typically, global political economy experiences periodic crises that take the following form. The prevailing techno-economic paradigm of one era gives way to a new set of innovations and economic procedures.[17] The lead economy associated with the older paradigm is in relative decline. So, too, is its ability to protect the networks of exchange and production developed in the preceding era. Other economies may be generating

---

[16] This statement is not necessarily one that will hold for all time. The costs of military conquest and the attractions of economic development and trade appear to be chipping away at this propen-sity. See, for instance, the argument and evidence in Rasler and Thompson (2005b).

[17] The emphasis on techno-economic paradigm is borrowed from the highly compatible "Sussex school's" approach to long waves of economic growth (see, among others, Freeman and Perez (1988).

economic challenges in the form of new innovations and new techno-economic paradigms. The pecking order of the global layer is destabilized. The ability to make policy and rules for the global layer is up for grabs. The crisis, therefore, is whether, when, and in which direction a new political-economic status quo will emerge.

The Twin Peaks model is emblematic of the combination of the emphases on systemic leadership and long waves of economic growth. The timing of economic long waves is such that there is a marked propensity for each period of systemic leadership to encompass two k-waves or innovation clusters. That is, each system leader pioneers at least two long waves of economic growth in the following sequence. A new wave and technological frontier are pioneered by a state, thereby propelling that state toward the pinnacle of the systemic hierarchy. The resulting instability in relative systemic positions, usually set up by a long period of decline on the part of the incumbent system leader, provokes the onset of a period of systemic crisis or global war—periods of intensive combat waged by all or most of the major powers in the system. There is always a complex of motivation, but the primary prize in these contests is the winner's ability to assume the mantle of systemic leadership for global concerns and to make policy for global affairs.

Innovation surges are propelled by identifiable commercial and industrial sectors that lead the way to extending the technological frontier. Representatives of leading sectors in history are subject to a two-phased sequence of preparation and actualization that is summarized in table 2.6. The asserted pattern of innovation surge–global war–innovation surge seems well documented in the table.

Table 2.6 The Timing of Leading Sector Growth Surges and Global War

First high-growth surge	Global war	Second high-growth surge
Portugal		
1460–1494	1494–1516	1516–1540
Netherlands		
1560–1580	1580–1609	1609–1640
Britain		
1660–1688	1688–1714	1713–1740
1763–1792	1792–1815	1815–1850
United States		
1873–1914	1914–1945	1945–1973

One state profits immensely from the global war. That same state emerges with a relative monopoly of global reach capabilities built up as part of the global war effort. This state also was a leading contender for the lead economy status prior to the outbreak of war thanks to its lead in introducing a cluster of prewar economic innovation. With its rivals exhausted by global war and its own political-military-economic capabilities expanded by participation in global war, the lead economy emerges as the new system leader. As the world economy's leading innovator, the new system leader is in an optimal position to usher in, and also pioneer in, a new round of technological innovation—the development of which was in turn accelerated by the global war effort.

The twin peaks of this process, therefore, are the spurts of radical technological innovation that precede and follow periods of global war. The first spurt helps to stimulate global war. The consequent global war helps to stimulate a second spurt of technological innovation. A new period of systemic leadership is thereby facilitated by the first peak and the global war. The subsequent peak in systemic leadership is coterminous with the second peak of technological innovation. Again, it must be emphasized that throughout this process, systemic leadership is not to be equated with global hegemony. One state has a decisive edge in commercial-industrial productivity and in naval capabilities. It has considerable global reach but it also has significant limitations in what it can do with its global reach, depending in part on the number, nature, location, and timing of its opponents.[18] In some centuries, systemic leadership has enjoyed something of an extended global honeymoon without much competition (for instance, Britain's nineteenth-century Pax Britannica). In others, the opposition emerges or re-emerges quickly (as in the Dutch-Spanish rivalry of the first half of the seventeenth century or the US-Soviet rivalry of the second half of the twentieth century). The system leader never rules the world. It only has a position of pre-eminence in global political economy for a finite period of time that is geared to the superiority of the techno-economic paradigm and global reach capabilities that provide a platform for a preponderance in affluence and influence.

The Twin Peaks model is not simply an abstract set of generalizations. It has been tested empirically over the past 500 years (Modelski and Thompson, 1996). In the past half-millennium, each successive system leader (Portugal, the Netherlands, Britain, and the United States) pioneered new commercial routes and industrial technology, generating a wave of leading sector growth. Global war followed and in each global war, an incumbent system leader emerged with 50 percent or more of the global system's pool of global reach capabilities (i.e., naval power). Subsequently, the incumbent system leader has pioneered and presided over a second round of leading sector growth. Diagrammatically, figure 2.4 summarizes the basic connections among the principal variables.

---

[18] Posen (2003: 22) advances the concept of "contested zones" or "arenas of conventional combat where weak adversaries have a good chance of doing damage" to intrusive system leaders.

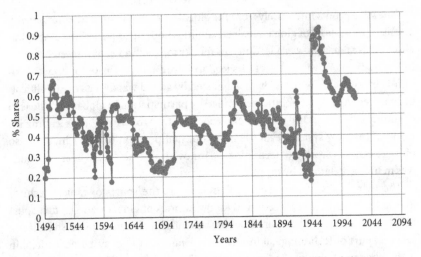

Figure 2.4 System Leader Share of Global Power Projection Capabilities, 1494–2018

Delineating Systemic Leadership Decline

Earlier sections in this chapter have delineated phases of global war bracketed by periods of growth surges in the lead economy. As it happens, the prewar phases also tend to be characterized by an alliance-making scramble among major powers. Old alignments are sometimes dropped, and new ones formed that figure to hold up better in the coming systemic crisis period of global war. The postwar growth surge period is also the one in which the lead economy/global system leader has the best chance to establish an order that best suits its preferences. All that is missing is a phase filling in between the postwar period of world order establishment and the coalition making in preparation for the next round of global war. That phase, labeled one of delegitimization of the order established after the last global war, is specified in table 2.7, which offers a structural calendar of "seasons" of political behavior.

One period is devoted to intensive fighting (1494–1516, 1580–1609, 1688–1714, 1792–1815, and 1914–1945) and the development of new or renewed leadership. The next period is characterized by optimal conditions for engaging in systemic leadership, especially in comparison to the next two periods of relative decline on the part of the system leader. Preparing coalitions for the next round of struggle tends to dominate the second of these phases (1560–1580, 1660–1688, 1763–1792, and 1873–1914).

The phase model doubles as a useful model for explaining the decline of systemic leadership. Figure 2.5 captures this dynamic. Global war leads to a macro

Table 2.7 Systemic Leadership Phases

Global system leader	World power	Delegitimation	Coalition building	Global war
				1494–1516
Portugal	1516–1540	1540–1560	1560–1580	1580–1609
Netherlands	1609–1640	1640–1660	1660–1688	1688–1714
Britain I	1714–1740	1740–1763	1763–1792	1792–1815
Britain II	1815–1850	1850–1873	1873–1914	1914–1945
United States	1945–1973	1973–2015	2015–2050	?

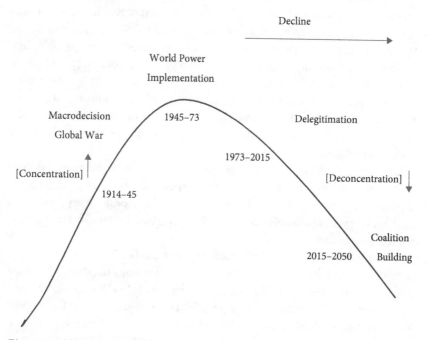

Figure 2.5 Systemic leadership decline

decision about whose preferences win and lose. In the next phase, the global war winners implement their preferred version of world order. By the third phase (delegitimation), the rules and institutions thought to be desirable toward the end of the global war phase no longer correspond very well to the type of global problems surfacing during phase three. For instance, in 1945 the main concerns were to reconstruct Western European and Japanese economies in order to revive the world economy and to discourage interstate conflict through collective security in the United Nations. Trade restrictions were negotiated downward and the International Monetary Fund (IMF) and the World Bank focused on restoring advanced industrial economies. NATO was designed to keep the Soviet Union at bay in Europe. Bilateral arrangements were made in East Asia in hopes of doing something similar to perceived USSR and Chinese ambitions.

Most of these goals were accomplished, although the collective security ambition did not work out as well. The fallback position was peacekeeping. UN troops would serve as buffers in situations in which warring parties no longer wished to engage in combat. In the next phase (delegitimation), the array of state actors was much different due to decolonization, and the nature of major global problems was vastly different as well. The IMF and World Bank switched their mission foci to underdevelopment. The United Nations attempted to intervene in civil wars with peacemaking troops less successfully than had been the case with peacekeeping interventions. Trade restriction negotiations began to run into greater resistance. NATO was transformed at least partially into an insurgency fighting organization operating outside of Europe. In phase four (coalition building), decision makers began to openly question their commitments to traditional coalition alliances, with the US president proving to be the most provocative in questioning the value of NATO. The two main global challengers, China and Russia, seemed to be flirting ever more closely with a formal alliance.

The upshot of figure 2.5 is that relative decline has been underway if deconcentration processes were at work. In some respects, one could argue that deconcentration begins almost from the outset of attaining a peak power position in the world power implementation phase. But it begins to become increasingly evident in phases three and four.

To the extent that the periodization captures the last half-millennium reasonably well and the pattern persists into the future, one can project the phase sequencing into the future. The last global war (1914–1945) was followed by a period of optimal systemic leadership (1945–1973). Various types of challenges to US system leadership were exhibited in the 1973–2015 phase. Coalition maneuvering should be observed in the present period (2015–2050). Some type of intensive conflict might then be anticipated, based on the past 500 years, in the 2050–? phase. However, it need not take the form of a global war along the lines of earlier global wars.[19] Assuming the fear of the implications of using nuclear weapons continues to prevail, something less than an all-out war might occur. But if global war is no longer imaginable and, as will be argued in chapter 8, if it is not clear that technological innovation and energy can be monopolized as it has

---

[19] The Thucydides Trap argument is discussed in chapter 9.

been in the past, it is also not clear that a singular lead economy or systemic leadership as we have observed will be possible either. The central ingredients that have been germane in the last half-millennium are or will be absent in coming years. If this is correct, these missing ingredients will necessitate the development of something novel in future decades. Exactly what novel form will take shape cannot be predicted with great precision, but it is conceivable that what is most probable can be discussed in general terms. That is the focus of chapter 10. Before we take that topic on, much more groundwork needs to be laid. The next two chapters are focused on the rise of the United States to pre-eminence and system leadership.

3

The Rise of the US Economy

The customary approach to accounting for the rise of the United States to global primacy is descriptive, American-centric, and heavily reliant on the distinctiveness of the ascent.[1] Once strictly a producer of raw materials in the world economy, the United States emerged as an increasingly competitive economy in the late nineteenth century and even managed to overtake the world economy's previous leader, Britain, well before 1945. As such, it is one of history's more remarkable illustrations of the possibilities of dependency reversal. Size, location, and resource endowment are often noted as causal factors in this move upward in status. After 1945, though, there was little doubt that the US economy was the world's most advanced center of high technology and manufacturing production. It also emerged in 1945 as the leading political-military actor and the head of a coalition of the most economically advanced states in the world system. Interwoven in the customary story are World Wars I and II—major wars in the late 1910s and early 1940s (from a US perspective). The United States entered the first world war late and had less impact than might otherwise have been the case. At this war's end, the United States is often thought to have retreated from the world stage. That was never the case, but it did enter the second one late as well but had more impact and, thanks in large part to the exhaustion of everyone else, emerged in 1945 as king of the planetary hill. In contrast to what happened after World War I, the United States, after World War II, assumed its pre-eminent role in world politics. More about the military-political side of this ascent is provided in chapter 4. In this chapter, the focus will be exclusively placed on the economic ascent.

---

[1] Parts of this chapter lean heavily on chapter 7 of William R. Thompson and Leila Zakhirova, *Racing to the Top: How Energy Fuels Systemic Leadership in World Politics* (New York: Oxford University Press) and William R. Thompson, "Global War and the Foundation of U.S. Systemic Leadership," in *America, War and Power, 1775–2000*, ed. Lawrence Sondhaus and James Fuller (New York: Routledge, 2017). Examples of quite useful treatments of American ascent and/or war impacts of the twentieth century include Milward (1977), Stein (1978), Kennedy (1980, 1999), Fearon (1987), Ambrose (1988), Higgs (1987), Shaffer (1991), Maddox (1992), Reynolds (1992), Watt (1992), Weigley (1992), Porter (1994), Koistenen (1997, 1998, 2004, 2012), Sherry (1997), Rockoff (1998), Phillips (1999), Zakaria (1999), Zeiger (2001), Katznelson (2002), Kennedy (2004), Mayhew (2005), Saldin (2010), and Pollack (2011). Most of these studies, perhaps except for Stein (1978), stress or seem to assume the uniqueness of the American path. Katznelson (2002), moreover, rightly notes that American political development analyses tend to overlook Gourevitch's (1978) "second image reversed" or the external environment's impact on domestic processes. This propensity further reinforces the exceptional interpretations of the American rise.

American Global Pre-eminence. William R. Thompson, Oxford University Press. © Oxford University Press 2022.
DOI: 10.1093/oso/9780197534663.003.0003

The economic ascent story is causal rather than descriptive, which is to say that the emphasis here is to explain the ascent in terms of the interaction among specific processes—as opposed to what happened decade by decade in the late nineteenth and early twentieth centuries. First, the background or combination of prerequisites for a lead economy must be identified, discussed, and shown to be interactive. Second, one of the more important processes is global warfare. The global war period, however, is 1914–1945. The two world wars that most people designate as occurring in 1914–1918 (or 1917–1918) and 1939–1945 (or 1941–1945) were not really separate wars but early and late phases of a period of systemic crisis. War's effects on development are absolutely crucial to US history but not as a monovariate shock or series of shocks alone. Wars, rather, are nested prominently within a complex of other drivers of change—as will be demonstrated in this chapter.

The ascent story is avowedly systemic-centric. No abstract and external *deus ex machina* caused the US ascent to global primacy to occur. Nor were some Olympian gods rolling dice to see on whom good fortune might fall. Rather, the ascent was the result of a conjuncture of favorable factors, including human agency. Some of these factors were unique to American history but some were not. Global system primacy had been achieved before in ways that paralleled the US ascent. It may or may not be the last time somebody follows this path to the apex of the system either. That is a topic that is explored further in chapter 8.

US economic growth can be differentiated into two overlapping types of processes (Wright, 1990, 1997; Nelson and Wright, 1992). Prior to World War II, the country's emphasis was a conventional amalgamation of innovation, unusually good access to inexpensive raw materials thanks to an extraordinary resource endowment, and a rapidly expanding domestic economy. The development of increasingly powerful and efficient machinery with relatively easy access to coal and petroleum was the hallmark of this era. After World War II, US economic leadership was increasingly based on a science-based technological leadership that focused on laboratory breakthroughs in chemistry and physics.

Figure 3.1 provides a summary overview of the connections among the main parts of this economic ascent story. The top cluster of variables refers to the more conventional contextual or background for ascent. In the absence of these six, or without major changes within their topical boundaries, ascent to the apex of the system would have been most unlikely. Possessing exploitable frontiers, expanding trade, and ample agricultural output, for example, were indispensable ingredients. So, too, were expanding transportation/communication networks, urbanization, and population growth. They established a resource foundation for the seven variables clustered in the bottom section that focus on transformations in business practices, science, technological innovation, and energy transitions.

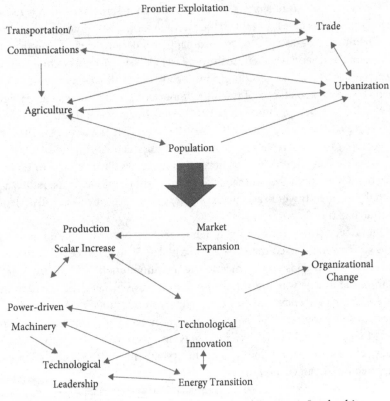

Figure 3.1 Factors Underlying US Technological and Economic Leadership

Without the top cluster, the bottom cluster would have been largely stillborn. Without the bottom cluster, the development of the top group would have been under-realized.

To clarify the model suggested in figure 3.1, some elaboration of the thirteen factors seems desirable. On occasion, some compression of the task at hand can be accomplished by grouping some of the factors—as opposed to dealing with each one separately.

Frontier Exploitation, Population Shifts, and Growth

The American frontier was exceptionally large. Ultimately, the frontier expanded to encompass territory more than nine times the size of the initial thirteen colonies. While the initial impetus was the expansion of agricultural land, it turned out that the land contained energy fuel and minerals that proved vital to late nineteenth- and early twentieth-century industrialization. This advantage was not simply a matter of access; it was also a matter of relative abundance near at hand that led to lower production costs. In 1913, the United States led the world in exploiting supplies of natural gas, petroleum, copper, phosphates, coal, zinc, iron ore, lead, silver, salt, and tungsten (Wright, 1990: 661). It was only the number two producer of gold. What transpired was the gradual diminishment of this raw material production lead. By 1950, the US lead in producing some of the materials was still evident, but it was rapidly diminishing by the 1970s and had vanished altogether by the beginning of the twenty-first century (Barbier, 2011: 485, 567). The new leading producers were former European colonies, now developing states. Access to raw materials had become more expensive and less reliable.

A large, relatively empty space once the original occupants had been removed coercively lured migrants with cheap land. That lure helped make population growth and the size of the domestic market greatly expansive in the nineteenth century. Some considerable portion of that empty space contained good agricultural land. The growing population could be accommodated by an expanding food supply, and as older agrarian areas diminished in productivity, new land could be brought on line.

Military protection costs were minimal thanks to the absence of strong, predatory neighbors and the usual weakness of native American resistance. The West was won largely by private initiatives reinforced by public cavalry units and isolated forts. Meinig (1993: 255) adds that despite the size of the frontier, it was quickly connected to the core by rail in the second half of the nineteenth century. Migrants could reach the frontier fairly easily, and their subsequent food production could also reach global markets.

Agrarian Development

US agriculture initially developed along a bifurcated geographical pattern. In the Northeast and early West (now the eastern portion of the Midwest), farming was carried out mainly by scattered settlers growing enough to feed their own families. Farming technology and the transportation infrastructure for moving farm product to urban markets was primitive prior to the mid-nineteenth century. In the South, subsistence farmers coexisted with plantations growing tobacco and cotton for British markets. The growing demand for cotton textiles produced in Britain was facilitated by the American supply of raw materials and the development of the cotton gin, which made the initial processing of cotton harvesting more efficient and less expensive. Accordingly, cotton dominated the southern region and also provided the principal export for the United States. The

Northeast was linked to the South through its own specialization in shipping and, later, its development of its own textile mills.

With the emergence of suitable farming and transportation innovations, the early US West expanded its specialization in food supply for the urbanizing Northeast. Mechanized plows, reapers, and combines enabled major labor gains and increased supply throughout the nineteenth century and beyond. The supply gains between 1800 and 1920 amounted to a thirty-five-fold expansion, a much higher rate than was associated with population growth. In addition to a greatly expanded surplus, another payoff was the reduced need for farm laborers, thereby releasing these workers for other lines of employment.

The US economy was highly agrarian at the outset of independence, with 80 percent or more of the population engaged in agrarian pursuits of some kind (Vedder, 1976: 227–228). Agriculture improved its supply and efficiency more than enough to feed an expanding population while, at the same time, generating surplus labor that could be enlisted for manufacturing factories. By 1850 the agrarian work force was down to 60 percent of the population, and it had dropped to 40 percent by the end of the nineteenth century. Twenty years later, only 26 percent of the population was linked to producing and moving agrarian products.

Urbanization

Despite the near continuous expansion of the frontier in the nineteenth century, urbanization was accelerated. From 1800 to 1840, the number of people living in cities increased by a factor of six (Hacker, 1970: 103). In the 1850s and 1860s, the numbers nearly doubled again in each decade. One-fourth of the population lived in cities by 1870. These expansions fed ongoing growth in food supply and manufacturing through greater demand which, in turn, increased the demand for labor in the cities. The complementarity of these processes created a virtual spiral of increased demand, supply, and productivity.

The locus of urbanization was initially situated in the Northeast on the Philadelphia-to-Boston axis. New growing cities (Pittsburgh and Chicago) emerged in the Midwest in the second half of the nineteenth century, during which time another Midwestern city, Detroit, expanded and was joined by a Southern city (Atlanta) and four Western cities (Los Angeles, Houston, Dallas, and Seattle). By the last third of the twentieth century, rapid city growth was more likely to be found elsewhere—five of the top ten urban centers were found in eastern Asia. Britain still had five of the top ten in the years 1800–1850 if we count Bombay as British. In the period 1970–2005, only one US city broke into the top ten fastest growing cities, and the prominence of

Washington, DC, is not predicated on economic production (Taylor, Hoyler, and Smith, 2012: 28).

Transportation and Communications

Neither the original colonies nor its population were particularly well connected in 1783. Road construction and river traffic were the mainstay of the first four decades following independence. This emphasis gave way to a then more efficient way to move cargo, namely the canals that simulated rivers. Steamboats were added to the transportation inventory relatively early in the nineteenth century. Railroads, less restrained by geographical obstacles and climate, increasingly took over in the mid-nineteenth century. Hacker (1970: 234) credits the new "iron horses" with stimulating iron, steel, and coal production, the opening of the Western Plains territory, and the facilitation of a national market in goods and services. By moving from iron to steel and increasing speed, US railroad costs came to be much lower than the British pioneers in developing moving steam engines on land.

In the 1860s, US rails, then concentrated in the East-Midwest, constituted half of the world's rail infrastructure. Yet the rail network was to expand sixfold in mileage in the next four decades, largely attaining its maximum size (Atack and Passel, 1994: 429, 432). The scale of this operation, in turn, greatly facilitated the possibility of growing other equally large and national corporations.

Railroads also made good use of the new telegraphs after the 1840s to coordinate and regulate their expanding traffic. Information could be moved quickly over long distances. The initial utility of the telegraph also led to a sequence of important innovations in communications. The telephone was developed to supplant the telegraph, and radio was initially designed to challenge the communications monopoly held by the telephone.[2]

International Trade

Unlike many of the earlier system leaders, US economic leadership was not heavily dependent on trade. Trade was a major consideration in the first half of the nineteenth century, thanks to Southern cotton and American shipping.

---

[2] Something similar took place in the transportation sector. Wagons built to support canals in the first quarter of the nineteenth century were converted to convey settlers throughout the West (Buck, 2015). The standardized parts turned out by wagon factories in the Midwest foreshadowed the later automobile concentration in the Upper Midwest. One wagon factory even morphed directly into an automobile factory (Studebaker).

Gray and Peterson (1974: 161) even nominate it as the key factor in economic development prior to the Civil War because it generated a surplus on which subsequent development could be based and because shipping and commerce provided a later foundation for manufacturing in the northeastern states. But after the Civil War, cotton's significance as the main US cash crop declined, as did the prominence of New England shipping. The advent of steamships had returned the long-distance shipping edge to Britain. Trade, of course, never disappeared, but its role in US economic development diminished.

Technological Innovation, Fuel Innovation, and Power-driven Machinery

Technological innovation, fuel innovation, and power-driven machinery are the core drivers of the first two industrial revolutions. They interacted to radically transform the trajectory of economic development in the modern world. The new technologies, fueled by coal, petroleum, and natural gas, generated new levels of machine power to accomplish a variety of tasks in transportation, communications, and economic production. Klein (2007: 83) captures these effects for US economic growth in the following passage:

> It hastened the settling of the continent, multiplied the productivity of a people short on labor, and became the indispensable engine driving material progress. Between 1870 and 1920 American consumption of energy increased about 440 percent, and its sources changed dramatically. In 1870 wood accounted for about 73 percent of all energy used, with coal supplying nearly all the remainder. By 1920 wood provided less than 8 percent of energy used, coal soared to 73 percent, oil contributed 12 percent, and natural gas chipped in 4 percent. By the 1880s a growing proportion of energy went into producing a new source of power that became the most vital technology of the twentieth century: electricity. Without new sources of power, the industrial revolution would never have occurred. Without plentiful new sources of fuel, the power revolution would have stalled out. (Klein, 2007: 83)

It is sometimes argued that industrial revolution might have been accomplished by relying on traditional fuels. But the number of trees to provide wood for burning and/or the number of animals needed to substitute for machinery in order to attain the levels of horsepower in place by the early twentieth century simply exceed any semblance of reality. By 1920, the forest acreage needed no longer existed. To feed the hundreds of million animals that would have been necessary, more pasturage than was conceivable would have been required. After

1920, the equivalent demand for raw materials and animal power only escalated. Some form of industrialization certainly might have been achieved with traditional sources of power, but the heights of economic growth attained could never have been maintained.

Jones (2014: 73) captures the dilemma succinctly. US energy consumption heated homes and factories, fueled ships and railroads, and smelted iron. In the absence of carbon-based fuels, the US economy might have handled one of these three types of activity, but taking care of all three would have been impossible.

Initially, coal was a useful substitute for the traditional reliance on wood and running water sources of energy—especially where one or both were not readily available. But the abundance and power of coal not only permitted industry to expand geographically, it also facilitated the movement to larger-scale manufacturing and corporations (Licht, 1995: 110; Atack, Bateman, and Margo, 2008: 189). In the late 1890s, US coal consumption exceeded the volume of consumption in the economy that had initiated the industrial revolution a century or more earlier. A quarter of century later, US coal consumption was twice the rate exhibited by the British economy.

New energy sources were fundamental to American economic growth but new applications were also needed. This is where technological innovation came in. In 1860, the top six leading industries in the US economy were cotton goods, lumber sawing, boots and shoes, flour and meal, men's clothing, and machinery. By 1920, the leading industry lineup had changed to machinery, iron and steel, lumber sawing, cotton goods, ship building, and automobiles (Atack and Passel, 1994: 462, 467). Two of the older consumer industries, lumber and cotton goods, were still thriving but they were now embedded in an economy that specialized in producing various kinds of iron and steel machinery.

Switching from cotton goods to machinery as the leading industry does not quite capture the distinctiveness of the transformation in the US economy. Some observers consider the half-century leading up to World War I as the most concentrated surge of economic innovations ever experienced. Smil (2005) lists a number of the representative changes in table 3.1 as evidence of this assertion. It also helps explain the ascent of the US economy into world manufacturing leadership during this period.

Gordon (2016) adopts a stance that overlaps somewhat with Smil's. His temporal emphasis is broader. Innovations before 1870 and after 1970 are asserted to have been less revolutionary than the ones focused on electricity and the internal combustion engine between 1870 and 1970. The initial emphasis of the first industrial revolution stressed the development of steam engine applications. The information technology–intensive third industrial revolution in the last half-century has had an equally narrow impact because of its application to entertainment and communications. The post-1970 innovations have also struggled with

Table 3.1 Smil's Selected List of 1867–1914 Inventions and Innovations

Years	Innovations
1867–1880s	First practical designs of dynamos and open-hearth steel-making furnaces, introduction of dynamite, definite formulation of the second law of thermodynamics, telephones, sound recordings, lightbulbs, practical typewriters, chemical pulp, reinforced concrete
1880s	Reliable incandescent electric lights, electricity-generating plants, electric motors and trains, transformers, steam turbines, gramophone, popular photography, practical gasoline-fueled four-stroke internal combustion engines, motorcycles, cars, aluminum production, crude oil tankers, air-filled rubber tires, first steel-skeleton skyscrapers, pre-stressed concrete
1890s	Diesel engines, X rays, movies, liquefaction of air, wireless telegraph, discover of radioactivity, synthesis of aspirin
1900–1914	Mass-produced cars, the first airplanes, tractors, radio broadcasts, vacuum diodes and triodes, tungsten lightbulbs, neon lights, common use of halftones in printing, stainless steel, hydrogenation of fats, air conditioning, Hammer-Bosch ammonia synthesis for fertilizer.

Source: based on Smil, 2005: 22–25.

other negative changes in the environment (an expanding number of retirees, inequality, and debt, accompanied by a relatively undereducated working force).

Klein (2007: 89–103) and Smil (2013) stress the significance of the shift from steam to electric motors in the late nineteenth and early twentieth centuries. Steam engines transformed production and transportation possibilities in the nineteenth century but they did so with many flaws that could be improved upon. Electric motors were less complex, smaller, less noisy, portable, and less dangerous. But these advantages depended on determining how to convert electricity into mechanical power, how to produce electricity in large quantities, and how to transfer electricity from one place to another. False starts and dead ends had to be dealt with, just as older innovations had to be moved aside (electric trolleys replaced horse-drawn vehicles, and electric lighting replaced gas lighting). The new infrastructure had to be built and extended.

These changes took time (and warfare demands) to be worked out. The percentage of US industry powered by electric motors provides one benchmark: 1899: 4 percent; 1910: 10 percent; 1914: 39 percent; 1918: 50 percent; 1919: 55 percent; and 1929: 75 percent (Schur and Netschert, 1960: 187; Jones, 2014: 287). Residential usage largely paralleled this progression. Between 1908 and 1930, the proportion of US households with access to electricity climbed from 8 percent to 68 percent (Smil, 2013: 51–52). A similarly timed process

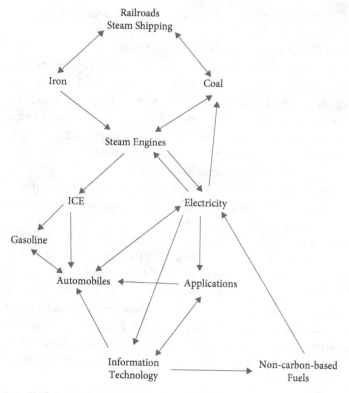

Figure 3.2 Coal, Steam, Iron, ICE, Electricity, and IT

characterized the development of the automobile industry. In 1920, over 8 million autos were operating in the United States compared to fewer than 200,000 in the United Kingdom, the next closest automobile consumer. By 1950, the contrast was over 40 million in the United States and a little over 2 million in the United Kingdom, at that time still the second leading auto consumer. This lead was predicated on early leads in factory electrification, equally early commitments to assembly line production, plentiful access to petroleum, and a large population.

Figure 3.2 sketches the technological/energy trajectory of the US economy over the past two centuries or more. The US economy initially copied the first British industrial block based on coal, iron, and steam engines.[3] It then proceeded to lead the way through the second block configured around electricity, internal combustion engines (ICE), and petroleum. The third development block is now focused on information technologies and, ultimately, non-carbon-based fuels.

---

[3] The development block conceptualizations are found in Kander (2013).

Business and Science Transformations

The trajectory outlined in figure 3.2 can be translated into a three-phase process of American economic preponderance (Smil, 2013). By the end of the nineteenth century, the economic ingredients were in place and expanding/diffusing throughout the economy. The decades leading up to World War I consolidated these innovations. In World War II and the two and a half decades that followed, technological (and energy) dominance was achieved. This dominance was neither inevitable nor unprecedented. It hinged on one lead economy bringing together the critical elements well in advance of the rest of the world. A large population, frontier, and ample resource endowment certainly facilitated and reinforced the emergence of this technological-energy predominance for a finite period.

In conjunction with the technological-energy transformation of the US economy, large firms emerged to cope with the extensive scale of operations associated with manufacturing (table 3.2). Capital had to be raised in ways that required a larger pool of investors than had previously been the case. Administrative complexities encouraged the emergence of professional and specialized managers to replace traditional family dynasties. Vertical integration was encouraged by profit and market control considerations. Horizontal integration was also encouraged until trust busting came into vogue early in the twentieth century.

Expanding the market meant that the large corporations increasingly operated on a multinational scale. Even so, headquarters, management, and profit repatriation tended to remain nation-centric. In sync with the rise of the United States to global leadership, US corporations encountered initially only limited resistance and competition in the aftermath of the second world war. Gradually,

Table 3.2 The Evolving Nature of Firms in the American Economy

Phases	Rough dates
Mercantile/Craft	1840s to 1890s
Factory-based Industrial	1890s to 1940s
Corporate Mass Production	1940s to 1990s
Entrepreneurial, Knowledge-based	1990s to –

Source: Atkinson (2004: 30).

European and Asian competitors emerged or re-emerged. As they did, the predominance of American multinationals also receded.

The US lead in science was very much a third phase phenomenon. University and corporate laboratories came into their own after 1945, although they had been in place since the late nineteenth century. World War II had been a tremendous stimulus and governmental support for research continued after the war ended.

World War II did more than super-organize American production capabilities. Equally significant to this pre-eminence story is the transformational nature of a commitment to basic science that began to emerge just before the United States entered World War II. To solve looming military problems involving technology, the US government constructed a new model that focused on grants to university scientists to work on physics, chemistry, and medical research. From 1940 to 1964, federal funding for research and development increased twentyfold. At its peak in the mid-1960s, this spending amount was around 2 percent of annual gross domestic product—roughly one in every fifty dollars in the United States was devoted to government funding of research and development (equivalent, relative to GDP, to almost $400 billion today). The impact on our economy, on Americans, and on the world was simply transformational (Gruber and Johnson, 2019: 6).

Gruber and Johnson (2019) go on to argue that this scientific transformation was not entirely premeditated. The immediate problem was to respond to military needs such as how to detect incoming bombers or track submarines. The military did not have the technological infrastructure or appropriate personnel to take on the task. Private industry knew how to create new products and improve old products, but these processes tended to rely on applied science and engineering. Basic science and scientists could be found in a few universities, but their labs were greatly underdeveloped and understaffed. The solution was to fund leading public and private universities, hitherto largely devoted to teaching, to expand their research role to better serve the war effort. But in contributing to the war effort, a number of innovations emerged that had initial military applications but also subsequent wider applications—as exemplified by radar, jet engines, transistors, and computers.

At the end of the war, this government-university model might have been retired after having served its immediate purposes. But it was not. Instead, it was expanded in the context of coping with the threat of massive unemployment in a postwar era by the GI Bill, which sent a large number of former soldiers to universities. Skill levels were improved and universities were expanded further, just as federal funding of university research continued to expand to about 1964. A world devastated by intensive war, moreover, had created a fertile demand for American economic products embodying new technology.

Technological Innovation

Taylor (2016: 75–106) suggests five "pillars" for governmental fostering of economic innovation:

1. Create and enforce property rights in science and new technology;
2. Increase research and development subsidies to lower the costs of innovation;
3. Improve formal education in science and technology to increase skills in using, and the demand for, new technology;
4. Encourage science and technology-oriented research universities in which innovations are developed; and
5. Expand international trade in order to expand contacts with foreign ideas, increase competitiveness among domestic firms, and take advantage of production economies of scale.

US participation in World War II and its immediate postwar policies focused on four of the five pillars. The property right pillar was already in place, but even it was later strengthened by postwar legislation. Federal grants and the GI Bill operated like subsidies to research universities, which made them better research platforms as well as contributing to their enrollment expansion. A free trade perspective facilitated the expansion of US exports.[4]

Subject to a substantial lag, the US dominance in Nobel prizes in chemistry and physics became most evident in the late 1960s. In that same decade, the United States had two to three times the per capita number of scientists and engineers at work than other developed economies possessed. Since then, parts of Europe and East Asia have converged on or exceeded the proportional number of US workers in research and development. Spending on research and development still favors the US economy, but convergence in that sphere is also in progress.

These problems have been aggravated by the loss of access to inexpensive energy beginning in the early 1970s. Imported petroleum meant increased costs for industries dependent on it and its derivatives. Industrial responses to the changed raw material environment were less than adequate. Major losses in the critical automobile and steel industries ensued. Other industries pursued

---

[4] Gradually, the once-favorable context for expanding investment in basic research began to sour. Environmental concerns about industrial and nuclear byproducts began to emerge. The Vietnam conflict (1965–1973) was an expensive governmental undertaking for nearly a decade. Political resistance to federal government size and expansion began to increase, leading to increasing polarization between Republicans and Democrats. One of the casualties was publicly funded basic research because it seemed relatively easy to cut. Chapter 6 has more to say about these changes.

cheaper labor costs by moving abroad. Smil (2013) characterizes this fourth, post-1973 stage as one of retreat especially from traditional manufacturing leadership. While fracking has lowered the cost of energy in recent years and encouraged talk of offshore manufacturing, little has materialized in a concrete fashion.

US relative decline is thus a combination of others catching up and US lagging behind its own earlier efforts. As noted, Smil and Gordon converge on the distinctiveness of the special nature of the innovation surge that pushed the US economy into the forefront of the world economy. They disagree, however, about the future, in the sense that Gordon expects slow growth to predominate while Smil does not rule out new innovation surges that could match or exceed the ones introduced in the late nineteenth century. Yet the general point remains that the US ascent was based on an unusually impactful set of innovations that may never be matched again, either in the US economy or elsewhere. These innovations of the late nineteenth and early twentieth centuries have now run their course.

Whether any new surges of innovation can replicate this distinctive feat remains to be seen. It seems conceivable that the interactions between information technology not centered on social media and non-carbon energy could bring about as radical a transformation as we have seen in the past. But these interactions are still very early in their maturation and have yet to overcome the usual vested interest obstacles to radical economic change.[5] Even should these obstacles be overcome eventually, there is also the question of whether any single economy will be able to monopolize the impacts of the new technology and energy for long enough to construct a strong and persistent lead economy. It took decades for part of the world to catch up to those momentous innovations of the late nineteenth and early twentieth centuries. Will it take decades to catch up to the coming changes in information technology applications and new energy sources?

It is difficult to say yes or no to such a question at this point. It is not difficult to be skeptical about the likelihood of one economy getting as far ahead of all the others, as the US economy had done by the mid-twentieth century. The future monopolization of high-tech advantages and non-carbon-based energy fuels seems less likely than in the past. Whatever lies in the future, it should be clear that the US economy is currently struggling with the difficulties of moving from one type of economy to another (see table 3.3.). Its relative decline as a lead economy will continue, at the very least, until it manages to stumble through this transition period. Moreover, getting through the transition period will not guarantee a reversal of relative decline if other large economies are able to make the transition more or less simultaneously.

---

[5] For instance, petroleum and coal producers resist obsolescence, unions resist factory automation, and automobile producers are reluctant to move away from combustion engines.

Table 3.3 The Largest (in Value) Global Companies in 2008 and 2018

Rank	2008 Companies	Founded	Value US billions	2018 Companies	Founded	Value US billions
1	PetroChina	1999	728	Apple	1976	890
2	Exxon	1870	492	Google	1998	768
3	General Electric	1892	358	Microsoft	1975	680
4	China Mobile	1997	344	Amazon	1994	592
5	ICBC	1984	336	Facebook	2004	545
6	Gazprom	1989	332	Tencent	1998	526
7	Microsoft	1975	313	Berkshire	1953	496
8	Royal Dutch Shell	1907	266	Alibaba	1999	488
9	Sinopec	2000	257	Johnson & Johnson	1886	380
10	AT&T	1885	238	J. P. Morgan	1871	375

Source: based on information in Startup Genome (2019: 11).

It is one thing to list a number of factors that contributed to US economic ascent. It is another to accord appropriate weights to the significance of their contribution. One factor—participation in World War II—stands out, however, as a crucible with great significance in turning a growing and wealthy state into something else: a scaled-up powerhouse.

World War II as a Critical Juncture

The crux of the Twin Peaks interpretation (introduced in the last chapter) that situates global war in between two phases of leading sector growth is that ascension to systemic leadership takes place in a very specific context. It does not happen randomly. Nor does it take place in a totally unique manner. The probability of systemic leadership ascension is most probable after a fundamental change in techno-economic paradigms and related acceleration in economic growth has destabilized the world economic, and therefore, the world political pecking order. Global war is likely to ensue as challengers compete for pre-eminence in world politics. The state most likely to ascend to systemic leadership at the end of the global war interval is the state most closely linked to the fundamental and radical innovations in political economy paradigms that are ultimately responsible for destabilizing change.

In the twentieth-century case, radical changes in political economy initially helped create a threat environment that emphasized the potential for systemic leadership transition and replacement. Once this threat/opportunity was in progress and not resolved immediately, we can draw on Porter's (1994: chapter 6) excellent argument that defeat in World War I essentially encouraged or facilitated the emergence of fascism and communism in states attempting to catch up quickly to the more economically developed winners.[6] The takeovers of Russia, Italy, Germany, and, to a lesser extent, Japan by adherents to these formulas for rapid and militarized economic development made the systemic crisis all the more acute. World War II, along with other combat in the interwar years, was the outcome and amounted to a showdown between diametrically opposed approaches to organizing regional and global orders.

The British industrial revolution of the late eighteenth century initiated a sequence of industrial changes that proceeded in multiple waves. The late eighteenth-century revolution focused on changes in the mass production of textiles and iron. The next wave, also British-led, was built around the many implications related to introducing steam engines as a principal source of propulsion. Steel, chemicals, and electricity, beginning in the second half of the nineteenth century, led to the introduction of a new cluster of revolutionary industries in which the United States and Germany were the leading pioneers.

Table 3.4 captures the destabilization implicit to the late nineteenth-century changes in the political-economic sphere. Britain's manufacturing lead was surpassed by the United States in the last two decades of the nineteenth century. Germany, well behind the United States in many respects, had also caught up to the British position by 1913. A long era of Pax Britannica had to give way to some new organizing principle. World Wars I and II were waged to determine who would supply the new organizing rules—the United States or Germany.

The fourth industrial wave was predicated on interchangeable parts and automobile assembly lines as a production mode that revolutionized manufacturing, gas engines that became the new principal source of propulsion, and

---

[6] Minimally, Porter's argument can be read as suggesting that World War I setbacks made it less likely that wartime regimes would survive. More maximally, participation in World War I demonstrated dramatically the need for new strategies in competing with other major powers. "Defeat" in World War I is used elastically. Russia would have been on the winning side if it had avoided or survived its revolution. Russian defeats early in World War I, however, made German-assisted revolution more likely. Italy was also on the winning side, but Italian opinion that none of its war aims had been achieved was widespread. Porter's focus is on the European powers, but the rise of more aggressive regimes in Japan can also be traced to the World War I–intensified perception that Japan required access to Manchurian resources.

Table 3.4 Shares of World Manufacturing Output (%s)

	Britain	United States	Germany	France	Russia	Italy	Austria-Hungary
1880	22.9	14.7	8.5	7.8	7.6	2.5	4.4
1900	18.5	23.6	13.2	6.8	8.8	2.4	4.7
1913	13.6	32.0	14.0	6.1	8.2	2.4	4.4
1928	9.9	39.3	11.6	6.0	5.3	2.7	
1938	10.7	31.4	12.7	4.4	9.0	2.8	

Source: Bairoch (1982: 296).

petroleum as the new central and increasingly primary energy source. These developments are sometimes labeled "Fordist" in honor of the entrepreneur who began assembling Model Ts in Detroit, Michigan, prior to World War I.[7] Unlike the late nineteenth-century innovations in steel and chemistry, the Fordist mass production changes in manufacturing were very much an American development. The automobile itself initially had been a European innovation but one characterized by more traditional craftsmanship.[8] The mass assembly changes in Detroit changed all of that and much more. For instance, it gave the United States a pioneering monopoly in the early twentieth-century's best-practice manufacturing technology, as suggested by the American lead in motor vehicle production reproduced in table 3.5. Equally impressive is the increase in production volume. Automobile output increased by more than a factor of ten between 1910 and 1920. Between 1940 and 1950, it almost doubled.[9] The success of the Model T also virtually ended the experimentation going on in different modes of automobile propulsion. Steam

[7] Naturally, the radical technological changes that were introduced in the early twentieth century were not the work of a single individual. Nor was Henry Ford necessarily directly responsible for the idea of the assembly line. But the Ford Motor Company did produce Model T's and they were the initial products of the new age of manufacture.

[8] Womack, Jones, and Roos (1990: 21–24) spend several pages describing the classical craft production system approach to automobile construction, which involved highly skilled specialists fitting non-standardized parts together one vehicle at a time relatively slowly and at high expense. Mass assembly of standardized parts simplified construction tasks, which, in turn, accelerated the process, facilitated the use of less skilled labor, permitted much greater production volume, and lowered costs as volume increased. These payoffs, of course, were not restricted to automobile production alone.

[9] Equally difficult to avoid is the diffusion of the Detroit assembly line to other advanced economies. Between 1960 and 1970, US automobile firms continued to produce about the same number of vehicles annually, but their share of world production had dropped dramatically. Table 3.5 understates the extent of contemporary diffusion by ignoring South Korean and Chinese auto production.

Table 3.5 Automobile Production in the Big Five Economies and China (Thousands)

	United States	Japan	France	Germany	United Kingdom	Total	China
1900	4.1						
1910	181			9.4			
1920	1906 (94.4%)		41		71	2018	
1930	2787 (86.3%)		194	77	170	3228	
1940	3717 (83.0%)	1.6	182	275	305	4481	
1950	6666 (86.9%)	1.6	257	219	523	7667	
1960	6675 (87.1%)	165	1136	1817	1353	11146	
1970	6547 (37.7%)	3179	2458	3529	1641	17354	
1980	6400 (29.9%)	7038	3488	3530	924	21380	
1990	6078 (25.3%)	9948	3293	4634	1302	25255	81*
2000	5542 (22.9%)	8359	2880	5132	1642	23555	605
2010	2731 (8.1%)	8311	1924	5552	1270	19788	13897
2020	1927 (5.6%)	6960	928	3515	921	14251	19994

*1991 data; U.S. share is based on "total" + China production.

Source: Mitchell (2003a, 2003b, 2003c); 2000 and 2010 information was obtained from the International Organization of Motor Vehicle Manufacturers at oica.net/category/production-statis-tics/2020-statistics/.

and electricity-based alternatives lost to the gasoline engines placed in Ford automobiles, thereby further reinforcing the twentieth century's gradually growing dependency on petroleum.

The control of appropriate energy sources is critical to this story. New technology does not always require new energy sources, but there is some probability of shifts in the need for more potent fuels. Global commercial expansion in the fifteenth through eighteenth centuries relied on sail power (along with gunpowder) to create Portuguese, Dutch, and English monopolies. Coal, abundantly available in Britain, fueled the steam power age. Not coincidentally, the United States began its ascent as one of the principal suppliers of petroleum.

War was extremely influential in this process. American discoveries in Pennsylvania immediately prior to the outbreak of the Civil War proved timely when Confederate maritime raiders were able to damage the Northern whaling fleets and reduce an important source of oil for lighting purposes. Electricity might have made oil much less significant if it had not been for the fortuitous emergence of gasoline engines in the late nineteenth century. Navies had begun converting to petroleum as their principal propulsion fuel for battleships prior to World War I but the first world war accelerated the wartime demand for petroleum in a number of ways. Navies had discovered that they could build bigger ships that were capable of staying at sea longer, more capable of being refueled, and able to travel longer distances if they switched from steam engines to gasoline/diesel engine and to petroleum over coal. Trucks (and even French taxicabs) became critical for supplying and ferrying troops during wartime. Gasoline-powered tanks were introduced as mechanized ways to break through stalemated front lines. Planes, initially used for scouting purposes, became fighters and bombers. All these new military fighting platforms depended on various types of gasoline engines. As they developed into the central weapon platforms of the twentieth century, access to the fuel that drove them added compelling national security incentives to the increasing industrial reliance on petroleum and petrochemicals.

But the predominant US role in oil production/distribution in the American Century was not simply a function of fortunate geological circumstances. It was an outcome that was strongly influenced by deliberate corporate and governmental strategies. Part of the US ascent to systemic leadership consisted of wresting away control over non-American oil from the preceding system leader, Britain, especially in the Middle East. Table 3.6 suggests that predominant US corporate control in non-American areas had not been achieved completely by the beginning of World War II. British and Dutch firms (note that the Netherlands was Britain's predecessor as system leader) still controlled most of the oil in the Middle East and Southeast Asia. Yet within a few years of the close of World War II, US firms, as summarized in table 3.7, were in control of a majority share of non-US/Soviet oil production.

This outcome is similar in significance to the estimate (Adshead, 1993) that the Mongols controlled over 50 percent of the world's horses in the early thirteenth century CE. Both the Mongols and the United States, for a time

Table 3.6 Control of Key Producing Areas outside the United States (%)

		Western Hemisphere	Middle East	Far East
1929	United States	58		5
	Britain/Netherlands	39	100	90
	Others	3		5
1939	United States	48	16	19
	Britain/Netherlands	36	78	73
	Others	16	6	8

Source: based on Shaffer (1983: 68).

Table 3.7 Acquisition of Control of Key Producing Areas outside the US and USSR (%)

	1938	1945	1953
United States	33	41	53
Britain/Netherlands	53	41	33
Others	14	18	14

Source: Schneider (1983: 36).

and in their respective eras, dominated the key to military propulsion. The United States went the Mongols one better by also controlling the production and/or distribution of what was to become the main industrial energy source of the twentieth century. The importance of this factor in the rise of the US economy as the system's lead economy is strongly hinted at in table 3.8, which records the ascent of US direct foreign investment (DFI) in petroleum-related assets. Table 3.8 cannot be read as a summary of petroleum's share of DFI, but it does underline the weight of petroleum investments abroad in establishing economic leadership in a techno-economic era heavily reliant on oil.

Another way of underscoring the importance of Fordist assembly lines, gasoline engines, and petroleum as the core package for economic ascent is provided by table 3.9's list of World War II war material production. One interpretation is that the US-led coalition won World War II because it was in a position to

Table 3.8 Percent Changes in US Direct Foreign Investment by Industry

1897–1914		1919–1935		1946–1970	
Other*	796	Utilities	688	**Petroleum**	1450
Utilities	504	Manufacturing	135	Manufacturing	1246
Mining/smelting	437	**Petroleum**	129	Other***	1114
Manufacturing	408	Other*	44	Trade	1000
Agriculture/timber	362	Mining/smelting	39	Mining/smelting	675
Petroleum	304	Sales	34	Public utilities	123
Sales**	198				
Railroads	77				

* mainly banks and insurance; ** excludes petroleum; *** includes sales organization and agriculture
Sources: Shaffer (1983: 36, 70, 83); Lewis (1938: 579, 588, 605); Wilkins (1970: 110; 1974: 329).

outproduce the opposing coalition.[10] We do not need to adopt this interpretation exclusive of other factors to recognize that the Allied victory was certainly facilitated mightily by the very strong Allied material advantage. If World War I fighting introduced petroleum-powered fighting platforms (tanks, battleships, and planes), World War II fighting was heavily dependent on these vehicles. The Allied side consumed twenty times the crude oil available to the Axis powers. One of the reasons is that the Allied side produced six times the number of military trucks, four times the number of tanks/self-propelled guns, and three times the number of combat planes.

The fourth column in table 3.9 calculates the US production share of this war material advantage. The US economy clearly did not generate all the war materials for its side and in some categories (tanks/self-propelled guns and artillery) was not even the leading producer. But the United States did contribute nearly 80 percent of the petroleum and military trucks, as well as about half of the aircraft. The rapid production of shipping was another US specialty. Since a respectable proportion of the non-petroleum US material contribution was generated via converted automobile factories using assembly line techniques, it follows that much of the "arsenal of democracy" was predicated on the same

[10] This debate about who or what won World War II is likely to go on indefinitely. An argument that supports the production interpretation is O'Brien (2015). Harrison (2016) is a balanced argument that contends that Russian infantry and Western air-sea production cannot be viewed in isolation. If one of the two factors had been absent, the war would probably have dragged on longer than it did.

Table 3.9 The Selective Production of War Materials, 1939–1945

	Axis	Allied	USA %
Coal	2624.9	4283.6	50.2
Iron ore	266.1	591.1	67.1
Crude steel	191.8	497.1	67.3
Aluminum	2503.3	4642.7	88.8
Crude oil	50.45	1043.0	79.9
Tanks/self-propelled guns	51845	227235	38.9
Artillery	179694	914682	28.1
Military trucks	594859	3060354	77.8
Military aircraft			
Combat	145584	417219	47.4
Trainers	28516	103578	55.6
Transport	4897	43045	55.6

Source: based on Ellis (1990: statistical appendix, 157).

Fordist-petroleum foundation that rocketed the US economy to its position of world pre-eminence.

Winning the 1939–1945 combat is definitely a part of the US ascent story. One does not have to denigrate the Soviet contribution on land to the World War II outcome to acknowledge US leadership in the planning, coordination, and supplying of the Allied side. If the Allies had not won World War II, US pre-eminence might have been restricted to the Americas at best. With the Allied victory over what may have been the last coercive attempt to unify Western Europe, US pre-eminence, reinforced by the very efforts to transform the American economy to provide an economic platform for victory, was guaranteed throughout what became known as the "free world." That systemic leadership after 1945 failed to encompass the entire planet is hardly surprising given the evolutionary trajectory of this form of global predominance.

In the early 1500s, Portugal, the first global system leader, managed to control parts of South America, some African coastline, and parts of the Indian Ocean, with other scattered bases in southeast and east Asia. The Dutch and British system leaders managed to build on this foundation and extend it in subsequent centuries, but there have always been areas beyond the reach (and often the interest) of global leaders primarily concerned with commerce. US systemic leadership has been more focused on industrial production than the Portuguese, Dutch, and first British eras but its geopolitical concerns with the defense of Western Europe, the "rimland" of Eurasia, and problem areas in Africa and Latin America would not have seemed all that remarkable to decision makers in earlier system leaders. They fretted about the same areas as sources of global policy problems.

What do these changes add up to? We have radical political-economic changes being wrought by major economic innovations. Their political-military implications alter the major power threat environment by creating an opportunity for systemic leadership transition that is traditionally fused with efforts to establish regional hegemony in Europe. Two of the most intensive wars ever fought, thanks in part to the new technology, were waged to decide the leadership succession issue. In the process, major power military organization and weaponry were organized around weapons platforms that reflected the technological changes (battleships, aircraft carriers, submarines, tanks, fighters, and bombers).[11] That is another way of saying that political-economic changes encouraged co-evolution in the threat environment, war, military organization, and weaponry. Only political organization seems omitted in this model.

That is an oversight that is easily remedied. Prior to the twentieth century, the US government was typically characterized as a federal system with a weak center. There were occasional lapses, as in the American Civil War, but, in general, the federal government reigned but did not rule the American political system. The co-evolutionary changes of the twentieth century changed all that. The US central government expanded in size and political clout primarily as a function of its wartime participation. The basic pattern was the well-known ratchet effect in which spending and personnel numbers go up and, later, do not return to their earlier levels. Political systems engaged in war must mobilize resources and personnel. The more intensive the war participation, the greater is the demand for resources and personnel. Governmental intervention and coordination of the war effort, as a consequence, is all the greater and more essential. Moreover, technological changes scope and range, and more civilian participation in the war effort (both in factories and as military targets).

Once the war fighting had ended, some movement back to prewar conditions was feasible, but it was unlikely that the prewar status quo would be regained. In the US case, federal revenues more than quadrupled between 1910 and 1920,

---

[11]   Military organization agents first choose which weapons platforms they feel will be most efficacious for their mission. Once chosen, however, the weapons platforms will influence the organization of the military services. This effect is seen in the ascendancy and decline of groups within each military organization (e.g., tank versus infantry commanders in the Army, bomber versus fighter pilots in the Air Force, and battleship versus aircraft carrier versus submarine commanders in the Navy). Much the same can be said about doctrine and strategy.

before declining to a level roughly triple the 1910 level by 1930 (see table 3.8). Between 1940 and 1950, federal revenues increased by a factor of six and never returned to anything resembling pre–World War II levels. Lest these numbers be dismissed as ignoring inflation, which also tends to ratchet upward in wartime situations, table 3.10 also reports data on public debt per capita and number of military personnel. Public debt, a device innovated by earlier system leaders to pay for global wars, expanded on a per capita basis by a factor of nineteen during World War I. World War II brought about another fivefold increase. Standing military personnel almost tripled as a result of World War I. The increase between 1940 and 1950 was closer to a quadrupling. In the case of this indicator of governmental size, the Cold War ensured that the numbers began to rise again after initially retrenching from the heights of 1945.

Prior to World War I, local and state governmental revenues claimed most governmental financial extractions. World War I almost created a 50:50 situation, but only temporarily. Depression, a second world war, and the ensuing Cold War permanently changed the federal role in the US political system.[12] The greatly increased centralization of the federal government was of course highly convenient for a state in a position to assume systemic leadership.

Table 3.10 The Expansion of the US Central Government

	Federal revenues	Public debt per capita	Military personnel (thousands)
1900	$653	$16.60	125.9
1910	962	12.41	139.3
1920	4261	228.23	343.3
1930	2634	131.51	255.6
1940	7000	325.23	458.4
1945			12123.5
1950	43527	1696.67	1460.3
1960	99800	1584.70	2476.4
1970	205562	1811.12	3066.3

Source: US Department of Commerce (1975).

[12] In this perspective, the world depression of the 1930s was a function of the intermittent introduction of new technology. Each new wave of technological change requires greater or lesser adaptations. The more difficult the transition from one wave to the next, the deeper is the downturn in economic growth (i.e., depression).

But it was not just the federal government that became more centralized. Within the federal layer, the division of power among the three nominally equal main branches had also been altered. War and crisis had brought about what Schlesinger (1989, 2004) has termed the Imperial Presidency—or a centralization of political power within the executive branch vis-à-vis Congress and the Supreme Court.[13] Schlesinger's argument has an attractive evolutionary flavor. If the original constitutional system created a web of checks and balances on the three branches of the federal center, the likely outcome was governmental stalemate unless one branch seized the initiative. Crises and external threat favored the presidency becoming the supreme branch because the executive branch could claim to be the best informed and was most prepared to act coercively in response to perceived attacks or opportunities. Thus, the more acute the sense of external threat, the greater is the power of the presidency.

Although Schlesinger does not use the ratchet metaphor, it seems as appropriate here as it did in reference to revenues, debt, and military size. Between the American Civil War and immediately prior to World War I, the US federal government is usually characterized as congressionally centered. Foreign (and domestic) policy problems in the twentieth century have swung the central governmental role toward the office of the president. This movement has not been inexorable. Crises come and go creating opportunities for greater congressional influence in "the troughs" of relative tranquility. But each successive twentieth-century crisis further expanded the powers of the presidency to the extent that it has become difficult to expect much in the way of genuine checks and balances in the US federal government—especially when it comes to dealing with crises and threats.

Conclusion

The argument that has been advanced here is that the ascent of the United States to world pre-eminence is not as exceptional as is often imagined. That the ascent of the United States marked a major sea change in world politics is without question. How it came about is a more controversial issue that, no doubt, will continue to be debated from different perspectives. The perspective adopted here is that the Twin Peaks model, based on a leadership long-cycle reading of the past millennium's developments, and with the assistance of an auxiliary,

---

[13] The argument and outcome were predicted by de Tocqueville (1969: 126) when he wrote: "If the Union's existence were constantly menaced, and if its great interests were continually interwoven with those of other powerful nations, one would see the prestige of the executive growing, because of what was expected from it and what it did."

co-evolutionary process interpretation, is quite capable of constructing a strong explanation of what transpired—and why things worked the way they did.

Fundamental change in the political economy sphere led to long-term economic growth and destabilization of the world's political hierarchy. A new threat environment emerged that was focused on the dangers associated with systemic leadership transition, and subsequently compounded by fascist and communist strategies and political takeovers in some major powers. Global war ensued. Military organizations and weaponry were transformed to correspond to the assembly-line/gasoline engine/petroleum-related technological changes that were radically modifying the way things worked in the twentieth century. Political organizations were also transformed to better correspond to the new times. Winning World War II set the stage for a new round of techno-economic change—one in which much of Western Europe was allowed to catch up to the US lead in a number of respects. The stage was also set for the next paradigmatic shift tied to information technology that became most evident toward the end of the twentieth century, even though its main carrier, the computer, first emerged in World War II. mid these changes, the state that was most responsible for introducing the radical innovations underlying the technological changes benefited most. Its economy expanded greatly and became more advanced than any other economy for a time. For better or worse, its political system became more centralized and more capable of acting on the world stage. It not only made money in waging global wars, but it used its material advantages to finance, supply, and increasingly coordinate victorious coalition warfare. Winning the global war made it likely that its own preferences (as opposed to the preferences of the losing side) would be pre-eminent in the postwar era. Finally, it was the superiority of its economic technology and global reach that conferred systemic leadership on the United States and not the context of general exhaustion on the part of friends and foes alike—although this certainly did not hurt. It also helped that US elites were more prepared to accept this role in the 1940s than they had been in the 1920s.[14] All things considered, the Twin Peaks story appears to work well as a guide to these structural changes.

Throughout American history, war figures prominently as a shaper and driver of change (Shefter, 2002; Anderson and Cayton, 2005). This generalization holds equally well in the first half of the twentieth century as it does for earlier periods. Yet war does not take place in a vacuum. Wars are embedded in fields of political, economic, and military processes. Wars are made more (or less) probable by other political, economic, and military factors that may be in flux. In turn, wars may also reinforce the direction taken by the larger complex of interrelated

---

[14] Generational changes is one of several processes that we have not yet integrated very well with other factors such as war and technological change.

changes that are underway. There is no reason to take away from the significance of war-induced changes—a generally under-recognized process in its own right—in suggesting that wars are part of a larger explanatory package. At the same time, wars, and especially World War II in the case of the US economic ascent, are hardly minor factors in the bigger picture.

Nor is the impact of World War II restricted to economic ascent. The next chapter focuses on its parallel role in vaulting the United States into a diplomatic and military-political move to first place. Indeed, the advent of system leadership is hard to imagine in the absence of a destructive and intensive global war.

4

Structure, Agency, and Grand Strategy

Why did the United States not assume a more internationalist stance and pre-eminent leadership role after World War I but did do so after World War II?[1] In a field often characterized as lacking in theory, we have multiple theories about this event. Legro's (2005) answer is that policymakers were disillusioned by the aftermath of World War I and reverted to more isolationist policies until the perceived external threats became too great to ignore in the late 1930s. Narizny (2007) argues that new strategies reflect changes in preference and influence of economic sectors. Southern farmers wanted a stable, peaceful Europe while New England/Midwestern manufacturers were more interested initially in do-mestic market expansion and then peripheral intervention, not European core concerns. Gradually that changed as European markets became more important to manufacturing exports. Braumoeller (2012) contends that US popular interest in Europe was geared to the perceived threat to the international distribution of power. The German threat in the 1930s was easier to downplay before the fall of France. As the German threat came to be perceived as greater, the US response, appropriately, was increasingly in favor of doing something about it.

There were definitely changes in strategic approaches, perceived threats, and export expansion but none of these explanations, singularly or combined, fully explains the transformation in the United States' positional shift from a poten-tially powerful if somewhat aloof state to the most powerful and central state in the system. One reason for the incomplete explanation is that most of the theo-ries that take on this question "normalize" the United States' shift for theoretical reasons. They treat it as a movement from a form of isolationism to greater in-ternationalism. That kind of approach reduces to asking why the United States became more actively interested in the outside world after 1945 than before. It is a perfectly reasonable approach if one's theory is geared to explaining national movements on an isolationist-internationalist continuum. Such an approach, however, falls short of capturing what was at stake in the US shift. It is like asking why do some children stay relatively marginal to recess fun and games while others are quite active? The United States shifted from relatively marginal to

---

[1] This chapter first appeared as William R. Thompson, "The 1920–1945 Shift in U.S. Foreign Policy Orientation: Theory, Grand Strategies and Systemic Leader Ascents," *Foreign Policy Analysis* 12, no. 4 (2016): 512–532.

American Global Pre-eminence. William R. Thompson, Oxford University Press. © Oxford University Press 2022.
DOI: 10.1093/oso/9780197534663.003.0004

not only quite active but also became the center of free world "fun and games." Explaining a new orientation to greater activity for a center of the universe is a bit different from accounting for why some children become more extroverted and popular on the playground.

A second reason for disappointment in the types of explanations produced has to do with the state of agent-structure disputes. Explanations in international relations have come to appreciate very greatly the role of agents as significant causal mechanisms. Lip service is paid to the interactions between agents and structure, but only agents are viewed as making things happen. Structures at best and often somewhat obscurely constrain agential behavior. Consequently, if one does not privilege agents in an explanation, as most analysts argue now, there is in fact no explanation—or at least, no satisfactory causal mechanism.

Both problems suggest the need for a greater appreciation for structure. Contemporary analysts have largely discarded structure to highlight the role of agents. But there is no parallel need to throw agents out with the proverbial bath-water in order to better highlight the role of structure. Agents and structures do interact, and our theories should reflect that reciprocal interaction more than they do. An alternate answer to the rise of the United States to systemic leader-ship question, then, is that the structural ingredients that had come together by the early 1940s were not yet in place as of 1919–1920. The United States was a sig-nificant actor in 1919–1920. By 1945, it was the most significant actor. It seems rather difficult to overlook this remarkable structural shift in accounting for a changed US approach to world politics. Might the United States have withdrawn from global centrality after 1945? The answer is yes, but structural changes had made the retreat from centrality far less likely in 1945 than had been the case in 1920. Put another way, there was less to retreat from in 1920 than there was in 1945. Or, if one prefers, the structural constraints were much greater in 1945 than they were in 1920.

It is of course one thing to criticize extant theories for missing an important variable. It is another to make the case for including it and then demonstrating how it might be included. The three theories being used as illustrative stalking horses are first outlined and then subjected to critique with an emphasis on how each one treats structure. A fourth theory is then advanced that allows a greater explicit role for structure.

Legro's Theory and the 1920–1945 Puzzle

In its most basic form, Legro (2005) contends that events happen, and pre-vailing ideas are either found to fit or not. When ideas no longer seem to apply, there is some potential for change. Legro envisions three basic strategies for a country to relate itself to the rest of the world.[2] States can embrace the outside world (integration), remain aloof (isolationism), or attempt to change it radically in some way (revisionism). Movement toward or away from one of these positions involves a two-step process. Shocks create opportunities for change in prevailing collective ideas but hardly guarantee that new ideas will be adopted. If the prevailing idea is found to be less than adequate, its appeal should collapse. A second phase of consolidation around some new collective idea should then take place. If the consolidation effort fails because no single alternative is articulated or adopted, the old orthodoxy is likely to re-emerge as the default option.

The first phase of collapse hinges on an interaction between expectations and outcomes. If the prevailing idea predicts a strategy that works or suggests that a deviation from strategic orthodoxy is likely to fail that then does fail, we should anticipate the survival of the prevailing collective idea. Even if there is a deviation from orthodoxy that is successful, no collapse is probable because the legitimacy of the older idea(s) is unlikely to be challenged sufficiently. Only when decision makers adhere to the prevailing prescribed strategy and fail is there some potential for collapse and a search for new strategies.

In the second stage of consolidation, the absence of any acceptable substitutes or a plethora of them, none of which gains much support, is likely to default to the previously prevailing strategy. Default may also occur if the new strategy does not appear to work very well. Consolidation around a new strategy is predicted only if some alternative gains enough support and seems to work well.

Thus, new grand strategies are thought to depend on a combination of external shock that alters the policy environment, recognition of the failure of the prevailing strategy, rallying around a new strategy, and the perceived success of the new strategy. Otherwise, little in the way of ideational change is anticipated. Inertia should prevail in the absence of factors overriding it.

Power and strategic circumstances play a vague, auxiliary role in possibly influencing perceptions about whether old or new strategies are succeeding. For instance, a state may be encountering failure or success because it possesses or does not possess enough capabilities to achieve its goals. Interest groups influence the number and success of replacement strategies in the consolidation phase. They focus criticism on prevailing ideas that do not seem to be working

---

[2] For Legro, grand strategy is a collective idea about the most effective approach to gaining the ends in which states are most interested. He borrows a railroad metaphor from Weber in which ideas function like the switchmen who direct trains in various directions by altering the tracks they utilize. In doing so, they send a train in one direction and preclude various other alternative paths.

and mobilize support for the consolidation of new ideas. In other words, relative power and interest groups are spear carriers in an opera focused on shocks and ideas as the diva performers.

One of the tests of his grand strategy theory focused on the 1920–1945 puzzle. Legro asks why did the United States refuse to lead, or even follow, after World War I despite its dominance in the international hierarchy only to embrace alliances and international institutions after World War II? His answer is that the American entry into World War I had defied the prevailing strategic consensus to avoid European entanglements and decision makers had little to show for their actions. The probability was that American decision makers would revert to their previous strategic position that had counseled against more internationalist behavior. By the early 1940s, however, the strategic environment had changed sufficiently such that more isolationistic policies no longer were viewed as appropriate. A pronounced internationalist stance led to victory in World War II and was maintained in the postwar environment.

His test hinges on when US decision makers gravitated toward an altered stance to external behavior. Focusing primarily on annual presidential State of the Union messages, Legro finds recognition of a changing political environment and the role of the United States in it prior to World War I. But there were clear taboos on becoming involved in European affairs other than commercial transactions. Some of this discourse changed toward the end of World War I, but only temporarily. Thus, there is some oscillation between isolationism and accepting the need for military alliances (about halfway on the isolationism-multilateralism scale) between the early 1900s and the outbreak of World War II. Only in the late 1930s is a consistent trend toward greater US integration/external activity manifested. The trend continues through the war years and culminates in a persistent commitment to multilateralism at the top of the scale at the end of the war.[3]

Legro uses this evidence to buttress several points. One is that there were a number of occasions at which shocks (World War I, Great Depression, and the Cold War) and changing relative power positions (or structural changes in domestic politics) might have been expected to lead to some changed stance toward external commitments. Yet only the lead-up to, and the participation in, World War II appears to have had a discernible impact of some duration. Legro views this outcome as strong reinforcement for his theoretical expectation that change is contingent on shocks plus some evaluation of the fit between outcome and ideational prescription/proscription.

---

[3] Busby and Monten (2008: 462) have updated the series to 2006 and show some gradual movement away from the peak in the early 1950s, with the lowest scores in the Bush II years.

Narizny's Theory and the 1920–1945 Puzzle

Narizny's (2007) theory aims to take on the peculiar analytical insistence on unitary actors pursuing national interests in security studies when the rest of political science is more likely to focus on efforts to capture the state in the pursuit of activating policy preferences. Narizny first narrows his focus to three types of sectoral groups identified primarily by the nature of their relationship to the international economy. There are groups with no linkages to the outside (labeled "domestic"), groups that depend on exports to or investments in the great powers ("core"), groups that profit from trade and investments in the periphery, and groups (bureaucrats, military, defense firms) that depend on governmental spending ("military-colonial").

Domestic interest groups have no interest in the world economy and opt for isolationism. Core interest groups prefer to avoid major power frictions and promote treaties, international law, and internationalism. Peripheral interest groups are not interested in internationalism but are willing to entertain the selective use of intervention and imperialism in the periphery. Military-colonial interests should be supportive of whatever strategy promises to maximize governmental spending.

Since sectoral groups have different preferences for identifying national interests and developing grand strategy, they choose to support politicians who adhere to their preferences. When those politicians become decision makers, their grand strategy inclinations have already been formed prior to the ascent to national office. Changes in national grand strategy thus depend on changes in the nature of the coalitions, electoral or otherwise, who capture control of the government.

There are caveats to this straightforward process. Domestic constraints, such as heavy national debt, recession, or monetary instability, work to inhibit international commitments and hard-line stances. Political coalitions are often not pure representations of one sectoral group and may reflect some intra-coalitional contestation over whose preferences will predominate. Once in power, they may be forced to compromise with other coalitions from time to time. Coalitions may also back political leaders whose views are not fully known or who only approximate their preferences. Political leaders may even change their minds once in office if circumstances are altered greatly. But if one grants too much leeway to these various qualifications, the theory will collapse. Thus, it makes more sense to expect leaders to follow the preferences of the coalitions that supported their ascent to office.

Within this framework, almost a century (1865–1941) of American foreign policy orientation reduces to a running conflict between Southern farmers and Northeastern manufacturers. The South produced cotton that was sold in Europe.

Therefore, they preferred core stability and internationalism. Manufacturers initially were focused solely on domestic markets until the 1880–1890s and therefore isolationist. Increased exports and investments in the non-European periphery moved the Northeast toward selective interventionism and greater rivalry with European great powers toward the end of the nineteenth century.

Democrats, anchored in the south, stood for internationalism and advocated that their presidents should also be internationalists. Republicans, strongest in New England and the Midwest, gradually moved from isolationist tendencies toward non-European intervention and a willingness to compete for markets with European powers. After World War I, a highly internationalist, Democratic president (Woodrow Wilson) was thwarted by a Republican Senate that wanted to avoid internationalist commitments in Europe. In the run-up to US involvement in World War II, a more cautious internationalist and Democratic president (Franklin D. Roosevelt) pushed for US participation in the European warfare despite considerable domestic opposition. After Pearl Harbor and Hitler's declaration of war, isolationist resistance was easily overcome.

Braumoeller's Theory and the 1920–1945 Puzzle

Braumoeller (2012) wants a theory that privileges neither "systemic top" nor "individuals bottom" but integrates their interactions while also providing an analytical microfoundation for explaining international politics. He starts with constituency worldviews and preferences. Any state has a constituency—those individuals who have some capability to pressure governmental decision makers—and they have worldviews that generate interests and preferences. Constituencies use their interests and preferences to interpret the state of the external system and to demand political action from their own governments. The heart of the argument is that

> The further the present structure of the system is from the state's ideal point and the greater the salience of the issue, the greater the constituents' level of dissatisfaction, and the greater their desire for action to redress the present situation. (Braumoeller, 2012: 40)

Constituency demands are registered by governmental leaders who proceed to act on them. Whether they are successful depends on the resources leaders can access and what other states choose to do. The activities and interactions of leaders change the structure of the system. Constituents evaluate the new system and may make more demands of their leaders. So, the basic sequence is that readings of the international structure generates dissatisfaction → constituencies demand their leaders do something to improve the external system → leader responses in different states → systemic structural change → constituent dissatisfaction and demands based on the revised system. The greater the issue salience and status quo dissatisfaction, the more likely it is that governments will respond to the demands. Whether their activities change the international structure depends in turn on the scale of activity, the capabilities of the states involved, and, again, the salience of issue and how much dissatisfaction with the status quo exists.

One of Braumoeller's tests is a brief case study of the end of US isolationism. His interpretation stresses the largely noninterventionist popular opinion prior to mid-1940. Depending on how the question was posed in opinion surveys, popular support for intervention in Europe or even aiding France and Britain remained below one-third of the people surveyed into the summer of 1940. Once France surrendered in August, the support for intervention or assistance (mainly the latter) doubled well in advance of Pearl Harbor. Great popular support was matched by increased US government activity to expand its defense spending. Defense appropriations for 1941 were six times the size of the spending in 1940. A peacetime draft, lend-lease, and other forms of cooperation with Britain followed quickly. Although no state of war between the United States and Germany was declared until later, German submarines had begun sinking American shipping by May 1941 and US ships were assisting British naval operations in the Atlantic.

Braumoeller points out that this response to an increased German threat did not stem from domestic changes in political power, interests, or preferences. Rather, it was a response to increased systemic threat. Early German military successes changed the distribution of power, and its radical ideas and defeat of democracies challenged the distribution of ideological preferences. The US response to the shock was a decidedly abrupt shift from isolationism to a belligerent form of internationalism as it became involved in an undeclared war. Vindicating his theory, constituents responded "in a very straightforward way to the stimuli provided by the system by demanding action in proportion to their dissatisfaction" (Braumoeller, 2012: 42).

Evaluating the Three Arguments

This is not the place to focus in any detail on one or more of the three arguments. Space does not permit it, and it would not serve the immediate purpose of this chapter. Suffice it to say that, collectively, their arguments underscore some problems encountered in addressing the 1920–1945 puzzle. But it should also be noted that none of the three are attempting to explain systemic leadership ascent per se. Legro seeks to understand ideational shifts as decision makers abandon one grand strategy for another. Narizny wants to explain how sectoral shifts lead to shifts in grand strategy. Braumoeller is most interested in how constituencies react to changes in the external power distribution and support or demand changes in foreign policy behavior. Yet all three do share an interest in US policy changes during the 1920–1945 interval. Therefore, their choices on what to emphasize remain highly germane to the present inquiry.

There are three elements in these arguments worth reconsidering. Two of the theories (Narizny and Braumoeller) emphasize domestic politics at the expense of the international system, although Braumoeller would argue that relative capability is at least represented in his approach. The third (Legro) claims to integrate ideas, interest groups, and structure but primarily stresses ideas. Thus, one element of criticism involves a relatively neglected international structure or, possibly, an exaggerated domestic politics/ideational emphasis. We need more balance in bringing together the essential ingredients.

Despite their variable explicit appreciations for domestic politics, all three models end up curiously downplaying how domestic politics matter. In Legro's model, everyone that counts presumably realizes that it is time to jettison old ideas and to adopt new ones. Agents tend to be black boxed in his approach. In Narizny's and Braumoeller's models, sectoral interests and constituencies, respectively, communicate their preferences to a unitary actor executive who, in turn, translates the preferences into an appropriate strategy. Whatever the convenience of these assumptions for modeling purposes, it would be both more accurate and more useful to view domestic politics as a contested arena in which different actors compete to see whose ideas and policies will win out. Chief executives are normally part of this competition, as are parties, legislators, agency heads, voters, pundits, interest groups, and sometimes even professors of international relations. The irony here is that we really need greater provision for domestic politics in influencing grand strategy adoptions, not less.

All three tend to treat the United States as either a normal state or great power when, in fact, its circumstances had vaulted it to lead status. This normalizing proclivity is understandable for theory-building purposes and could also be viewed as an extension of the neglect of systemic hierarchy but, as a second problem area, it leads to underexplaining what transpired in 1920–1945. The United States did more than merely swing from isolationism to internationalism in its foreign policy orientation. It also moved from being a relatively marginal great power to the central state in the global power hierarchy. It is rather difficult to focus on one at the exclusion of the other. Third, too little appreciation is paid to the role of global warfare—World Wars I and II. Two of the arguments peg their approach on bestowing preponderance to the United States as a result of

World War I. Yet awarding a preponderant position to the United States in 1918–1920 is premature. It took World War II, the greater shock of the two, to establish global preponderance, among other things.

These three elements—internal/external balance, normalization, and global war—tend to overlap in the 1920–1945 case. More explanatory balance is needed because the circumstances were less than normal—external developments, domestic politics, and their interactions were important—and because global warfare played an important causal role. It is difficult, therefore, to treat the three elements entirely separately. A different model is needed that permits their blending.

There is also an opportunity to question some of the debatable interpretations that emerge from the applications of the three earlier models. Legro's version, for instance, argues that the United States was dragged into World War I toward its end and that Wilson complicated the war entry by justifying it in terms of eliminating autocratic threats to democracy. Yet, traditional imperialism, as evidenced by the mandate system, prevailed in the postwar era. A limited US impact led to the evaporation of support for external commitments and a reversion to the traditional inclination to stay clear of European politics. Axis threats in the 1930s, Pearl Harbor, and a major war effort in the early 1940s made it clear that the United States could not revert to isolationism in a postwar world—at least to most policymakers. Therefore, the disillusionment experienced after World War I was avoided and a more solid base for consolidating the new grand strategy was established.

Narizny's focus on strategic change causes him to depreciate systemic changes in preference for the coming together of Northeastern manufacturing and Southern farming in the New Deal era. But surely there was more to the US ascendance than simply a revised domestic coalition? At best, a new, more internationalist domestic coalition would have pushed for greater US participation in world politics. What happened in 1945 went considerably beyond that benchmark.

Public opinion was indeed becoming more sympathetic to the European plight prior to Pearl Harbor, à la Braumoeller, but the US president still depended on an error by Hitler (declaring war on the United States after Pearl Harbor) to bring about US participation in the European theater. Nor is it clear that more supportive public opinion accounted for increased US participation in the Atlantic/European war theater prior to Pearl Harbor. Roosevelt had been operating ahead of his constituency in this respect engaging in undeclared war activities in the Atlantic theater for some time. Finally, the ascendance of the United States involved a bit more than merely a response to a short-term increase in the system's power concentration after the fall of France. If that is all that was at stake, one would have expected normal multipolar maneuvering as a response. Instead, an even greater concentration of systemic power emerged in the form of US systemic leadership prior to and after 1945.

Borrowing from Kingdon's (1995) agenda-setting arguments, it is possible to develop a fairly simple and straightforward argument that provides space for balancing internal and external considerations, facilitates evading the normalization straitjacket, and has a prominent role for variable shocks, as manifested in global wars. The model also helps focus attention on the ascendance of the United States to global systemic leadership, as opposed to its movement toward more internationalist policies or merely responding to perceived changes in the distribution of power. Yet it remains a general model for shifts in grand strategy—and not one restricted to states rising to superpower status.

An Alternative Theory of Grand Strategy Shifts

The Kingdon problem is that policy problems and advocates for policy change are present for long periods of time. Only some policy problems are addressed at any given point in time. Only some policy changes are adopted. Why is that the case? Kingdon (1995) sees new policies emerging from conjunctions of three separate and independent process streams involving problems, policies, and politics. The basic principle is that policy change is more probable when ideas fit or best correspond to the nature of the problem and the political environment. Translating this perspective into changes in grand strategy formulations does not require much adjustment.[4] The problems for grand strategy include changing international environments that combine new (or declining) threats and new (or declining) capabilities to cope with them. For instance, an ascending state becomes more powerful and is likely to make new enemies. Leading states become less powerful and may need to do different things in order to remain competitive with challengers. In either case, older strategies are likely to be providing less and less correspondence to the altered international circumstances. Strategies that are no longer corresponding to international circumstances afford some opportunity to contemplate changing the prevailing grand strategies. But a perceived misfit is not likely to be enough.

The third stream of politics is also critical. Within this stream are several different sub-processes. External shocks, policy entrepreneurs, interest group preferences, and public opinion can play roles here. The value of external shocks is to galvanize policymakers into searching harder for alternative strategies.[5]

---

[4] Legro's theory says much the same but it does not follow through on the prescription.

[5] The importance of shocks is that prevailing strategies and institutions are thought to be characterized by a great deal of inertia. Something must overcome the inertia and an abrupt shock creates an opening for possible changes. As Gourevitch (1986: 21–22) puts it: crisis challenges prevailing policy approaches and makes "politics and policy more fluid" until some resolution is achieved that

This is the "rethinking" process. But it is one thing to recognize that the outside world (or the inside world of the state's ability to cope with the outside world) has changed. It is another to need to do something concrete in relatively short order in response to something like an external attack (Pearl Harbor, 9/11). Policymakers are expected to act in such situations and may have more leeway to try something different—at least for a while.

Interest groups and public opinion speak to the domestic political support or opposition to new strategies. To this cluster we should add political parties, which are, after all, designed to aggregate, albeit selectively, interests and opinion. Policy entrepreneurs play intermediate roles in articulating the nature of the problem at hand, promoting new policies/strategies, and organizing support or diminishing opposition to new strategies.

> New ideas do not exert influence on their own. . . . To compete successfully against rival beliefs and acquire political power within a government, new policy ideas must first win over experts on the basis of their theoretical appeal and practical relevance, by offering a persuasive explanation for past shortcomings and solutions to current challenges. They must then accommodate or overwhelm the intellectual biases within state bureaucracies. . . . Finally, to be put into practice, the new ideas must mobilize political coalitions or serve the agendas of ruling parties. (Patrick, 2009: xxiv–xxv)

These are the multiple tasks of policy entrepreneurs—to sell ideas and to get them put into practice. Yet, as Kingdon notes, policy entrepreneurs rarely control the process of policy formulation but must work within the parameters set by events, windows of opportunity, and institutional structures.[6]

---

closes the system until the next crisis occurs. Thus, the windows of opportunity created by the crisis or shock are delimited in time (Dueck, 2006). They do not remain open indefinitely. The need for shocks to overcome policy inertia suggests that major strategy shifts are likely to occur abruptly, as opposed to gradually. Finally, as Hermann (1990: 12) notes, shocks are events that cannot be ignored. Without them, there is less incentive to contemplate policy changes. Major shocks thus have the potential to change the nature of external problems to which some actors feel the need to respond.

[6] This type of approach tends to dodge the question of learning in foreign policy (see, among others, Tetlock, 1991; Levy, 1994; Malici, 2008). Do actor belief systems change because of external changes? We know, for instance, that decision makers in 1945 were committed to avoiding some of the errors of 1919–1920, which would suggest actor-level learning. Alternatively, are belief systems so entrenched that one must wait for new regimes that are less committed to old policies to initiate genuine changes? These questions are certainly worthwhile, but they are subordinated in this framework as secondary issues. That is, some actor belief systems may change while others do not. Sometimes, grand strategy changes are more likely if there is a regime change, but they can also occur in the absence of regime changes. The causal mechanisms that are highlighted in the Kingdon-type model are not psychological in nature but rather timing and pressures for and against policy change.

Thus, the theoretical argument is that new strategies must be seen as conforming to perceived problems in the international environment, which can be basically reduced to the perceived fit between threats, opportunities, and relative capability. Second, major shocks are probably critical for new strategies to have some chance of being adopted. Presumably, the greater is the shock, the better are the chances for somebody to do some rethinking. Policy inertia is more likely to prevail in their absence. Third, new strategies are more likely to be adopted to the extent that they benefit from adept policy entrepreneurs and do not face strong and entrenched political opposition that is greater than the domestic support for such a shift. Fourth (as in Legro's two-phase approach), the consolidation of new grand strategies is more probable to the extent that they appear to be successful. Perceived success reinforces the inclination to stick with the new strategy.

More specifically, and as highlighted in figure 4.1: the probability of new grand strategies emerging (e.g., ideational shifts) is a function of the perceived fit between the nature of the problem and the state's capabilities for addressing the problem + shocks + policy entrepreneurs + the balance of support and opposition in domestic politics + successful reinforcement. The stronger the presence of these five factors, the more probable is a shift in grand strategy.

Should all five of these factors be equally weighted? The answer is no. It is conceivable that the relative weight of each factor could vary from case to case. For instance, one case might involve a moderate shock and very persuasive entrepreneurs, while another case might be linked to a very severe shock and relatively mediocre entrepreneurs. Other things being equal, they might have

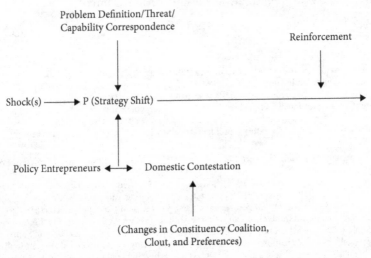

Figure 4.1 An Alternative Approach to the Probability of Grand Strategy Shifts

similar outcomes. The point remains that both shocks and entrepreneurs are likely to be present in most cases, albeit in varying packages.[7]

None of the factors taken in isolation is considered sufficient to change strategies. Perceptions of problems and capabilities vary in accuracy. Shocks vary in intensity. Some policy entrepreneurs are more gifted or lucky than others. Exactly how much external change or domestic support must take place is unclear. Reinforcement should be critical to helping the new strategy stick, but how much reinforcement or consensus about reinforcement is needed may be expected to be perceived somewhat differently from case to case. Hence the evasion of great precision by suggesting that when these factors come together (and when more of them come together), a shift in grand strategy is more likely.

The lack of precision is certainly not ideal. But the imprecision is saved somewhat by requiring the five different factors to occur in close sequence. The theory does not simply contend that some policy entrepreneurship is helpful to obtaining a shift in grand strategy. That would not be much of a theory, especially since it is rather difficult to imagine a strategy shift without policy entrepreneurship. But the theory does say that while policy entrepreneurship is helpful, it is not sufficient if some mix of the other four factors is not present in something. Even if they are all present in weak form, the conjoined probability of a shift might remain weak. The probability of a change becomes stronger as the factors themselves appear in greater strength.

Changes in the environment are conducive to ideational innovation. Shock leads to experimentation by policy entrepreneurs and a fumbling search for policies that seem to fit the political landscape—both in terms of the nature of the problem, capabilities, and domestic evaluation. The alternative is a looser theory but perhaps one that better fits the craggy analytical landscape. Whether that is the case in the US mid-twentieth century shift remains to be seen in the next section of this paper.

Assessing the External Realm

Changes in the system are critical for establishing first a weak (1917–1920) and then a strong (1930s–1945) context for changes in grand strategy. World War II and the distribution of power in its aftermath are critical ingredients in

---

[7] Compare this approach with Dueck's (2006) theory of grand strategy adjustment, which focuses on the conjunction of international conditions, domestic politics, political leadership, and strategic culture and possesses considerable theoretical overlap with the approach developed in this chapter. However, Dueck sometimes seems to emphasize international conditions, which, in his approach, tend to be fused with window-of-opportunity creating shocks, while his discussion of his cases seems to privilege the political leadership component filtered by the constraints of strategic culture.

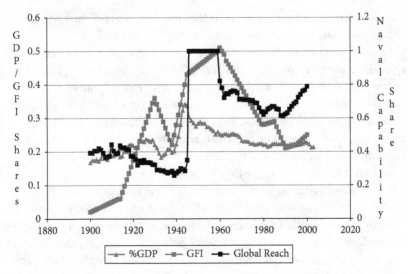

Figure 4.2 Shares of Economic, Financial, and Military Capability

accounting for the rise of the United States. Thanks in part to the US wartime role as the "arsenal of democracy" and the devastation wrought on most of the war's participants, the United States emerged in 1945 as a superpower with a very strong edge in economic wealth and military weaponry. Nothing very similar happened in 1918.

The US ascent in world politics had begun in the nineteenth century, but even after World War I it still had some way to go before attaining the level, unprecedented in some respects, achieved during and immediately after World War II. Some evidence is helpful on this score. Figure 4.2 plots three series. One is the US share of world gross domestic product (GDP).[8] A second series captures the US share of gross financial investment.[9] The third index represents a measurement of US relative global reach focusing at different points on a combination of battleships, naval expenditures, aircraft carriers, and various attributes of nuclear submarines and ballistic missiles at sea.[10]

Superimposed on one another, the three series look similar. The global reach share pushes upward in the vicinity of World War I and then declines for two decades. It peaks after World War II and then declines from about 1960 to the

[8] The US share of world GDP is calculated from data made available in Maddison (2007). The original data are expressed in 1990 international Geary-Khamis dollars utilizing PPP (purchasing power parity) converters.

[9] The US share of gross financial investment is based on estimates supplied in US billion $ for selected years between 1825 and 2000 by Obstfeld and Taylor (2004: 52–53).

[10] This index is the leadership long cycle index for global reach based on naval capabilities and described in Modelski and Thompson (1988), and later revised and updated.

mid-1980s, before improving with the collapse of the Soviet Union. The GDP share index moves upward and peaks just before the Great Depression, then declines into the mid-1930s before peaking again during World War II. The relative decline of the GDP share is quite consistent after the second peak. The investment share index climbs quickly in the aftermath of World War I and peaks around the mid-1930s, before declining to 1940. It then peaks roughly in the early 1960s before experiencing a descent that is not reversed prior to the 1990s.

More specifically, the GDP share moves from .188 in 1910 to .219 in 1920, about a 3 percent increase. By 1945, the US share had climbed to .338, almost a 12 percent increase. The US investment share in 1910 was .05, increasing to .174 in 1920 and an even stronger .430 in 1945. The global reach share indicator actually shows decreases from 1910 (.442) to 1920 (.371) and then 1945 (.350), but this is a bit misleading. The 1910 share is exaggerated due to British-induced changes in dreadnought technology around that time. If World War I had lasted longer, there is some possibility that the United States would have outbuilt the British and ended up with the largest navy. The 1945 US share picks up a waning commitment to battleships while the 1946 share (1.00) is more indicative of the postwar US relative share in global reach capabilities, reflecting a strategic shift away from battleships to carriers and, later, submarines.

Thus, two of the capability share series experience some movement upwards around the time of World War I. But all three series possess more impressive peaks that are linked to World War II and its immediate aftermath. It is not too fanciful to see something like a capability step ladder at work. World War I was an initial step. World War II was a second, much higher step upward. Put another way, the United States' relative capability position improved much more after World War II than after World War I.[11] Figure 4.3 demonstrates something similar. In this figure, US relative naval capability changes are contrasted with Legro's 6-point scale of internationalism.[12] Some relatively minor movement in internationalism (toward and away from contemplating the wisdom of alliance-making) oscillates around a high but less than commanding and gradually declining naval position prior to the advent of World War II. With the advent of

[11] As Krasner (1978: 343) notes, "It is not clear that during the interwar years the United States had the power to construct a new global order." By this statement he meant that even though the United States was the strongest economic power in the system, it had rivals that were not that far behind—unlike the situation after World War II in which the economies of the other major powers had been damaged badly. Put another way, Wilson sought to create a new global order without the material clout to pull it off. The failure to sell the League of Nations idea at home was only part of the failure.

[12] Legro (2005: 200) operationalizes the isolationist-internationalist continuum in terms of a 6-point scale in which the highest point states that "the security of the United States depends on actively constructing international institutions and relationships that tie it to other major powers, and to which it gives political-military backing." The data in figure 4.3 are based on content analyzing presidential State of the Union messages.

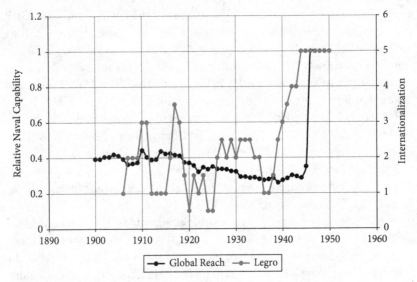

Figure 4.3 Internationalization and Naval Capability Preponderance

the second world war, both US positions (first the internationalism and then the navalism), as coded in the figure, more than double.[13]

For the United States, World War II stands out as the most significant sustained military shock of the twentieth century. It cost sixteen times as much as World War I (which in turn cost about what the Korean War cost).[14] Four times as many armed forces were killed in World War II as in World War I. The US economy was mobilized for war in the early 1940s to a much greater extent than in 1917–1918 and with much greater societal impacts. Just as important is the lead role assumed in planning the Western war effort on multiple fronts in World War II. One can argue that everything is relative and that World War I was certainly a significant shock compared to the Spanish-American War. But even the first world war (for the United States) paled in comparison to the second world war for mobilization, expense, lethality, and coalition leadership purposes.

Figure 4.2 demonstrates that the US relative position in GDP, gross financial investment, and global reach capabilities benefited from World War I. The United States made money on the war, supplanted Britain to some extent as the

[13] One might wish to argue that an internationalist foreign policy and naval expansion are closely related, and, in some respects, they are. But naval expansion (in absolute terms) during World War II preceded the commitment to systemic leadership after the war. In challengers, there are groups that advocate the link between naval expansion and systemic leadership aspirations, but they do not necessarily control challenger foreign policy making.

[14] The cost estimates are Daggett (2010), available at Sgp.fas.org/crs/natsec/RS22926pdf. The death counts are from DeBruyne (2017) at census.gov/history/pdf/ww1-casualties112018.pdf.

leading source of capital investment, and expanded its naval arsenal for greater global reach.[15] A number of European states had become indebted to the United States as a source of wartime loans. But in each case a much stronger claim can be made for World War II boosting the US relative position. Thus, US ascension to the center of world politics was clearly underway in the first two decades of the twentieth century but was better realized by the fourth decade.[16]

Relative capability position interacts with the different types of US war participation in 1917–1918 and 1941–1945 (Cohen, 1994: 433–434). In World War I, the US forces arrived late to the fray but were instrumental in supplying fresh meat for the trench warfare and in blocking German initiatives, especially in 1918, and played a strong role in the Allied counteroffensive in the second half of 1918. US forces did not always operate autonomously but were sometimes distributed, albeit reluctantly, among the British-French forces already in the field and technically were under French command. When it came time to hammer out peace proposals and the postwar order, Wilson was able to influence the outcome as one of several Allied leaders but hardly the leading figure. The US war effort deserved political acknowledgment but not excessive deference. Nor were the British, French, or even the Italians rendered prostrate by the war effort.

Contrast this situation with the World War II war effort. The United States arrived late again but not as late and at a time when both the British and the Soviets were reeling from early defeats. The French were already out of the picture. The US economic and military contribution to the war effort was much greater than in 1917–1918.[17] US political leadership was more manifest in Anglo-British negotiations. Allied troops in the West this time were under American command. At the end of the war, Britain and France were not in much position to oppose US preferences. The Soviet Union was in a better position to resist in some parts of the world but lagged in atomic weapons and the ability to project force over long distances. Its opposition was manifested primarily on the Eurasian fringe (Eastern Europe and Korea) and, ultimately, by withdrawal from full participation in the world economy and, on occasion, global institutions.

In terms of problem definition considerations, the 1940s were a far more likely window of opportunity for changing grand strategy. Even the shocks of

[15] Fordham (2007) suggests that so much money was made on exports to the Allies during the early part of the war that German attacks on US shipping became much more probable and so too did American intervention on the Allied side. Quite literally, the United States could not afford to remain neutral.

[16] Cassis (2006), for instance, notes that New York did not become the world's premiere financial center until after 1945.

[17] For instance, in World War I, only half of the planes flown by American pilots were made in the United States, and European artillery was relied upon heavily by American units (Cohen 1994: 433). Between 1939 and 1945, the United States produced 50.6 percent of the aircraft, 87 percent of the major naval vessels, and 39.5 percent of the tanks constructed by Britain, the Soviet Union, and the United States (based on my calculations from annual production figures in Overy (1995: 331–332).

Pearl Harbor and the second world war effort were vastly different in magnitude than the sinking of US ships and the first world war effort. World War I was much different from what preceded it but, with the advantage of hindsight, it was not quite enough to bring about changed ideas about grand strategy on its own strength. Domestic politics successfully resisted the implications of the World War I shock.

The postwar strategic problems were also quite different. In 1919–1920, the problems consisted of questions on the order of what to do with conquered territory or how punitive reparations should be. External threat perceptions, at least from the US perspective, were virtually nonexistent. There was some confused intervention in the Soviet Union's civil war; yet there was no immediate threat of Bolshevik expansion into Europe. The aftermath of World War II was much different. The fear of a Soviet threat of control in Western Europe and elsewhere was substituted for the vanquished German threat. Markets in Europe and Japan not only needed to be rebuilt so that they could consume US products, but they also had to be protected from internal subversion and external attack.

It should also be kept in mind that US grand strategy did not change abruptly in 1945. As Miscamble (2009) argues, the changes in US grand strategy emerged somewhat haphazardly between 1945 and 1950. Postwar developments such as British collapse and Soviet expansion were not really part of the grand strategizing by the Roosevelt administration during World War II. Roosevelt's preference for great power condominium gave way to global containment as the nature of the strategic problem shifted.

Similarly, the nature of perceived threats differed vastly in the two occasions. Prior to 1917, it was conceivable that the United States could remain aloof from the war in Europe. An American sense of interdependence with the rest of the world had become greater, as had American profits from supplying resources to the European war effort. But a German victory in 1917–1918 would not have had obvious implications for American security. Initially, the Germans had backed away from attacking US ships supplying its opponents. If it had persisted in this strategy, US involvement would have been much more difficult to sell at home. That Germany chose to re-escalate the war at sea on commercial shipping reflected a decision that it might be able to win the war in Europe before US capabilities could be mobilized for an infusion of new resources. That German miscalculation still falls short of a future German threat of military expansion in the Americas. The post–World War I threat environment was even more benign; no serious threat was apparent prior to the 1930s (Cohen 1994: 440). Thus, the sense of strategic threat was less than acute immediately before and after World War I. The same cannot be said immediately before and after World War II.

The Realm of Domestic Politics

Even so, the post–World War I window of opportunity might almost have been enough for change, but Wilson's world order ideas proved a bit too hard to sell at home. It is not obvious that the idea of joining an international organization was simply too radical. Republicans, after all, had first raised the idea of some type of postwar peace league.[18] Wilson, himself, seems to have thought (or at least said) that membership in the League would be unlikely to require much in the way of US involvement in European problems.[19] Most commentators on the fight to market the League of Nations membership to Congress and the American public believe that a weaker form might have been negotiated domestically.[20] Wilson had compromised in his negotiations with Britain and France over postwar settlements, but he declined to compromise at home initially and thought he could rally public opinion to overcome Republican-dominated Congressional opposition.[21] He was wrong and suffered an incapacitating stroke while attempting to do an end run around his domestic political opponents. He might still have compromised at the very end but was either no longer capable of seeing the necessity of doing so or preferred not to do so.

In contrast, Roosevelt ultimately faced a much more favorable domestic setting with far less explicit opposition for the war effort and the need to do

---

[18] According to Cooper (2001: 11–13), the idea was first raised by Theodore Roosevelt in 1910 and subsequently endorsed by Henry Cabot Lodge, of all people, and former president William Howard Taft in 1915. Lake (1999) stresses that the Republican senatorial opposition encompassed "conservative internationalists" who were open to a nonbinding European alliance and "irreconcilables" who preferred to remain as distant from European problems as possible. A looser collective security organization, therefore, was politically possible if a compromise could have been worked out between "progressive" and "conservative" internationalists.

[19] Ambrosius (2002: 51–64) argues that the League commitment was not a radical move away from traditional US isolationism in that the commitment was general (as opposed to the entanglements of a specific alliance with a European great power) and that Wilson did not expect that collective security would require military coercion to make it work. Even it did, he once described US troops as too far away to be called on for European problems. Clements (1999: 219) adds that Wilson once also explained that the United States would always have an effective veto on the use of force to maintain security guarantees in Europe and elsewhere.

[20] This comment is based on a reading of the pertinent passages on the League of Nations campaign in the United States in McDonald (1968), Wells, Ferrell, and Trask (1975), Knock (1992), Cooper (2001), Ambrosious (2002), and Eckes and Zeiler (2003).

[21] To obtain British and French support for the League, Wilson had had to accept major German reparations and French control of the Saar (Brands, 2003: 116). Dueck (2006: 55–75) devotes some consideration to this issue and argues that the failure of the United States to accept League of Nations membership was not due to tactical errors or personality flaws on the part of Wilson. The US strategic culture's tradition of limited liability meant that a full commitment to collective security was unlikely to generate much domestic support. Hence Wilson's preferences were literally doomed from the outset. But, surely, Wilson might have been expected to appreciate this problem, especially when several policy initiatives had been blocked by senatorial opposition. Wilson's ultimate refusal to compromise must be judged an entrepreneurial failure given that there did seem to be some possibility of securing US membership in the League, with some concessions on the nature of collective security obligations.

something different after the war. The level of perceived external threat had risen through the 1930s. Authoritarian regimes seemed likely to expand on most continents. From the US perspective, not only were European affairs becoming more menacing, but Asian and Pacific interests were also increasingly threatened by Japanese actions. The odds of the United States remaining aloof from a second world war were much smaller than they had been some twenty years earlier. In this respect, the prewar definition of the strategic problem had changed considerably. Pearl Harbor sealed the deal.

The Pearl Harbor shock was hard to ignore, but US public opinion had become more favorable to the idea of an expanded American role in world affairs even before December 1941. In the late 1930s considerable resistance to moving away from isolationism could be found in survey data. An October 1941 poll, however, indicated that 61 percent of the people surveyed preferred a more internationalist US foreign policy after the war in Europe had ended. The numbers continued to climb—67 percent in December, 75 percent in January 1942, and 83 percent in June 1943 before dropping in to 71 percent April 1944 and then increasing again to 81 percent in March 1945. Public support for more activity in foreign policy may have dropped by 1947 but remained about 75 percent until Vietnam.[22]

Roosevelt, at one time an enthusiastic disciple of Wilson (and later more cautious in expressing internationalist preferences), operated in a working environment much different than Wilson's.[23] Wilson's political opponents controlled Congress. Roosevelt's party retained control of Congress. Adopting a more internationalist stance before 1917 was much easier to debate than in 1941. It continued to be debatable after 1917 but much less so after 1941.

Focusing on the main political entrepreneur for grand strategy shifts, Wilson was incapacitated at a critical political juncture; Roosevelt had polio but it did not incapacitate his political maneuvering.[24] Whereas Wilson was initially forced to respond tentatively to German prewar initiatives and, later, make issue-by-issue, postwar bargains with the British and French, one biographer (Black, 2003: 504–505) credits Roosevelt with a personal 6-point grand strategy as early as 1939, if not before: overcome the depression by rearming, win a third term as a peace candidate, develop US military strength, take advantage of authoritarian aggression to draw the United States into a second world war, win the war and usher in

---

[22] These public opinion numbers are discussed in Page and Shapiro (1992: 176–177) and are characterized by the usual problems associated with different polling organizations asking different questions over time.

[23] As a vice presidential candidate in 1920, Roosevelt argued that the League was needed as a fireman to put out fires and that the United States would be the fire chief (Kinsella, 1978: 18).

[24] Whether Wilson would have been more open to domestic compromise if he had not had a major stroke will never be known.

an era of Pax Americana, and, finally, realize Wilson's goals of postwar restructuring with the assistance of a US-led international organization. The biographer in question provides no evidence that Roosevelt was entertaining all these goals in the late 1930s but one can certainly see how it is possible to give Roosevelt more credit for manipulating and controlling his environment than was the case with Wilson. That he was in a much better position to do so in a reopened window of opportunity is equally clear, and that is all that really matters for our present purposes.[25] Hence, the 1940s enjoyed an edge in effective political entrepreneurship and the relative absence of sizeable domestic opposition in contrast to the immediate post–World War I years.

More structurally, Gourevitch (1986) contends that the 1930s Depression weakened the Republican, nationalist business leadership hold on policy, creating an opening for a New Deal coalition that included internationalists. Frieden (1988; see also Ferguson, 1989) also argues that change toward a more internationalist stance in and after World War II was more likely than in World War I because the balance between two opposed domestic coalitions of corporations and banks had swung in favor of actors who preferred greater international involvement by 1940. Trubowitz (1998), as in Narizny's later interpretation, argues that Northeastern business interests were not enough. One must add Southern regional sectoral interests that also gravitated toward a more international position. Thus, it was a Northern-Southern political coalition that facilitated the advent of internationalism in the 1940s and thereafter as long as civil rights were kept out of the picture. Narizny (2007) accounts for the shift in terms of partisan foot-dragging in which Republicans committed to isolationism and realpolitik were sufficiently powerful to block Democratic internationalism prior to 1941, but not after.

All these arguments, often overlapping with one another, seem plausible to varying extents. We really do not have to choose between them at this point. They represent various explanations for diminished domestic political opposition to a more internationalized American foreign policy stance. All we need to establish for our own immediate purposes is that there was much less domestic resistance to a new grand strategy in the 1940s than in the 1910s and 1920s. There seems little controversy about the outcome even if we continue to disagree about the specific causes. Inasmuch as these arguments point to exogenous shifts in domestic politics that seem to have facilitated the change to a more internationalist position during and after World War II, all are quite compatible with the generalization that favorable domestic politics make a grand strategy shift more likely in 1945 than in 1920, other things being equal.

---

[25] It had to help that Roosevelt had already lived through Wilson's earlier iteration or window of opportunity.

Reinforcement

Reinforcement comes into play after a shift in grand strategy has occurred, although non-shifts can be reinforced as well. In 1920, the Democratic ticket, with Franklin D. Roosevelt as the vice presidential candidate, was repudiated at the polls. It is not clear that the League or grand strategy were all that prominent in the election, but Republicans viewed their victory as a popular mandate to avoid European collective security entanglements. The 1920s were hardly peaceful but strategic threats to North American interests were not particularly prominent. Nor was US policy all that isolationist. It did continue to play a role in European politics, especially on the question of German reparations in which the United States was a critical player. The point is that nothing took place in the immediate aftermath of World War I and the postwar settlement to suggest that things might have been different if the United States had joined the League.[26] In this sense, the non-change in strategy was reinforced until the nature of German and Japanese ambitions became more evident in the 1930s.

In the 1940s, participation and leadership in the United Nations were bundled with several other Bretton Woods–type organizations designed to provide an institutional infrastructure for the new American-led world order. US-Soviet relations may have fluctuated from time to time, but the US perception of Soviet threat did not waver in the aftermath of World War II. Collective security proved difficult to operationalize in a bipolarized world, and not all the organizations created in the 1940s retained US support indefinitely. Still, there was little to suggest in the 1940s through 1960s that the United States had much choice but to assume systemic leadership and a more internationalist stance than had ever been the case in the past. The 1940s shift was therefore amply reinforced as well.

The Ingredients for Strategy Changes

Table 4.1 summarizes how the new theory fares in comparing the two opportunities for grand strategy change. In terms of problem-capability correspondence, the pre- and post–World War I era was less threatening than was the case in the 1930s and 1940s. It was much easier to entertain a preference for evading European entanglements in the first two decades of the twentieth century than a few years later. The US relative capability position had improved coming out of World War I, but it was not quite a first among equals in 1920. It had played a critical military role toward the end of World War I but not one that overshadowed

---

[26] With the advantage of hindsight, it seems most unlikely that interwar international relations would have been all that different even if the United States had joined the League.

Table 4.1 The Application of the Theory to the Two Cases

Theoretical Factors	1920	1945
Problem definition and state capability correspondence	Weak	Strong
Shocks	Relatively moderate	Strong
Policy entrepreneurs	Handicapped	Strong
Contestation in domestic politics	Strong	Weak
Reinforcement	Inertia reinforced	Change reinforced

the military contributions of Britain and France. The US navy had expanded, yet it was still roughly on a par with the British navy. US commerce and finance were developing a stronger and more widespread profile, but it was not as predominant worldwide as it was later to become.

All these tendencies became more prominent and pronounced in the second case. The US military role in the Second World War did not compare to Britain's or France's. Britain became a subordinate ally and France was defeated before the United States entered the war. Neither state was in much of a position to resist US preferences during or after the war. In contrast, the United States in 1945 was more than a first among equals—it was truly predominant and had greatly benefited from the war effort, unlike its allies. The war enemy in 1945 had been defeated more definitively than had been the case in 1918. Moreover, the Soviet Union was fast emerging as a new external threat in 1945. A more malevolent world in 1945 than in 1919–1920, accompanied by a more significant enhancement in relatively capability by 1945 than had been the case by 1919–1920, meant that the problem and capability fit for a shift in grand strategy was much better in the 1940s than in 1919–1920.

German attacks on neutral US shipping and participation in World War I had shock impact, but the shocks sustained between 1941 and 1945 were much more severe than in the 1916–1918 interval. The US mobilization effort was more intense and longer lasting in the early 1940s than in 1917–1918. The socioeconomic and psychological impact on the home front was correspondingly more severe in World War II than in World War I.

As a chief policy entrepreneur, Wilson proved adept at compromise in the Versailles negotiations. His campaign to sell US participation in the new League of Nations was not doomed to inevitable defeat, and much of the failure must be credited to his rigid approach to dealing with Republican opponents in the US Senate. An incapacitated president proved unable to make the deal that was essential to congressional ratification. However far-seeing Roosevelt was, he retained his political skills despite an illness that might have been incapacitating. He also had less domestic opposition and events worked in his favor. The Japanese attack and German declaration of war meant he did not have to persuade people to join the war effort. Some type of postwar international organization, controlled by the United States and its allies, seemed likely from early on as part of a postwar restructuring effort.

Domestic opposition was quite significant in the first case. The Republicans controlled Congress as of 1916. The Democrats controlled the presidency. Almost regardless of why this was the case, it was a political context that was highly conducive to impasse in the absence of adroit maneuvering and compromise—neither of which was forthcoming on the League issue.[27] In contrast, Roosevelt had won an unprecedented third (and later a fourth) term. The Democratic majority persisted in its control of the presidency and Congress. A different elite (and mass) generation, and one that was more open to international initiatives by most accounts, was in power in the 1940s.[28] It remained in power through much of the threatening Cold War environment that followed the end of war in 1945. Whatever else the Cold War was, it was not a rivalry designed to discourage high levels of US participation in world politics. Reinforcement was almost a given.

Table 4.1 indicates that all five factors emphasized by the new theory were relatively absent or weak in the World War I column. All five factors were present and strong in the World War II column. Such a dichotomous outcome would seem to provide good initial support for the theory's utility. In the spirit of Kingdon-like models, the things that were important had not come together by 1919–1920 but had by the early 1940s. Therefore, no change in grand strategy took place in the first case. Quite significant changes occurred in the second case.

Ideas about how to avoid future wars or avoiding entangling commitments were certainly part of the shift, but only a part. Ideas helped shape actor preferences, and actors justified their preferences in terms of ideas about what institutions and behavior might best advance future security. Yet the ideas, subject to evolution themselves, hardly operated in a constant structural vacuum.[29] Structural change was highly significant to the World War I/II systemic leadership puzzle. So, too, were the quality of political entrepreneurs

---

[27] One irony is that Wilson made his academic reputation initially on a book on Congress, albeit without ever observing the institution at first hand.

[28] The whole question of the role of generational change in foreign policy shifts remains underdeveloped.

[29] By the 1940s, Dallek (1979: 56) argues that Roosevelt valued the United Nations as an institutional device to help camouflage the great power condominium at the center of his postwar world order concept.

and the domestic political context for resistance to new strategic ideas and behavior.

Conclusion

Problems, threats/relative capabilities, shocks, policy entrepreneurs, domestic politics, and reinforcement interact in various ways to bring about shifts in grand strategy. All seemed to be in play in a more facilitative way in the 1940s than they were in 1919–1920 and help account for the ascent of the United States in 1945. It remains to be seen whether all cases of grand strategy shifts involve all the possible factors equally. It may be that different mixes of the factors (e.g., strong entrepreneurship overcoming considerable domestic opposition in some cases while in others weak domestic opposition means that even tepid entrepreneurship can succeed). More cases will need to be examined to determine just how many different paths to grand strategy shifts there may be. Yet grand strategy shifts with one or more of the five factors completely absent would invalidate the theory as currently framed. More case studies are needed in any event to assess whether the new theory's mix of factors are the right ones for wide applications across time and space. But we should be able to say under what conditions change in grand strategies are most probable. When external problems and relative capabilities correspond, shocks create openings, policy entrepreneurs generate enough support, domestic audiences constrain their opposition, grand strategy change is most probable. If the new strategy seems to be working, it has some probability of persisting into the future and acquiring its own characteristics of policy inertia.

This argument has been developed with an eye toward explaining the rise of the United States to systemic leadership in 1945, as opposed to 1920. But the model has been purposefully left as generic as possible to make it applicable to a variety of grand strategic changes—not just the rare systemic leadership ascents. At least that was the intention. Whether the model is as broadly applicable as intended remains to be tested. However, the model does allow for a balanced combination of external and internal factors. Neither the outside nor the inside is privileged, even though it may well be the case from time to time that the influences of one realm may trump the influences emanating from the other arena.

There is no need to force very large structural changes into isolationism-internationalism boxes. Movement on this continuum may well be accompanied by other types of changes that we should be reluctant to overlook. Finally, global war plays a critical role in this application, but other types of shocks that have variable impact on actor calculations may be equally important.

The last two chapters have tried to explain how the United States rose to pre-eminence in the mid-twentieth century. The next three chapters are focused on different dimensions of its relative decline. Chapter 5 looks at the external nature of positional decay, while chapter 6 zeroes in on the internal nature of decline—in this case, a dysfunctional political system in the throes of a variety of trans-formations. Chapter 7 looks at some of the confusing aspects of assertions about the United States' unipolar "moment."

5

The Relative Decline of the United States

The re-emergence of relative decline as a topic in US political discourse is hardly inappropriate, but its intermittent appearance—not unlike a whale breaching occasionally—is misleading. The occasional debate and discussion about decline over the past few decades suggests that it is a handwringing lament that is put forward periodically by various overly pessimistic critics of contemporary policies and affairs. The reaction is that the unwarranted pessimism will go away if you take two aspirin and outwait it.[1] Yet one of the misleading aspects of this problem is that the relative decline of the United States has been ongoing fairly consistently for some time. That its recognition is intermittent tells us more about our different assumptions about world politics, or perhaps the analytical role of optimism and pessimism in international relations, than it does anything else.[2]

Another misleading element is that the relative decline has been slow and may even have hit an unusually high floor. Other system leaders have declined either quickly or slowly, but the extent to which they have declined has been more definitive—at least in retrospect. These characteristics of US relative decline facilitate differing and diametrically opposed interpretations of what the US relative position might be in any given year. The very term of "decline," of course, also suffers from overly negative reactions from some analysts who view raising the issue as akin to assaulting motherhood and apple pie. The opprobrium associated with the concept only undermines our ability to deal with the phenomena of rising and falling positions. Rising and falling status is the natural order of things. A truly static position in world politics would be the anomaly.

Moreover, the analysis of decline also tends to get caught up too quickly with the related issue of who might be catching up with whatever state is thought to be declining. The relative decline of system leaders does imply that others are catching up to a once preponderant position, but credit for the declining position should not always go only to the states that are ascending. Nor, if one

---

[1] See, for instance, Huntington (1988) and his discussion of five waves of declinism in contemporary US foreign policy discourse. Joffe (2009) states that US declinism reappears every ten years.

[2] Edelman (2010: xiii) notes that the positions of anti-declinists have been reinforced by the consistent errors of the declinists—by which he means that declinist positions are repeatedly shown to be premature by subsequent events. His lead example is the discussion about US decline in the late 1980s immediately prior to the emergence of a widely perceived period of unipolarity. My position is that if there was analytical error, the unipolarity claims are more deserving of the label than the decline discussion has been. See chapter 7 for more on this topic.

American Global Pre-eminence. William R. Thompson, Oxford University Press. © Oxford University Press 2022.
DOI: 10.1093/oso/9780197534663.003.0005

demonstrates that the states catching up have a long way to go, does that imply that the descending state, therefore, really is not in decline. For system leaders, the root causes of relative decline are not due primarily to increasing external competition or even to the much-vaunted concept of overstretch; the root causes of relative decline tend to be internal and due principally to S-shaped technological trajectories. In this respect, system leaders rise and fall on their own "swords." The technological edges that undergird their rise are neither static nor perpetual. They come and go. This facet of relative decline—the why dimension—often gets lost in the debates about who is on first base in the international system in any given year.

This chapter is designed to address these issues by focusing on data on military and economic capabilities. The military data examine strategic capabilities that have been developed to operate in the global commons (as introduced in chapter 2) and thus encompass naval, air, and space arenas. The economic data evade some of the problems of the typical gross domestic product–based indices by looking at the identity of the top 100 multinational industrial corporations at selected points in time over the last 100 years. The military data support the interpretations of anti-declinists, while the economic data support the interpretations of declinists. Reconciling these perspectives empirically and theoretically will give us a better-grounded view of the extent of US relative decline that emphasizes technological change and energy transitions. In brief, it is hard to deny that net relative decline has taken place. The real questions are associated with what we should make of it.

Focus

One problem with discussions of relative decline is that they can encompass all sorts of activity ranging from economic growth through guns-butter trade-offs to questions of ethics and morality. It is important to specify at the outset what is most germane to a discussion of the relative decline of system leaders. We should begin with the concept of systemic leadership.[3] Regional systems often have leaders, but relative decline issues are most often focused on the elite states that predominate at the global level. Such a statement, in turn, implies a distinction between global and regional activities and their associated elite players. Regional international relations are circumscribed by geography and distance. Regional leaders often predominate based on bulk characteristics such as size of

---

[3] Khong (2013) reminds us that Americans tend to favor the "leadership" term over "hegemony" for political/public relations reasons. That may be, but its employment here is more a matter of stressing the limitations on what the lead global state can do or dictate. At the same time, no claim is made here that the global system leader should be viewed as particularly benevolent.

population, economy, and military force. They are the 800 pound gorillas of their local neighborhood. Global leaders predominate on the basis of developing lead economies in the world economy.[4] A lead economy is not necessarily the largest but it is the most active, the most innovative, and, quite often, the most affluent economy in the world because it is operating on the technological frontier.[5] They led in developing new trade routes when that mattered in the age of sail; it now leads in developing new industries (such as railroads, automobiles, and information technology) and exploiting new fuels (coal and petroleum) that diffuse in a highly uneven fashion throughout the system.

When the focus of discussion is the relative decline of system leaders, the hegemonic term may be used as a synonym but only as long as it is not meant to connote coercive domination by military force as typically found in imperial systems. System leaders certainly use military force, wisely or otherwise, but their predominance is based primarily on the extent to which their economies are technologically more developed than their competitors. When they lose this edge, they lose their claim to systemic leadership, albeit subject to some perceptual and other types of lags.[6]

It has been argued elsewhere that systemic leadership is a function of a triangular relationship among three variables: innovative leadership in producing commodities that are highly valued and technologically sophisticated, a leading share in the production of these leading sectors, and a leading share in military instruments of global reach that defend the home base and long-distance trade alike.[7] The three variables do not operate independently or proceed simultaneously. Leading sector

---

[4] Note the implicit distinction between predominance and domination. System leaders rarely dominate. Regional leaders sometimes do.

[5] Consequently, the popular focus on which economies are the largest in the world seems misplaced. As it happened, the US lead economy overlapped with the United States possessing the largest economy for a time, but this coincidence is more an exception than a rule. Historically, very large states such as China and India have often possessed the largest economies, while only on occasion (e.g., Song Dynasty China) have they also been able to claim the attributes of the system's lead economy. Even an indicator such as which state trades the most demands careful interpretation. As of 2012, China secured the lead in the trading of goods (but not services), but that still falls short of qualifying China for the system's lead economy. The question is what is produced and traded, not the overall volume of all economic commodities. At the same time, the hopes linked to what is sometimes referred to as "Saudi America," an incipient boom in North American hydrocarbon production, are likely to prove less tangible than promised in the longer run. Even as more petroleum and gas become available, it is less clear that it will suffice to end American dependence on non–North American energy sources or even lower energy prices in North America. Of the two (energy independence and lower energy prices), the lower energy prices in the abstract would be critical to a resurgence in US economic innovation. But less expensive hydrocarbon costs might only delay the transition to new fuels.

[6] The relative decline in the pre-eminent military capabilities developed to protect the systemic leadership tends to lag behind the relative decline in economic innovation. Cultural pre-eminence also tends to lag behind economic innovation.

[7] One could certainly add legitimacy as a fourth foundation variable, but it is not clear that it is necessary or as necessary as the other three. Legitimacy facilitates the system leader's contribution to global governance, but its absence would probably not preclude system leadership activity. Thus, it seems better to view it as an important but associated variable.

innovation tends to lead high shares of leading sector production, and both of these leads, in turn, predict to the creation of a predominant share of global reach capabilities.[8] Analyses of system leader relative decline should thus focus foremost on high-tech production and the ability to project power around the world. These are the keys to success at the global level where the emphasis is on inter-regional interactions—in distinction to intra-regional interactions.

Accordingly, the focus here will be placed on global power projection and technological leadership. Global power projection can be viewed most effectively by examining the distribution of weapons that are used for long-distance purposes. Technological leadership has been examined before by looking at the national share in the production of selected, leading sector industries (such as automobiles or jet airplane production). In this examination, however, the emphasis will be placed on national shares of multinational corporate (MNC) sales. The assumption is that MNCs control most of the world's business wealth, innovation, and trade. Systemic leadership, at least in the twentieth century, was strongly and positively correlated with MNC share. Which country's MNCs are doing best, therefore, serves as a proxy for both innovation and market share.

Nonetheless, our immediate concern is not with polarity. Table 2.4 in chapter 2 suggests that the relative US global power projection peaked in the 1950s. This observation does not ignore the great strides made in absolute projection capabilities since 1950, but others have enhanced their capabilities as well. After the peak in 1950, US relative capabilities at the global level declined through the Cold War era. They rebounded with the disintegration of the Soviet Union but are likely to resume a relative decline trajectory in the twenty-first century. At the same time, no one else has come close to the US relative position in the early twenty-first century, just as no one else came close to the U.S. relative position in the 1945–1990 period. It is probably safe to say that no one is likely to approximate the US military power projection capability soon (or the next decade or two), if then.

One can say, therefore, that the share of US global reach capabilities has declined over the past sixty to seventy years. But the rate and pace of decline have been quite slow. No other modern power has ever managed to approximate the US lead in this dimension. It may be some time before it is even imaginable that some other state could approximate the preponderance the United States has maintained in global power projection capabilities. Hence, the relative decline in this category must be judged to be negligible in substantive meaning to date, and probably into at least the next decade. It would not be prudent, however, to assume that this lead will be maintained at the same level forever or even more than a decade ahead.

---

[8] These assertions are supported by empirical analysis in Rasler and Thompson (1994) and Reuveny and Thompson (2004).

The Chinese Military Challenge

As also demonstrated in chapter 2 (table 2.4), China's ability to project military capability over long distances has a considerable way to go to catch up with the United States' power projection capability. The problem is that China does not need to catch up in order to fight to gain objectives in or near its home region. Rather, it needs to develop military superiority in its back yard. The United States, on the other hand, does need to project military capability around the globe. Only some of its coercive capability can be committed to East Asia. As discussed earlier, the preoccupation with the Greater Middle East over the past few decades has meant that its tactical concerns have focused on low-intensity warfare and not fighting great powers. Thus, a challenge over regional hegemony in East Asia requires a more selective comparison of the two rivals' capabilities. Which side is likely to predominate in a clash in East Asian waters given capabilities assigned to the theater?

Fortunately, somebody else has already examined this question for the 1996–2017 period. Heginbotham et al. (2015) look at ten components of East Asian maritime combat for two scenarios—one involving amphibious conquest of Taiwan and another a contest over the control of the somewhat more distant Spratly Islands. The first four components focus on air warfare. Which side can establish air superiority (#2)? Which side can damage the other sides air defenses and bases (#1, 3, and 4)? The next two components relate to maritime warfare. Can the Chinese destroy US warships (#5)? Can the United States destroy Chinese amphibious capability (#6)? Components 7 and 8 involve one side's ability to deny the use of the other side's satellites. Component 9 asks a similar question related to which side is more likely to use cyberwarfare successfully. Finally, the tenth component is about the possession of second-strike capability—which side can survive a nuclear attack and still retaliate?

Table 5.1 summarizes the outcome for a Chinese attempt to retake Taiwan. In 1996, the United States had major advantages in seven of the ten combat components.[9] By 2017, the United States could claim a strong advantage in only one of the ten (second-strike capability). Of course, it is presumed that an attacker should have a major advantage to make a successful attack feasible. Table 5.1 suggests that the Taiwan theater remains problematic for China, but less so with the passage of time.

The Spratly Islands are farther away from the Chinese mainland than Taiwan and, therefore, more difficult for Chinese operations, even with artificial islands being built to overcome some of its disadvantages. In 1996, the United States had a major advantage in nine of the ten areas (adding the second-strike information from table 5.1). Gradually, this overwhelming advantage has deteriorated with

---

[9] An advantage means that the side with the advantage can be expected to attain its battlefield goals while the other side is much less likely to do so.

Table 5.1 Taiwan Scenario

Conflict components	1996	2003	2010	2017
1. Chinese Attacks on Air Bases	US	US	parity	china
2. Air Superiority	US	Us	us	parity
3. US Airspace Penetration	us	parity	parity	parity
4. US Attacks on Air Bases	parity	US	us	us
5. Chinese Anti-surface Warfare	US	us	parity	parity
6. US Anti-surface Warfare	US	US	us	us
7. US Counterspace	china	china	parity	parity
8. Chinese Counterspace	US	us	parity	parity
9. US vs. China Cyberware	US	US	us	us
10. Confidence in Secure Second China Strike Nuclear Capability US	Low High	Low High	Low High	Medium High

Source: based on Heginbotham et al. (2015: xxix). Strong leads are indicated by capitalized and bold identifications of the leader; weak leads and parity are expressed in lower case letters.

improvements in Chinese weaponry. In 2017, the United States could claim a major advantage in only two or three of the ten components. US-Chinese parity is observed in four areas. Hence, the situation is not quite the same, but the trend line is similarly biased in favor of improving Chinese military capabilities in its adjacent seas (see table 5.2).

Table 5.2 Spratly Islands Scenario

Conflict components	1996	2003	2010	2017
1. Chinese Attacks on Air Bases	US	US	US	parity
2. Air Superiority	US	US	us	us
3. US Airspace Penetration	US	US	US	us
4. US Attacks on Air Bases	US	US	US	US
5. Chinese Anti-Surface Warfare	US	US	us	parity
6. US Anti-Surface Warfare	US	US	US	US
7. US Counterspace	china	china	parity	parity
8. Chinese Counterspace	US	us	parity	parity
9. US vs. China Cyberware	US	US	us	us

Source: based on Heginbotham et al. (2015: xxix). Strong leades are indicated by capitalized and bold identifications of the leader; weak leads and partity are expressed in lower case letters.

Table 5.3 Sixteen Selected Indicators of Chinese Technological Catch-up

Indicator	As % of US	Values
	2004–2010	2014–2018
Total R&D as % GDP	52	76
Basic R&D as % GDP	13	26
Researchers as % workforce	22	25
University quality in top 500	9.5	28
Number science/engineering articles (average across fields)	14	33
Citations of scientific articles (three years post-publication)		
Average	44	68
Top 1%	27	52
Share of innovation companies in Global 100	8.3	11.5
High-tech production value added	30	77
IT production value added	50	145
IT services production value added	13	31
Commercial knowledge intense value added	21	53
Supercomputers among top 500		
Number	4.7	208
Performance	1	82
Industrial robot usage		
Robots/worker	10	49
Robot installations	81	416

Source: based on data reported in Atkinson and Foote (2019).

Note that the outcomes associated with scoring the relative advantages and disadvantages of the two rivals in East Asian waters are similar to those found subsequently in table 5.3's summary of Chinese gains in technological innovation and production. Neither the technological nor the military spheres are arenas with constant relative capabilities. Whether China can expect to become predominant in all ten components at some point in the future remains an open question, but China is making explicit headway in overcoming its local theater disadvantages.[10] For China, the local theater seems to have higher military priority than the global arena.

---

[10] See, as well, O'Rourke (2021), which views Chinese naval modernization gains as a major challenge to US Indo-Pacific forces.

Economic Preponderance

Yet military capabilities, especially at the global level, are predicated on the economic foundation that sustains them.[11] Modern system leaders first acquire the lead in technological innovation (not the size of the economy) and, in the process, develop expanded security concerns and the economic surplus to pay for the increased costs of not only of defending the homeland but also of policing the world economy.

There are several ways to measure leads in technological innovation. One that is not especially labor-intensive but that is definitely tricky due to the likelihood of misinterpretation is to look at the lead in gross domestic product share (Maddison, 2003) as reflecting one of the byproducts of a lead in innovation. Figure 5.1 captures the shape of the US rise in the world economy reasonably well. The US trajectory rose to and peaked around World War II, declined until around 1980, and then remained at a relatively stationary level into the current era.

Gross domestic product, nonetheless, is a treacherous indicator for technological leadership. The bulk size of the economy does not tell us anything necessarily about the quality of economic production. It only indexes how much economic activity is going on. As the Soviets discovered, gains in gross domestic product can be achieved by making nails too large to use, just as they can be generated by producing nails that are differentiated for a variety of uses. Similarly, gains in gross domestic product can be made by building houses, just as they can be achieved by building computers and green energy devices. The ability to build concrete blocks for housing is not to be denigrated, but it is not equal to also being able to produce products at the technological frontier. Moreover, while figure 5.1 may capture the shape of the US relative economic trajectory, it greatly underplays the extent of economic preponderance achieved by the United States in the twentieth century.

A better, even if still general, approach for our purposes focuses on shares of world manufacturing. Figure 5.2 portrays an updated version of Bairoch's (1982) well-known data for Britain and the United States.[12] Two arcs are shown. Britain's economic leadership arc had peaked by 1880 and moved toward a

---

[11] It is difficult to imagine this not being the case in the contemporary era. It certainly applies to the Portuguese, Dutch, and British system leader predecessors of the United States. There was a time when it was possible to seize wealth with military force, but that sequence has become increasingly improbable over the past few hundred years.

[12] Bairoch's (1982) data have been updated using World Development Indicators (WDI Online) of value-added manufacturing, substituting "high income" aggregations for Bairoch's "developed world" categorization.

Figure 5.1 US Share of World GDP

more "normal" share. The more impressive US arc peaked in 1953 and while it declined, it has yet to dip below a still "abnormal" 15 percent share. Again, these trajectories appear to possess "eyeball" validity in terms of their overall shapes. Britain's onetime advantage as the factory of the world, no doubt, is probably not demonstrated all that accurately given that Bairoch's focus on manufacturing did not discriminate between high- and low-tech production. Britain's initial advantage lay in spearheading the industrial revolution in the manufacture of textiles and iron products, subsequently linked closely to the utilization of coal and steam engines. If we were to focus exclusively on higher-tech manufacture, Britain's lead would look more impressive than what is shown in figure 5.2.

Perhaps one of the more reassuring elements of the threat of Chinese catch-up to the United States is the idea that China's economy has been quite proficient at basic manufacturing processes but still lacks the capability of innovating new industries and techniques. Most economic growth of states considered less developed a generation ago have failed to make the transition to this high level of production complexity. The middle-income trap does not prevent low-income economies from moving up the ladder to the next level, but a high-income economy seems out of reach for most states. Exactly why this trap is observed so

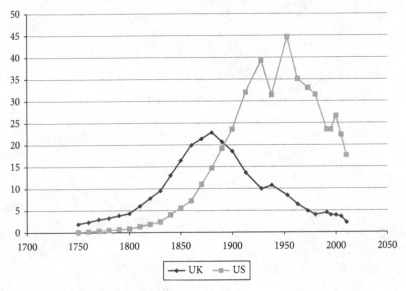

Figure 5.2 Shares of World Manufacturing

often is disputed, but it means that most economies are denied moving toward an ability to generate new technology on their own—as opposed to borrowing, buying, or stealing more advanced technology from other states. It also leads observers to be skeptical that a state like China might move from low-income status to become a leader in the production of radically new high technology. Historically, the odds have been against very much just such a transition, especially within a few decades.

On the other hand, a passage through the middle-income trap is not out of the question. One only needs to point out that England was once primarily an exporter of wool to European textile mills, early US exports were dominated by cotton destined for British textile mills, and Japan was not that long ago made fun of as a place that produced cheap toys and tourist items. It is possible, if rare, to ascend the technological gradient to the very top of production complexity. The question is whether China is a candidate for such an upward climb.

Brooks and Wohlforth (2015) are representative of analysts who are highly skeptical of China's ability to move beyond low-tech production. They note that the United States leads China by a vast margin in receipts for the use of intellectual property, triadic patents (patents registered in the United States, Europe, and Japan), the proportion of science and engineering citations in the top 1 percent of those cited, and the number of Nobel laureates in physics, chemistry, physiology, and medicine. These are all good indicators of technological superiority, and there has been equally good reason to be skeptical of China's ability to evade the middle-income trap. The problem is that those vast margins are shifting in China's favor. The US lead in intellectual property receipts remains daunting. China's share in 2018 was less than 5 percent of the US share.[13] It will also take some time for the cumulative number of Chinese Nobelists to catch up with the US share, but that is also a lagging indicator in the sense that awards are made for breakthroughs usually made sometime in the more distant past.[14] The Chinese numbers of top 1 percent citations have about tripled between 2000 and 2016, while the US increase over the same time period was about 6.2 percent.[15] The triadic patent data also demonstrate some gap diminishment. Not only has Japan passed the United States, China, and is already close to the German position, it seems to be slowly closing the gap with the United States, as shown in figure 5.3—assuming it stays on a trajectory similar to what has been observed in the past.

We can do better than looking at four indicators thanks to work done by Atkinson and Foote (2019). They looked at a large array of technological indicators in order to compare the Chinese share as a proportion of the US share in the first decade of this century with the second decade. On every indicator (table 5.3), the Chinese share in the mid-2010s was higher than it had been in the mid-2000s. On a few indicators, the Chinese share had surpassed the US share. None of this means that the Chinese economy has caught up to the US economy in matters of advanced technology. It does suggest, however, that the trendline is heading in a direction favorable to the Chinese catching up at some point.

A third approach follows this theme of moving from gross calculations (GDP) to more specific perspectives by examining the distribution of MNC activity around the world. MNCs have become the core of the world economy—a development ushered in earlier by US technological leadership in the first place. Not all MNC activity is certainly high-tech in nature—not when Walmart leads in Global 500 sales. But by examining the national identity and market share of the most pre-eminent MNCs, we can gain an appreciation for how the world

---

[13] In 2018, US receipts exceeded 128 million US dollars. China's receipts approximated 5.5 million dollars. See the World Bank's World Development Indicators for the source of these numbers.

[14] Taylor (2016:50) enumerates the nationality of Nobel Prize winners (1950–2015) to highlight the predominance of American laureates. However, if one calculates the decadal proportion of winners, an American share peak was registered in the 1990s (70 percent), declining to 55 percent over the period 2010–2015. Obviously, 55 percent remains a disproportionate number, but the question is whether the negative trend persists into the future—something that is hardly inconceivable.

[15] Author's calculations based on data reported in National Science Foundation (2020).

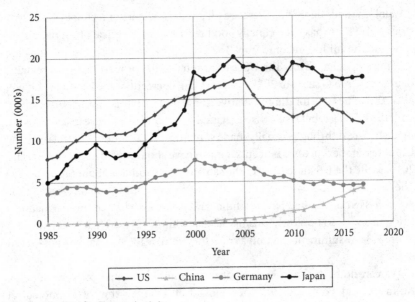

Figure 5.3 Triadic Patent Activity

economy is either tilted in favor of some states or an even playing field. MNCs have also become the core focus of research and development investments that lead to technological innovation and superiority.

Annual data on MNC activity have been generated by *Fortune* magazine for over half a century.[16] We can harness this information to estimates made for the pre–World War II period to sketch a dynamic picture of the rise and fall of US corporate activity in the twentieth century and beyond.[17] To make the data as comparable as possible over time, only industrial corporations are examined.[18] Thus, the increasing prominence of service corporations, and especially financial services, is underplayed.

---

[16] *Fortune* (1957) was the first time information on non-US firms was added to the Global 500 emphasis on US firms.

[17] The 1912 data are found in Hannah (1999). The 1937 data are supplied in Schmitz (1995).

[18] The pre-1945 estimates are restricted to industrial corporations. Therefore, the post-1945 estimates need to be similarly restricted for this analysis. The pre-1945 estimates are also restricted to the top 100 firms in the world or fewer (a 1937 estimate looks only at the top 50), which suggests that the post-1945 estimates should be similarly restricted. Finally, the pre-1945 corporate rankings are based on the size of assets controlled, which is viewed as a proxy for sales shares. In the post-1945 era, it is possible to look directly at sales. In this case, then, the pre-1945 approach is not followed in the post-1945 period.

Table 5.4 and figure 5.4 provide overviews of the US share of the top 100 industrial MNCs since 1912.[19] The preponderance of US corporations resembles the post–World War II preponderance held in global power projection capabilities, at least through 1970. The US share was between three-fifths and two-thirds of the top 100 firms through the pre–World War II era. The 1956 figure is much higher (.796) and it does not require much imagination to guess that the US lead in MNCs approached 100 percent around 1945. Assuming the MNC lead peaked at some point between 1945 and 1956, the trajectory of the MNC share has been a fairly steady decline down to about a one-fourth share in the last twenty years—very much like what is portrayed in Bairoch's manufacturing share data in figure 5.2.

Here again, we have uncontestable evidence for relative decline (and a high floor).[20] The predominance the United States maintained in industrial multinationals up through as late as 1980 is no more.[21] It is hard to imagine a return to the level of MNC predominance that was maintained through much of the twentieth century. While the US share lead in 2010 is still twice as large as its nearest competitor, that is not the same thing as the kind of gap that characterized earlier years. For example, in 1956, the nearest competitor position was roughly one-eighth of the US position. In 1980, the ratio was still about 5:1. Not only is it conceivable to imagine the combined Japanese-Chinese MNC share surpassing the US position in the near future, the Japanese share of the top 100 did pass the US share in 1995. The Japanese MNC catch-up turned out to be short-lived, and the United States share lead can be expected to persist for a while longer. But the economic capability configuration is clearly multipolar and has been for several decades. Nor is the US lead in MNC activity unsurpassable. At the same time, though, there does not appear to be any reason to expect the US

---

[19] As noted previously, the exception is the 1937 information which is based on the top 50 global corporations.

[20] However, Starrs (2013) contends that a focus on MNC shares underestimates US economic power because US investors disproportionately own parts of non-US corporations and because globalized production processes and related divisions of labor complicate the assessment of who actually profits from product manufacture and marketing. But even to the extent that he is right, the substantial decline demonstrated in figure 5.4 would seem to be able to withstand charges of exaggeration.

[21] One possibility, of course, is that by concentrating only on the top 100 firms, the outcome is biased toward older, larger, and rich firms, which would benefit US scores and disadvantage relatively new Asian firms. If so, the extent of US decline might be underestimated in table 5.3. However, Biswas's (2013: 46) calculations suggest that there may be some bias, but perhaps that it is not too distortional. He provides information on the unweighted numbers (not the sales) of MNCs in the 2011 Fortune Global 500. Japan's share is .136 and China's share is .122, whereas table 5.3 gives them a combined .204 share. Biswas's count for the United States would put the US share at .266, while table 5.3 indicates .261. Comparing weighted and unweighted numbers is awkward and it is logical that new firms are likely to enter at the bottom of the top 500, but the comparison suggests that we are not dealing with two entirely different universes in focusing on the top 100 as opposed to the top 500 firms in the world.

Table 5.4 National Identity of Top 100 Industrial Multinational Corporations (weighted by revenue)

State	1912	1937	1956	1970	1980	1995	2010	2019
United States	.608	.644	.796	.654	.466	.248	.261	.348
United Kingdom	.155	.219	.104	.078	.097	.025	.043	.044
Germany	.096	.067	.033	.081	.111	.108	.100	.081
France	.044			.036	.069	.061	.044	.033
Netherlands	.023	.043	.054	.048	.069	.029	.039	.034
Belgium	.007				.007			
Switzerland			.008	.011	.015	.031	.033	.007
Italy			.004	.021	.046	.024	.030	.013
Russia	.016						.018	.025
Luxembourg	.004						.007	.005
Norway							.008	.006
Denmark						.012		
Finland						.037		
Sweden						.005		
Spain							.015	
EUROPE	.345	.329	.203	.275	.414	.283	.386	.247
Japan				.071	.071	.423	.124	.095
South Korea						.035	.067	.029
China						.005	.080	.217
Thailand							.007	
India							.006	.012
Taiwan							.011	.013
Malaysia							.007	
Singapore								.013
ASIA				.071	.071	.463	.302	.379
Mexico	.006				.010		.015	.006
Canada		.027			.011			
Brazil					.010		.019	.007
Venezuela					.013	.005	.010	

Table 5.4 *Continued*

State	1912	1937	1956	1970	1980	1995	2010	2019
South Africa	.040							
Australia					.005		.006	
Saudi Arabia								.026
OTHER	.046	.027			.049	.005	.050	.039

Note: The numbers in each cell represent the proportional share of MNC assets/sales of each country.

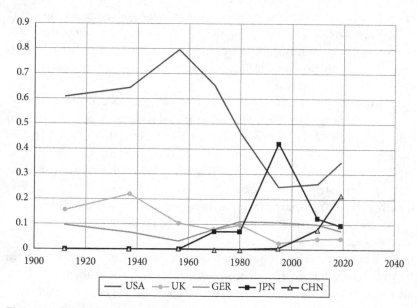

Figure 5.4 Top 100 Industrial MNC Sales Shares

MNC share to soon fall below a quarter share of world MNC activity. This is a high floor, and it has taken some time to decline to that level.[22]

But a skeptic might wish to argue that an emphasis on manufacturing is passé. The world economy is becoming increasingly service oriented, especially in its most affluent neighborhoods. To look only at manufacturing unduly penalizes

[22] Moreover, the US share of the world's foreign direct investment has increased in terms of inflows from slightly less than 10 percent in 1970 to close to 22 percent in 2018. The US outflow share has declined from 37.5 percent in 1970 to about 20 percent in 2017. Thus, the US disproportionate share of investment flows seems likely to persist as well. These calculations were computed by the author using World Bank WDI data expressed in current US dollars. Trends in US FDI are discussed in Jackson (2017).

the increasingly service economy of the United States. The charge is accurate. If we compare the US top 100 MNCs in 1956 with those in 2010, the proportion of service firms more than doubles. In 1956, US service firms accounted for 21.3 percent of the top US MNCs. By 2010, US service firms claimed 49.8 percent of the top 100 US MNC sales.

Alternatively, if we look at the more global picture found in the upper echelon (top 100) of the Fortune Global 500, we lack systematic information for non-US firms in 1956, but we can assume that they would not have claimed more than a very small share of the global top 100 MNC revenues.[23] Most of the US service firms in 1956 are found clustered near the bottom of the global (and US) top 100 firms. By 2010, service firms claim 44 percent of the global top 100 firm sales and US firms are overrepresented in this group (about 38 percent of the global service sales go to US firms). Expressed differently, almost exactly half (48.8 percent) of the US share of the global top 100 firms (regardless of type of economic activity) goes to service firms.

So, ignoring service firms clearly does affect calculations of the US share. But it does not alter the fact that US firms controlled roughly 80 percent of global elite corporate revenues in the mid-1950s and that by 2010 the US share had declined considerably. If we combine manufacturing and service firms in 2010 (as Fortune reporting does), the US MNC share of top 100 revenue was 34.5 percent. Approximately a third of global sales is certainly much better than approximately a fourth. Yet a movement from over two-thirds to one-third remains an impressive decline. It means the US share is still far more than disproportionate but not as predominant as it once was.

Thus, as suggested by various indicators, the US economic lead has survived for some time. It may well continue into the near future. It may also be that it has hit a floor beyond which it will not decline further—or not decline further for a few more years.

But it is a lead that is far less impressive than it once was. It is also a lead that has been challenged with some success. Further challenges are to be expected.[24] In this respect, the relative decline has substantive meaning. It is difficult to imagine its not having negative implications for the future of the US lead in power projection capabilities as well. If developments proceed as they have in the past, as the economic foundation shrinks, subject to some lag, we should

---

[23] Nor did Fortune magazine provide any information on insurance firms in its 1956 reporting.

[24] Biswas (2013: 57–58) suggests that the increasing number of Asian corporations, especially the Chinese firms, will (1) make it increasingly more difficult for Western firms to compete for the growing Asian market; (2) give Asian firms more funds to become more competitive in leading-edge technology; (3) favor Asian firms' competition for talented personnel from Asian countries on which Western corporations have been able to rely upon for the past fifty years as low-cost but high-tech labor; and (4) tilt the concentration of global capital flows generally toward Asian markets.

anticipate a system leader's willingness and ability to support global operations to diminish as well.

The More Things Change, the More They Remain the Same?

There is always the question of whether developments will proceed in the future just as they have proceeded in the past. Concentration in power projection and/or technological innovation may give way to perennial fragmentation. Power projection may become dependent on drones that are less expensive to build and operate, and therefore open to participation in by many state and even non-state actors. Technological innovation may no longer be clustered in time and space. For that matter, technological innovation in the future may never duplicate the transformation scale achieved in the past (Smil, 2005; Gordon, 2016). Advances in social media, after all, are not the same thing as introducing indoor plumbing or air conditioning. If nothing else, one can live much better without the former than the latter changes.

Observations such as these are not unrelated to the relative decline question. An ascent based on building assembly lines, autos, and jets and undergirded by petroleum and electrification probably cannot be sustained by information technology changes as experienced to date. That is to say, the overall change is less radical than were the ones experienced in the late nineteenth and early twentieth centuries. But that does not mean that future radical changes on the scale of the second industrial revolution are not still coming. It only suggests that they have yet to arrive.

These questions about future continuities are well asked but difficult to answer very definitively in the present. In the end analysis, we may simply have to wait and see. Nonetheless, the claim that we will never match the transforming innovations of the nineteenth century overlooks an important aspect of the relative decline question. In some respects, the question that is more important than whether or how much relative decline has transpired is what will be needed to ascend in the future. There is a strong clue on this issue in the MNC data. If we ask what these corporations do, and have done, should we expect a great deal of change or a great deal of continuity between 1912 and 2010?

The change/continuity question hinges on what is examined. There is no question that if the focus is placed on the names of the corporations, there will be substantial change. Few top 100 corporations in 1912 still existed in 2019.[25]

---

[25] Hannah (1998: 63) examines the history of the top 100 industrials between 1912 and 1995, tracing mergers, bankruptcies, and name changes. He finds that twenty of the original 100 survived in 1995. The survivors were largely concentrated in what were new industries in 1912.

Nor should we expect the same type of corporate specializations to survive for 100 years. Just as most of us no longer play vinyl records on turntables, the most affluent economies no longer consume coal or steel as they once did.

Oil and vehicle production and marketing remain important. Even in 1912, the oil category was the single largest type of corporate specialization. After 1912 the combination of the two categories never is less than 35 percent and reaches as high as 61 percent in 1980, thanks to inflated oil prices. Between 1956 and 2010, oil and vehicles claim slightly less than half the sales of the top 100 industrial MNCs. Other specializations rise and fall. Food and tobacco declines in large part because tobacco sales have declined in the global North. Coal and textiles pretty much drop out of the top 100. Chemistry peaked early and then declined. Metals (combining ore extraction and steel processing) do much the same. Aerospace enters dramatically and then decays. The production of products dependent on electricity trends upward. So does the production of information technology and telecommunications. But none of these new specializations has come close until recently to rivaling the interdependent oil/vehicles concentration in the American economy.

Thus, there have been changes. Some sunset industries have fallen out of the top 100, while some sunrise industries have entered the elite ranks. By and large, though, the predominance of the gas-driven engine dominates the top 100 MNCs through much of the twentieth century and continuing into the twenty-first century. What should we make of this continuity?

It is not implausible to anticipate continued improvement in prime movers, consequent changes in fuels, and new phases of technological innovation led by a lead economy. If so, the real question for analysts of world politics is not so much whether the United States' lead has declined or even how much it has declined. We can answer both questions concisely even though, no doubt, we will continue to disagree about their implications. The root of the problem is that there is no necessarily direct relationship between relative position and influence across the board. When the United States possessed a stronger relative position, it did not always choose to exert its predominance. Nor was it always possible to successfully apply its predominant position in all corners of the world. The relative position of system leaders does not guarantee political-economic outcomes. We can only say that stronger relative positions should be roughly correlated with outcomes preferred by the system leader. Similarly, weaker relative positions should be equally roughly correlated with outcomes not preferred by the system leader.

Nonetheless, the real question, ultimately, may prove to be who will be best positioned to capitalize on the likelihood of new prime movers, fuels, and technological innovation in the remainder of the twenty-first century. If one country successfully leads the way in this process, a new era of systemic leadership will likely emerge. If no single country assumes the leadership mantle, we will either need to develop new institutional practices to govern the world economy or we will be consigned to a relatively leaderless arena in which international competition could easily trump international cooperation.[26]

At this point, it is hard to tell which path the world system will take. The relative decline of US systemic leadership is real, but it has not yet proceeded to the point that the United States is out of the running for either remaining competitive or even resuming a strong lead. Other possible contenders for the systemic leadership role have yet to surpass unequivocally the US position in technological innovation. The European Union (EU) is far from being a monolithic actor. Nor does it (or, more appropriately, its component members) have a long track record of leading in economic innovations or global power projection since the nineteenth century. China has yet to develop much in the way of global reach capabilities. Its economy, for the most part, has yet to make the transition from specializing in inexpensive labor and mass production to specializing in high-tech production. Still, and despite variable handicaps, neither the EU nor China can be ruled out as potential system leaders. But it is also difficult to rule out completely the return of the United States despite a gradual and incremental loss of the requisite platform (leading sector innovation and market share plus global reach) for exercising global leadership. But if this analysis is on target, a US renaissance will depend on a greatly revived economic platform for systemic leadership. It will not come about through appeals for retrenchment, lower taxes, or reduced governmental spending—all symptoms of, as opposed to antidotes for, relative decline.

No doubt, we will continue to argue over whether the United States has really experienced much in the way of meaningful decline. It clearly has, but the decline is manifested far more clearly in the economic sphere than in the military sphere. The amount of relative decline experienced to date is not yet enough to have eliminated the United States' *primus inter pares* status. But being first among equals is a different proposition from being first among unequals. It is even conceivable that the United States might retain indefinitely a first among equals status without regaining the type of system leadership position it once held. That is one possible future scenario.[27] Other possible futures involve other states acquiring the lead economy and system leader status. In the interim, no doubt, we will continue to debate the existence and meaning of the incumbent system leader's relative decline. Perhaps only when the question has been resolved by the transition to a new global leadership structure—either of the traditional national

---

[26] New institutional governance practices are emerging, regardless of what is happening in the systemic leadership sphere. The question is whether they can stand alone or are more likely to work in a regime reinforced by renewed systemic leadership.

[27] See Rapkin and Thompson (2013) for five different scenarios for the future of global systemic leadership.

variety or some other, newer sort of institutional arrangement—will the question become moot.

Non-economic Decline Dimensions

As crucial as the economic foundation is to this question of system leader decline, it is not the only arena to consider. Political-military activities are also prominent at the apex of the global elite.

Go (2011) is interested in comparative imperial dynamics. One of his arguments about these dynamics is that global hegemons go through three phases: ascent, maturity, and decline. In the ascent phase, aspiring hegemons are energetic and aggressive in order to facilitate their continued rise and acquisition of a position of economic preponderance. In the ascent phase, competitors need to be defeated and subordinated. They use military force and acquire territorial control to achieve this singular structural unicentricity. Once economic preponderance is attained, there is less need for force and territorial expansion because economic competitors have been encouraged to accept a secondary status and because ascent hinges in part on a world war that also has the effect of reducing competitors and competition for a time. Now the global status quo must be maintained because that status quo is closely linked to the new hegemon's economic prosperity. Since the competition is reduced in strength, more indirect techniques can suffice in many cases. In the hegemonic decline phase, however, competitors are back and renewed in their competitiveness. More direct techniques are necessary to defeat them or to try to maintain the faltering status quo.

Go suggests that if this interpretation is correct, we should see different frequencies of territorial expansion/acquisition and uses of military force in different phases. The maturity phase should see the lowest frequency of direct aggression. In the ascent and decline phases we should observe higher frequencies of aggressive behavior. Table 5.5 tests these predictions. The top half of the table looks at British annexations of territory between 1765 and 1939. Controlling for the number of years in each phase, the annexation rate in the British maturity phase was about half that in the ascent phase and nearly a third of the decline phase in which competition has returned.

In the lower half of the table, comparable phase delineations are reported for the United States, but since colonies went out of fashion, the behavioral indicators are restricted to uses of military force, sketched over time in figure 5.5.[28]

---

[28] The British data are reported in Go (2011: 212). He also looked at the US case, but his analysis was limited to 2004. Table 5.5 uses Go's phase periodization for the United States but recounts the military use of force information, utilizing a similar but more recently published source (Torreon and Plagakis, 2021).

Table 5.5 Hegemonic Aggressive Behavior by Phase

British colonial annexation

Number of Years	Phase	Years	Colonies acquired	Annual rate
52	Ascent	1765–1815	39	0.75
57	Maturity	1816–1873	23	0.40
65	Decline	1874–1939	69	1.06

US use of force

			Uses of force	
65	Ascent	1874–1939	195	3.00
27	Maturity	1946–1973	47	1.95
45	Decline	1974–2019	264	5.87

Source: The data on British colonial annexation are taken from Go (2011: 212). The US use of force information is reported in Torreon and Plagakis (2021).

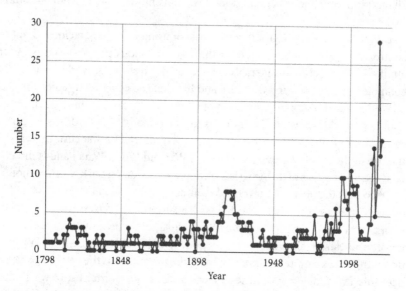

Figure 5.5 Instances of US Use of Force

A similar pattern to the one observed in the British case is discerned. The frequency of uses of military force were about 54 percent greater in the ascent phase and 201 percent greater than in the maturity phase. These frequency counts no doubt understate the amount of behavior involved. Landing forces on the Caribbean island of Grenada is not the same thing as a massive intervention in South Vietnam. Both interventions are counted the same way by the source in the sense that one year in Grenada equals one year in South Vietnam. But then so too is sending specialized armed forces to a number of different countries in Africa, Eurasia, and Latin America, which are reported as one incident if their application focus is the same because that is the way US presidents choose to report military activity to Congress. Thus, there are ways in which military interventions might be weighted in terms of number of personnel involved, deaths, or costs if those data were available but the bias associated with relying on frequency would not be restricted to any single phase. So, we might count differently but there is little question that the frequency of military intervention in the US decline phase would still be higher than in the earlier two phases.

The basic difference in phases is due to the amount and nature of competition. When competition is greater, more force is deemed necessary. When competition is limited, indirect influence is more attractive and less essential to get the job done. Go's argument is more nuanced than this one-variable-explains-all recapitulation but, essentially, that is what primarily changes from one phase to the next.[29]

Do these numbers suggest that the costs of using force have ballooned out of control and contributed to decline via the drain of military protection costs? After all, the United States considerably outspends the rest of the world on military equipment, personnel, and activities and has done so consistently since the end of World War II. But as a proportion of GDP, this does not seem to be the case. Table 5.6 provides a list of US war costs for the period 1775–2010. The numbers in column 3 are impressive. Column 4, however, controls for war costs in terms of the size of the existing economy. The Civil War and World Wars I and II did encompass large shares of the American economy. The wars since Korea have not.[30]

Of course, the post-9/11 wars and their costs did not end in 2010. The methodology used to construct table 5.6 is also admittedly conservative because it omits certain types of costs (veteran benefits, public debt interest, and assistance to allies). An alternative project, Brown University's the Costs of War undertaking, takes a more comprehensive approach and adds the veteran benefits, debt interest, and ally assistance to a calculation of a shorter list of wars—the 2001–2020 costs of wars in Afghanistan, Pakistan, and Iraq (Crawford, 2019).

---

[29] For instance, Go (2011) suggests that the high costs of colonial rule and the Cold War rivalry with the Soviet Union contributed to the US reluctance to exercise power directly and overtly in various instances. Yet these other restraints are not advanced as anywhere near equal to the fact that less force is needed in the absence of economic competition.

[30] The evaluation of war costs cannot be restricted to financial costs alone, but most of the human suffering since World War II has been borne by allies or opponents.

Table 5.6 Military Costs of Major US Wars, 1775–2010

War	Duration	Total military cost of war	War cost as % of GDP at peak of war
American Revolution	1775–1783	2.407 million	NA
War of 1812	1812–1815	1.553 million	2.2%
Mexican War	1846–1849	2.376 million	1.4
Civil War: Union	1861–1865	59.631 million	11.3
Civil War: Confederacy	1861–1865	20.11 million	NA
Spanish-American War	1898–1899	283 million	1.1
World War I	1917–1921	334 billion	13.6
World War II	1941–1945	4.104 trillion	35.8
Korea	1950–1953	341 billion	4.2
Vietnam	1965–1975	738 billion	2.3
Persian Gulf	1990–1991	102 billion	0.3
Afghanistan	2001–2010	321 billion	0.7
Iraq	2003–2010	784 billion	1.0
Total post-9/11	2001–2010	1.147 trillion	1.2

Source: slightly modified from Daggett (2010: 1–2). Note that Daggett does not count veteran benefits, war-related debt interest, or assistance to allies. Therefore, the numbers would be higher with a different accounting system.

Its $6.4 trillion estimate is almost six times the post-9/11 number reported in table 5.6. But that is over a twenty-year period, which makes it more comparable in some respects to the shorter Korean War costs. While it is disheartening to think about how such a sum might have been spent on something else such as infrastructure repair, climate change, accelerating an energy transition, or heading off a post-Covid-19 economic depression, even that large sum is not sufficient to account for relative decline. At the same time, it has not helped, especially in light of the marginal returns for the expenditure. That conclusion leads us to the topic of territorial traps.

Territorial Traps

Territorial traps (Thompson and Zuk, 1986) are sea power commitments to defend land bases. They are traps because sea powers, especially system leaders, are ill-designed to compete militarily on land. Their specialty is monitoring and policing the global commons. The technology for that function does not always translate readily into land operations that require boots on the ground, and, as often as not, large numbers of them.

Yet territorial commitments seem inevitable in the history of systemic leadership. Beginning with the Portuguese, strategic debates over whether to establish land bases or rely on offshore coercion were usually won by the land base advocates. It is not hard to see why. Offshore coercion has its limitations in Eurasia. It was not difficult for Europeans to dominate the Indian Ocean trade routes with their ship cannons. Those same cannons could also fire on coastal cities but not much else. Penetration inland was held up for several hundred years until advances in military firepower/tactics was improved and enabled successes in the eighteenth century in India and the nineteenth century in China.

Prior to the European military/industrial revolutions, European ships needed bases to repair, refuel, and maintain the ability to keep fleets at sea. Reliable access to markets was also an imperative. The initial solution was to build a network of European-style fortresses that could be relieved from the sea when they came under attack on land. Alliances were made with local rulers to provide some protection. The problems were threefold. Once land commitments were made, there was always a temptation to push defenses outward to improve security. More land threats on the frontier? Extend the security perimeter forward and reduce the threat to the home base. Of course, the extension of security perimeters was accompanied by the catch-22 of more territorial commitments that required defense.

A second problem related to the local alliances. Europeans always needed local alliances to enhance their land forces. But the local allies often needed defense, armament, and training to ensure their support. Gradually, the weaknesses of local rulers would drag in a greater European commitment. In many cases, the Portuguese, Dutch, and British simply took over local defenses when it became clear that indirect assistance would not suffice. But the third problem was that there were also constant pressures from European entrepreneurs to extend European military presence on land to protect commercial, religious, and political undertakings.

These three general tendencies encouraged successive iterations of European intrusions into Eurasian space. The Portuguese momentum peaked early in the sixteenth century but their operations were stymied when a large number of their military-political elite were killed, captured, or ransomed in a late sixteenth-century effort to conquer Morocco. The succession struggle that ensued enabled a Spanish takeover of the Portuguese empire that lasted several generations. The Dutch ended up greatly overextended in their gradual attempt to control Indonesia. Military costs came to exceed commercial profits in the eighteenth century. The British ended up with an extensive empire on which the sun never set and one that was never explicitly sought. It was also difficult for the British to relinquish control even though they had little choice given the costly problems they encountered in places such as India, Egypt, and Palestine. Initially advantageous, they became too costly as the metropole's ability to sustain imperial efforts declined. As such, they constituted secondary decline factors. That is, the "overreach" became evident after relative decline had already set in and thus was not a primary contribution to decline. But once decline was in progress, the increasing burdens of extensive territorial commitments could not help making the problems worse.

Whether the United States is imperial is something that continues to be debated. Extensive territorial expansion ended in the US case after its North American ambitions were realized. Occasional forays into Caribbean and Pacific holdings tended to be less than permanent.[31] Even so, indirect territorial commitments gradually expanded after 1945. The Soviet threat in Western Europe led to the NATO commitment and the stationing of troops in Europe to guarantee the US commitment to defending Western Europe. The Greek civil war vaguely extended the US commitment to parts of southeastern Europe and the Middle East. The Korean peninsula was initially written off as of marginal interest, but the attempt of North Korea to conquer the southern part of the peninsula led to US/UN intervention in 1950 and a long-running commitment to defend South Korea. An initial desire to avoid helping France control Indochina led ultimately to a long and large-scale US military intervention in Southeast Asia in the 1960s and 1970s. In the 1980s, the US focus was centered particularly on Central America and suppressing insurgent takeovers. The 1990s inaugurated the large-scale intervention in what is sometimes called the Greater Middle East (in this case, the first Gulf and Bosnian-later Kosovo interventions), followed by a retaliation against Afghanistan and a second Gulf intervention, Iraqi occupation for eight years, and a later return to combat the Islamic State.[32] Clearly, the second Gulf intervention distracted attention from Afghanistan, which almost guaranteed the protraction of the Afghan commitment. The same second Gulf intervention and subsequent occupation of Iraq set up the subsequent rise of the Islamic State phenomenon. Whether the premature if partial withdrawal of American forces and the betrayal of Kurdish allies will encourage the re-emergence of the Islamic State remains to be seen.

One observer (Bacevich, 2016: 362–363) had this to say about American adventures in the Greater Middle East:

Rather than keeping threats to US interests at bay, a penchant for military activism, initially circumspect but increasingly uninhibited over time, has

---

[31] The exceptions are Puerto Rico and Hawai'i.
[32] Smaller-scale interventions had begun in 1979 (Iran) and the early 1980s (Lebanon).

helped to foster new threats. Time and again, from the 1980s to the present, U.S. military power, unleashed rather than held in abeyance, has met out-right failure, produced results other than those intended, or proved to be largely irrelevant. . . .

Take whatever definition of purpose you want; after more than three decades of trying, for U.S. forces the missions remain unfinished. Indeed, "unfinished" hardly begins to describe the situation; mission accomplish-ment is nowhere in sight. Put simply, we're stuck.

Whether the United States remains stuck in the Greater Middle East, the point is that one thing seemed to lead to another in a semi-conscious fashion (with the advantage of hindsight) that resembled the territorial trap problems of earlier system leaders. Trillions of dollars and thousands of military casualties later, it is unclear what was accomplished other than to seriously aggravate the insecurity problems already manifested in the regions affected (see Al Mukhtar and Nordland, 2019; Malkasian, 2020; Reality Check Team, 2020). The status of Bosnia and Kosovo remains unclear, the Taliban rules in Afghanistan once again, and the instability of a pacific Gulf future seems probable. These territorial trap problems did not initiate US relative decline, but the difficulties the United States has encountered in trying to disentangle itself from the Middle Eastern tar baby persist. They also have interfered with focusing on the Chinese challenge.

Conclusion

It would be naïve to conclude that an examination of the evidence reviewed in this chapter will resolve the ongoing debate about the relative decline of the United States. There seems to be more at stake for many participants in the de-bate than would be suggested by what is otherwise a straightforward analytical question. Nonetheless, the evidence suggests that the relative economic position of the United States has declined in comparison to what it once was even if the relative military position of the United States has yet to experience much in the way of meaningful decay. Overall, the US systemic lead remains in effect, but its future seems more fragile and vulnerable than in the past. No other state is close to snatching the lead away. Considerable inertia characterizes the short term (the next one or two decades). Yet the net trend line, barring a US technological re-surgence which remains a possibility, suggests that the system is moving toward multipolarity in general and perhaps a sort of bipolar stalemate in East Asia—if it is not already there. It is there in terms of the distribution of economic wealth. It is not yet there in terms of the distribution of global reach military capabil-ities. But the history of the international system suggests that the distribution of military power should align itself eventually with its economic foundation for meeting protection costs. "Eventually," however, could be several decades down the road.

This record is confusing for several reasons. US decline gives off mixed signals that different analysts can choose to emphasize in entirely different ways. Analysts also come at the problem with widely varying ideas about what the foundations for pre-eminence are. Then, too, the ongoing decline of the overarching petroleum regime in economic production muddies the interpretative waters even further. Moreover, the relative decline of US systemic leadership is unlike those of its predecessors. Portuguese, Dutch, and British relative declines were all less ambiguous (at least in retrospect).[33] The weakened Portuguese were absorbed and subordinated by their Spanish neighbors for some sixty years. The Dutch and British financially exhausted themselves in global warfare. The Dutch naval lead was gone after 1713 even if its prominence in trade lingered a bit longer. The British naval lead did not quite disappear after 1918, but its relative position was increasingly tenuous and was gone within a few decades and its technological lead had long since evaporated in the mid-nineteenth century. In contrast, the United States has managed to hang on to its leads in both technological and global reach capabilities—although the latter is much more impressive than the former.

Still, the evidence implies that we should stop debating whether relative decline has occurred. It seems hard to deny that it has occurred. It is not impending. On the contrary, it has been ongoing for some time. US exceptionalism, whatever its claims, cannot be expected to bar typical positional changes. We should focus more on what the relative decline means, as opposed to spilling ink denying it, and contemplate seriously what else might be coming down the road.[34] Relative decline probably does not mean that the United States is about to become an ordinary country in world politics. It is hanging on tenuously to the system's lead economy and retains a clear lead in global military reach. But it is not the kind of lead your grandfather or father knew. The rest of the twenty-first century, so far, appears most unlikely to resemble the second half of the twentieth century, or even the first decade of the twenty-first century. The US relative position was once stronger than it is today even if the United States remains the most powerful state in the system. The ultimate questions are whether that means the same

[33] The exception to this generalization is Britain's first systemic leadership decline in the eighteenth century prior to the French Revolutionary Wars. This one was also more ambiguous, but it is also not acknowledged by most international relations analysts.

[34] Atkinson and Ezell (2012: 64–84) list twenty factors that British and US relative decline share. The twentieth factor is "reluctance by elites to admit relative decline." Their fundamental point is that it is usually easier to deny that there is a problem than to acknowledge that there is a problem and that something different needs to be tried to turn things around.

thing it once did, and do we have any reason to expect the United States to re-main the most powerful state tomorrow?

US relative decline means that it should be harder for the United States to "get its way" in world politics. It does not mean that US foreign policy initiatives will always fail. But the initiatives will be both more costly and less likely to suc-ceed. Whether the United States will ultimately be eclipsed by another power depends in part on whether US complacency gets in the way of reinvigorating its leadership in economic innovation. It also depends on whether another state can wrestle away the lead in economic innovation. That type of eclipse is not just around the corner, but it cannot be ruled out as a possibility for later in the twenty-first century. In these respects, most everybody in the US decline debate is partially right—but also partially wrong. Relative decline has occurred. But it has yet to eliminate the US lead. At the same time, nothing guarantees that the US lead will survive for long. The lead has been diminished considerably, especially in economic matters, and that makes it more vulnerable to being eclipsed by a challenger. Whether relative decline continues apace will depend on a variety of factors ranging from denial/complacency through dysfunctional political institutions to successful innovation in the United States, and their comparative absence elsewhere.

A few years ago, Brooks and Wohlforth (2016a: 91) had this to say about the United States' political future:

> Even though the United States' economic dominance has eroded from its peak, the country's military superiority is not going anywhere, nor is the globe-span-ning alliance structure that constitutes the core of the existing liberal interna-tional order (unless Washington unwisely decides to throw it away). Rather than expecting a power transition in international politics, everyone should start getting used to a world in which the United States remains the sole super-power for decades to come.

"Superpower" is a term that emerged toward the end of World War II to acknowledge that some great powers were simply vastly more powerful than other great powers were or had been. Brooks and Wohlforth were right about the economic erosion even if they overly discount its fundamental significance. They were also right about the persistence of global military superiority and the importance of an extensive alliance network. But all that global military su-periority is unlikely to be able to be focused on East Asia or any other region in which US influence is challenged. Nor is the gap in superiority guaranteed to persist forever. Challengers press to catch up and incumbent system leaders aspire to stay ahead but also need to contain costs. As a consequence, they tend to rest on their technological laurels as the gap between challengers and incumbents diminishes. Unfortunately, we have also seen how fragile the alliance structure is when Washington unwisely attempts to throw it away. It may be something that can be reconstructed to some extent post-Trump but allies will have good reasons to be even more wary of US trustworthiness in the future than they have had in the past. All that suggests the United States will be something less than the sole superpower for decades to come unless the superpower label is restricted only to a military lead.[35] And, as noted before, there is a difference between being ahead and being far ahead. The United States' capability foundation for systemic leadership is in the process of moving from once being far ahead of the competition pretty much across the board to something akin to just being ahead, and not necessarily in every area. As the superiority or primacy gap diminishes, so, too, does the space for exerting systemic leadership. At the very least, it makes successful leadership much harder and more dependent on clever diplomacy and allies.[36]

It is to a dysfunctional political process that we move to next. Explaining how domestic politics has been transformed over several decades has its own complexities. Not everything can be linked to external relative decline. Yet some of it can be linked without much doubt. Moreover, it is hard to see how anything substantial can be done to address external decline in relative position without a significant turnaround in the functioning of domestic institutions and processes.

---

[35] The implied persistence of unipolarity is a topic taken up in chapter 7.

[36] We have a tendency to single out various foreign policy agents who are considered to be above average in their ability to manipulate allies and foes at the negotiation table. Putting aside the accuracy of these categorizations, clever agents can work with a weak resource base, just as a superior poker player can win hands with poor cards on occasion. The point is twofold, though. The number of above-average foreign policy decision makers seems to be rather finite and bluffs are more likely to be called by other players with good or better cards. It is better therefore, not to rely on bluffs too often.

6

The Dysfunctionality of Domestic Politics

The last chapter focused on external relative decline—that is, falling behind in terms of gains made by other states. But there is also an internal type of decline that may or may not be autonomous from what goes on in international relations. The main questions that arise in this context are whether (a) there is evidence of internal decline and, if so; (b) to what extent is the relative decline linked to internal decline? There are several possible types of linkages. Relative decline may be variably responsible for domestic decay. Domestic decline processes may be variably responsible for external relative decline. Or domestic decline processes may be variably responsible for decision makers and stakeholders finding themselves unable to address the reasons for external decline. None of these possibilities are mutually exclusive. They might all be in play.

There is clear evidence of domestic decline in the US case. It is related to external decline but not a perfect reflection of it. That is, some of the domestic processes have their own motors and could have taken place with or without relative external decline. It is also unquestionable that domestic decline processes diminish the probability that domestic actors will be able to respond to external decline and turn things around. At the very least, domestic decline slows down and may block any effective responses to external decline. In addition, the generation of public goods at the global level requires domestic support to continue. If that support is increasingly less likely to be forthcoming, it is hard to imagine US presidents continuing in that vein—regardless of whether access to an adequate resource base for leadership activities is at hand. Either way, the likelihood of global leadership is reduced.

Domestic Political Dysfunction

One of the main obstacles to responding to American relative decline problems is domestic political dysfunction. Figure 6.1, based on Campbell (2018), offers a respectable summary of many of the factors pertinent to US internal decline even though its ostensible purpose is to explain the dependent variable of Donald J. Trump's ascent to the presidency. Although it is not reflected in the figure, it begins for Campbell with the demise of a golden age in postwar

American Global Pre-eminence. William R. Thompson, Oxford University Press. © Oxford University Press 2022.
DOI: 10.1093/oso/9780197534663.003.0006

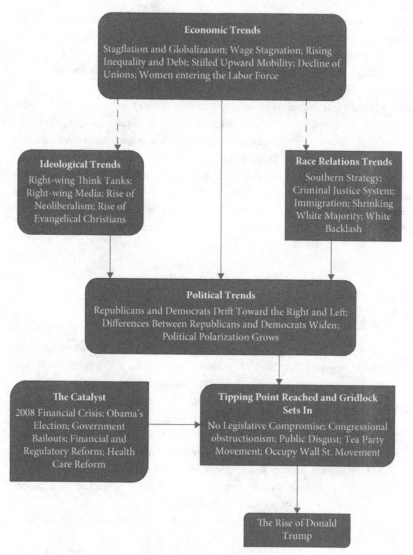

Figure 6.1 The Rise of Trump, based on Campbell (2018: 12)

economic/technological growth—thereby linking it to the earlier discussion of technologically inspired upswings and downswings in chapters 2 and 3. A combination of other economic, ideological, and political processes, with a catalyst in the form of acute recession and the election of an African American president, help explain the ascent of Trump. But Trump is not our dependent variable in this examination. He is both a symptom of US decline and an accelerator of it. Therefore, he is merely another factor in the ensemble of interacting processes that has brought the United States to where it is entering the third decade of the twenty-first century.

Changing the emphasis to internal decline also offers an opportunity to simplify what is most significant in explaining domestic dysfunction. Three sets of processes—political-economic, political, and race/demographic—interacting on intersecting trajectories encompass what is most at stake. All three handicap any efforts to respond to relative decline, let alone to address internal decline. Some of the processes probably would have evolved and proceeded in the absence of relative decline. That almost must be true because some of these processes predate the advent of relative decline in the early 1970s. At the same time, it would be hard to argue that these longer processes brought about relative external decline. Thus, it is important to be careful as the discussion proceeds to clarify how and which external and internal processes may be linked.

Politico-economic Processes

Technological Change and the End of the "Golden Age"

From an economist's perspective, the second half of the twentieth century divides neatly into two. The first period, which began in the rubble of World War II, saw an economic boom of extraordinary proportions across much of the world. A host of new international arrangements to assure steady exchange rates, ease restrictions on foreign trade, and provide economic aid to the poorest countries pointed to an era of global cooperation. As economic growth exploded, people could feel their lives improving almost by the day. New homes, cars, and consumer goods were within reach of average families, and a raft of government social programs and private labor contracts created an unprecedented sense of personal financial security....

The second period, from 1973 almost to the end of the century, was dramatically different. In Japan, North America, and much of Europe and Latin America, the warmth of prosperity was replaced by cold insecurity. International cooperation turned to endless conflict over trade, exchange rates, and foreign investment. White-collar workers grew nervous. Blue-collar workers could feel themselves slipping down the economic ladder. . . . Labor shortages turned into chronic unemployment, and young people were hard-pressed to find anything beyond temporary work. It was an age of anxiety, not an era of boundless optimism. (Levinson, 2016: 3–4)

The foregoing two paragraphs are rarely enunciated by economists. The idea that we go through periods of upswing and downswings lasting several decades is alien to the economics profession. Nonetheless, the night and day behavior of the two halves of the 1945–2000 era is hard to explain in any other way. Much later in the same book, Levinson (2016: 263) acknowledges explicitly that productivity and innovation tend to move in long cycles. The main reason is that the most advanced economies develop radical new technologies that fundamentally change the nature of their economies. As described in chapter 3, the US economy (Atkinson, 2004) has traversed a mercantile/craft era (1840s–1890s), a factory-based industrial era (1890s–1940s), and a corporate mass production era (1940s–1990s), and is still in an entrepreneurial/knowledge-based era (1990s–present). New waves of novel technological innovations alter production systems, how the economy is organized, and how firms are constructed. Economic productivity is strong and increasing in the earlier phases of the long cycle era and much less so in the later phases as the impact of the new innovations become more routinized.

The Twin Peaks model's argument is that systemic leadership is structured around, among other things, two phases of technological innovation spurts. The first one facilitates the creation of a capability foundation that proves critical in the ensuing crisis over global leadership and paves the way for a second spurt of technological innovation after the global crisis has been resolved. There is considerable, albeit less than perfect, overlap in the asserted periodicities of the four phased movements of the last two centuries. But, together, they suggest a highly parsimonious approach to summarizing technological/energy changes since the advent of the industrial revolution. Britain had its prewar surge in cotton textiles and iron production and its postwar surge in railroads powered by coal and steam engines. The United States' prewar phase emphasized steel, chemicals, and electricity, while its post technological surge that ended around 1973 stressed motor vehicles, petroleum, and semiconductors. Inexpensive fuel costs contributed to the rise of the US economy in both the prewar and postwar surges. Higher fuel costs have contributed something to lower growth rates in the post-1973 era, but it would be difficult to argue that slower growth is due only or even principally to increased fuel costs. Crude oil prices fluctuated at the beginning of the era in the 1860s and 1870s, stabilized at a relatively low price between most of the late 1870s and early 1970s, and began to fluctuate again and rise after 1973–1974. The oil shocks of the 1970s and thereafter were not simply random perturbations and intermittent drags on the economy. They were harbingers of even more fundamental transitions in both world order deterioration and an energy transition away from the dominance of petroleum and other fossil fuels.

These economic and price fluctuations were not simply fluctuations. They represented phasing in and out of strong growth periods and the adjustments from an economy based on one way of production to new ways of doing things.

Unfortunately, these adjustment periods can be long in duration. Old economies struggle to survive. New economies fight to break in. Much of the population gets caught in between—many with skills suitable for the old economy and few with skills for the next one.

New economic systems do not just easily and quickly pop into place with the old system going gently into the night. New technology systems take time to mature and diffuse, and the resulting institutional, political and personal transformations left in their wake take even longer. Before a new economic system can take the place of an old one, there has to be a transitional period during which the old system loses its propulsive force and progressive energy. The technology system becomes "played out" and it becomes increasingly difficult to wring advances and innovations from it, since most have already been figured out. Yet, during the transitional period the new economy technology system has not yet gained the critical mass needed to generate robust growth; it is too small, expensive, and weak, just as computers and telecommunications were in the 1980s. (Atkinson, 2004: 26)

Table 6.1 shows above average productivity growth through 1973 and then, reflecting the "played out" nature of the old economy and the "not quite ready" nature of the new economy, an abrupt fall-off into below-average productivity growth through 2001. There is a brief return to above-average productivity usually associated with IT impacts on efficiency in the 2001–2007 period. Its brevity is explicable in terms of how much the postwar innovations changed lifestyles in comparison to the more restricted impact of applying computer applications in office and social communications and by the possibility that the full impact of IT innovations is yet to come. So far, much of the apparent impact has been applied to more trivial activities, in contrast to the impacts associated with greater automation, transportation, and medical breakthroughs seemingly around the corner.[1]

Among the byproducts of fluctuations in productivity are fluctuations in economic growth. As shown in figure 6.2, economic growth is also wave-like, with the height of the waves linked to the scale of the productivity gains realized. If we add to that globalization and a change in economic paradigm as the US economy moves away from more traditional mass production, there is also a crashing

---

[1] We did not see much trivial applications of steam engines, but it did take at least a century before steam engines began to be transformative after first being applied to pump water out of flooded coal mines. The transformative effects of IT presumably will require something less than a century of experimentation.

Table 6.1 Nonfarm Business Sector
Productivity, 1948–2016

Time period	Growth Rate %
1948 Q4–1953 Q2	3.6
1953 Q2–1957 Q3	2.1
1957 Q3–1960 Q2	2.3
1960 Q2–1969 Q4	2.7
1969 Q4–1973 Q4	2.8
1973 Q4–1980 Q1	1.4
1980 Q1–1981 Q3	1.1
1981 Q3–1990 Q3	1.7
1990 Q3–2001 Q1	2.1
2001 Q1–2007 Q4	2.7
2007 Q4–2016 Q3	1.1
Average	2.3

Source: Sprague (2017).

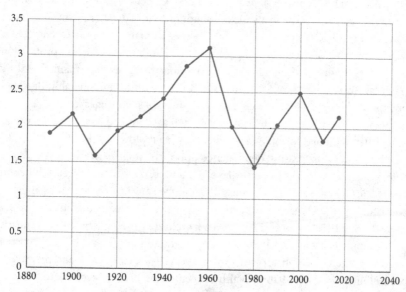

Figure 6.2 US Decadal Economic Growth Rate

Figure 6.3 Manufacturing Employment, 1939–2019

wave in manufacturing employment after the 1970s (figure 6.3), with numbers of people employed in manufacturing in 2017 approximating the number employed in 1941. Raw material prices increased, especially in terms of petroleum. Demand declined. Some firms moved south or to foreign sites to cut their labor costs in a time of declining affluence. Others automated to some extent. Either way the number of manufacturing jobs declined both overall and as a proportion of workers (Figure 6.3) even though the manufacturing sector remained healthy (Federal Reserve Bank of St. Louis, 2020). Labor union membership declined precipitously (figure 6.4), which helped businesses keep wages lower than they might have been. Although wages had increased in the immediate postwar years, they flattened for blue- and white-collar employees alike after the 1970s despite families' increasing dependence upon two wage earners (husband and wife) going to work. The lower the level of income, the flatter the series shown in figure 6.5. Only the highest income group enjoyed any income increases, thereby contributing to increasing inequality in the United States. Inequality, increasing since the late 1970s, approached levels not seen since the early twentieth century.

The point to be stressed is that wage stagnation and rising inequality were largely absent in the high-growth, postwar years to the early 1970s and very much present after the early 1970s. Wealth concentration became even more concentrated than income concentration. The bottom 90 percent of the population's share of wealth declined from 33 percent in 1989 to 23 percent in 2016. The top

Figure 6.4 Estimated US Union Membership as Proportion of Work Force, 1930–2019

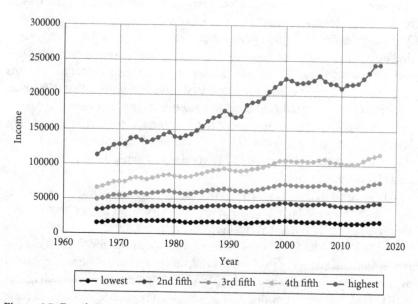

Figure 6.5 Family Income by Quintiles (2017 Dollars)

1 percent increased their share in the same period from 30 percent to 39 percent (Stone et al., 2020).

This increased inequality occurred despite the massive entry of women into the US labor force that characterized the postwar era. From less than 30 percent in 1950, the proportion of the work force occupied by women reached almost 47 percent in 2015 (Fry and Stepler, 2017). An expanded labor supply must be accorded some credit for expanded economic growth in the immediate postwar period. It should also have decreased inequality to some extent. Yet its effect has clearly diminished over time. Two-earner families have instead become the norm to make ends meet. Globalization clearly had something to do with this, particularly in terms of moving reasonably well paying manufacturing jobs to Chinese factories. Where those jobs were lost is, not coincidentally, where some longtime Democrats started voting for Republican candidates. Neither political party offered much economic support for the workers who got "left behind" by these structural changes (Alden, 2017). But Republicans claimed the job losses were due to immigrants stealing the jobs, governmental favoritism toward minorities, and corporations that had abandoned American workers for more profit from lesser labor costs.

Another byproduct of declining productivity and the transition from a period of upswing to one of downswing in economic growth are a number of increasing or decreasing trends in activities that reflect the changing economic context. Both tax rates for the highest personal tax rate and corporations have been in decline since 1960. One of the peculiar political ideas in Washington, DC, that survives the absence of evidence is the oft-expressed argument that tax rate cuts will pay for themselves due to the increased economic growth that will ensue. Tax rates cuts are appealing to firms looking to cut costs and voters. The trend in tax rates reflects a persistent pressure to cut them more that, intermittently, is successful in getting cuts implemented. Not surprisingly, the pressure to consider and enact tax cuts is greater in a period of economic decline than in a period of economic ascent.

Yet tax cuts rarely have much positive impact on economic growth, in part because they tend to favor the wrong set of taxpayers and in part because they simply do not have the intended effect. A case in point were the corporate tax cuts of 2017, which were sold as increasing the incentives for firms to expand production and hire more workers. Instead, many firms saved the money gained as cash reserves or used it buy back their own stock. Tax cuts for the rich do not tend to trickle down in any discernible way. Still, the political notion that these behaviors will have the announced effects live on as long-held Republican articles of faith or, as Krugman (2020) suggests, zombie ideas.

But tax cuts do reduce revenues coming into federal government coffers, which leads, in turn, to budgetary deficits and increases in public debt. For some, deficits and debt are evidence of fiscal mismanagement. Republicans (and especially members of the onetime Tea Party movement) are outraged when Democrats engage in these practices but much less concerned when their own party spends more on government policies than revenues would seemingly permit.[2] Aside from the increased propensity for polarization and occasional government shutdowns over the issues of deficits/debt increases, the implications of expenditures exceeding revenues depends on a long-term perspective, the interest rates the government has to pay to borrow money, and the likelihood that investors will continue to provide support for government borrowing. If interest rates stay low, economic growth persists, and investors continue to see US bonds as safe investments, the real costs of public debt can decline over time. If any of these three variables changes appreciably, the political-economic costs of deficits/debt are likely to increase and become more problematic.

In any event, deficit/debt behavior increases in periods of economic decline. Moreover, they are predicted to increase even more in future decades. The public debt trend suggests levels attained only in world war episodes in the past. Even if these high levels are not sustained over time, they probably encourage governmental spending behaviors that work against funding activities that seemingly can be deferred in the short run. Two areas that provide prominent examples are public infrastructure investment and federal investment in research and development. Figure 6.6 tracks the course of US public infrastructure investment since the late 1940s (see, as well, Davis (2016)). Fair (2021) suggests that the path of American public infrastructure spending, both defense and non-defense types, is inexplicable. Yet he suggests one partial explanation when he says that it is as though the United States government had given up worrying about the future decades ago. As an explanation, such a suggestion is not quite sufficient. We need to add that in periods of declining growth, some types of expenditure are more likely to be given short shrift in trade-offs with more pressing, short-term concerns. Putting aside public safety concerns, infrastructure investment is critical to keeping an economy functioning. The problem is that old bridges, roads, and equipment keep working until they fail. This phenomenon encourages decision makers to put off what most observers would acknowledge as necessary investments in sustaining the future of economic activities.

Figure 6.7 provides a graphic rendering of the shifts in federal and corporate research and development. The federal commitment to research and development, as measured by the federal share of the total, peaks in the 1960s, similar to figure 6.6. The declining trend thereafter continues without deviation. The

---

[2] Norris and Inglehart (2019: 333) nicely summarize the short-lived Tea Party as "a predominately white male movement of disgruntled anti-government social conservatives stoking racial resentment and welfare chauvinism, with a strong authoritarian streak." While short-lived, the Tea Party did help pave the way for Trump's version of outrage (Coaston, 2018; Peters, 2019).

Figure 6.6 US Public Infrastructure Investment

Note: The broad infrastructure series includes public investment in hospital and educational structures, highways, sewers, transportation facilities, and conservation and development.

Federal %   Business %

Figure 6.7 Federal and Business Shares of Research and Development Expenditures, 1953–2018

Source: calculated from data reported in National Science Foundation (2020: Table 6).

corporate research and development share, of course, does exactly the opposite (as it must, given the nature of the calculation). But here is the rub. Firms engage in research and development to improve the marketability of their products. The emphasis tends to be short-term and indiscriminate as to the significance of the product. From a profit perspective, breakfast cereal needs research and development just as much as decarbonizing coal or developing alternatives to fossil fuel energy sources. Federal spending on research and development tends to be relatively more long term and basic in focus. Putting money into university-based physics and chemistry research may not have any immediate application, but some of it will pay off twenty-five years down the road. Figure 6.7 suggests that the US government, wittingly or otherwise, has traded off a commitment to public basic research for private applied research. A fair amount of money still goes into basic research but as a priority, its significance has clearly waned. That is unfortunate in an economy geared to exploiting the next technology cluster that will be built on earlier basic breakthroughs.

The Opioid Crisis

An unanticipated and still debated byproduct of relative decline in economic growth and productivity is the ongoing Opioid Crisis. The debate is not so much about the causes of this problem but rather how best to distribute blame for the multiple influences at work. Opioids only became relatively common in the 1990s. Doctors overprescribed them for pain relief. Pharmaceutical companies oversupplied them while at the same time drumming up demand for their prescription through marketing ploys. Foreign suppliers, especially Chinese drug producers, also contributed to the oversupply problem.

Yet a root cause can be traced back to why people sought relief in the first place.[3] The crisis aspect was driven home by the information that the US population was no longer living longer thanks to improvements in health care but that populations in other affluent countries were continuing to prolong their lives on average.[4] The life expectancy problem was quickly traced to upward trends in the deaths of young to mid-life white adults without college degrees. People of similar ages with college degrees and/or of African American/Hispanic ethnicity were not experiencing similar trends. Why were blue-collar workers at greater risk of statistically premature deaths? Their mean incomes had peaked in the

---

[3] See, for instance, Case and Deaton (2017), Dasgupta, Beletsky, and Ciccarone (2018), Marichal (2018), DeWeerdt (2019), Scavette (2019), and Khazan (2020).

[4] Other countries, including the United Kingdom, Ireland, Canada, and Australia, have been experiencing similar problems with unexpected earlier deaths but not in a way that was comparable to the US record.

1970s. Globalization, automation, and the demise of labor unions restricted employment opportunities, which in turn brought despair to the unemployed and underemployed.[5] At the same time, traditional support structures—families, churches, unions—were eroding (Case and Deaton, 2017, 2020). Drugs, alcohol, and suicide became more attractive. A large proportion of former workers on some type of disability were already using pain killers heavily. Drug overdoses and death rates increased as a consequence, especially in areas hard hit by restricted employment futures.

Obviously, all the blame for opioid overuse cannot be traced to relative economic decline. Whatever proportion of the "credit" should go to the economic context in which it began, the crisis has contributed to continuing decline. Lives have been lost, worker participation in the labor force has declined significantly, health care and criminal justice costs have increased, and economic productivity has been sacrificed. The President's Council of Economic Advisers (2019) estimates a $2.5 trillion price tag for the 2015–2018 period alone, which puts it in a category similar to US warfare costs.

The Shrinking White Majority, White Backlash, and Immigration

In 2008, the Census Bureau began announcing the demise of the white majority in the United States by the 2040s (see table 6.2). It did not matter that Census Bureau data on race tend to minimize the number of whites in American society or that the expansion of mixed-race marriages and offspring are likely to dilute the significance of racial identity in the future (Alba, 2016). Simply talking about a shift in majority-minority population shares seems inflammatory to people

Table 6.2 Shifting Demographic Group Shares of American Society

	White	Black	Asian	Hispanic
2013	62.6	12.4	5.1	17.1
2060	42.6	13.2	7.9	30.6

Source: based on Ewert (2015).

[5] Ventatarmani et al. (2020), for instance, find an 85 percent increase in mortality rates due to drug overdose in areas in which automobile assembly plants closed in comparison to areas where they have not closed.

who identify closely with one of the groups involved (Tavernise, 2018). Whites fear supplantment as a ruling majority. Non-white minorities can expect that time is on their side.

While it is easy to see ethnic prejudice at work here, Jardina (2019) points out that the main political impact of information about declining majorities affects three different but overlapping groups. One group is racist and resents or fears other groups as less worthy compared to its own group. A second group values their own group but is primarily concerned about future losses of status and privilege for the group currently at the top of the societal hierarchy. Members of this second group may or may not hold racist views of other groups but still see their numerical changes as threatening in a zero-sum way. Finally, the third group combines the views of the first two groups—highly valuing its own group's existence at the top and despising non-white groups as of less value than its own. This third group is most likely to harbor white nationalists.

For some purposes, these distinctions are important. A person who fears loss of status for their group is not necessarily opposed to welfare programs that are perceived as favoring minorities, as opposed to a racist individual who opposes government discrimination in favor of minorities. But if a political entrepreneur can send supportive signals to all three groups almost simultaneously in the right context, a voting coalition encompassing the three groups becomes quite plausible. The argument is that Trump has managed to do that with talk of Mexican rapists flooding the border, chaos in inner cities, and there being good people on both sides of the 2017 march of white nationalists in Charlottesville. Some earlier American politicians had tried to make some of the same connections but gaining support from all three groups required a context that favored high threat perceptions by all three. Racist signals always work for some proportion of the population. Majoritarian fears of a pending shift had to emerge and to be stoked, as did perceptions of immigration problems on the US-Mexican border (Sides, Tesler, and Vavreck, 2018).[6]

The relationship of anti-immigration sentiments to the type of economic distress wrought by the Great Recession and white majority fears of becoming a minority is not hard to discern. Immigrants have long made easy targets for scapegoating. The availability of immigrants willing to accept lower wages

---

[6] Experimental evidence supports the generalization that voters who fear the loss of a white majority are more likely to vote Republican, espouse conservative views, and desire to see restrictions placed on immigration (Craig and Richeson, 2014; Myers and Levy, 2018). Curiously, though, it is possible to reduce the group status threat mechanism in experimental situations by exposing subjects alternatively to information about the values and likelihood of future multiracial diversity. That may suggest that it could be easier to reorient one of the three groups (the group threatened by a loss of status) than the other two, other things being equal and of course depending on just how highly people value their group identities.

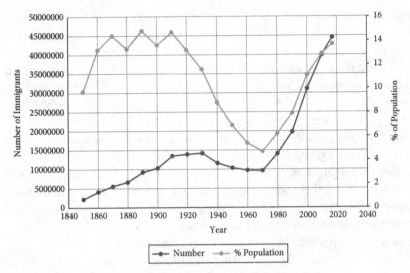

Figure 6.8 Immigration Numbers and as Proportion of Population
Source: based on data reported in Migration Policy Institute (2019).

is an easy explanation for the loss of jobs, especially if immigration numbers are increasing when well-paying jobs seem to be declining. Remove
the immigrants and somehow entry-level jobs will be more plentiful again.
Worried about the impending loss of a white majority? Stem the inflow of
non-white immigrants and the problem is at least postponed for a few more
decades. Immigrants from areas deemed antagonistic to US national interests
can be labeled as national security risks. Unfortunately, these views, whether
factually based or not, work very much against addressing the real causes of
decline because continued immigration is vital to continued US economic
growth and innovation.

Contemporary immigration to the United States may seem something like
a tsunami of foreigners entering the country to some but this impression is in
some respects due to relatively restricted migration prior to the 1970s. Since
then the number of migrants has increased in each successive decade, but the
proportional number of immigrants is only now returning to what was once
the norm in the long period between the end of the American Civil War and
the end of World War I (see figure 6.8).[7] However, Kaufmann (2019) suggests
from a comparative perspective that the political reaction to immigration in the
contemporary US case is something that should be expected when new groups

---

[7] The lion's share of the immigration facts in following paragraphs are drawn from National
Academies of Sciences, Engineering and Medicine (2017).

are perceived as entering in large numbers, even if the American response seems somewhat delayed given the tempo of increased immigration.[8]

Even so, figure 6.8 can be misleading. It charts the number of foreign-born as a proportion of foreign and native-born. Yet migration is not the only process at work. The more important driver is the declining fertility rate of non-Hispanic white females to below replacement numbers. Native-born numbers are thus declining over time, reflecting the role of affluence in discouraging the number of offspring. Without immigration, the American society would be aging or graying even faster than it is. Moreover, without immigration, the American economy would be in worse shape than it currently is.

These last two statements require elaboration. The percentage of seniors in the population, without immigration, is forecasted to increase by 75 percent in 2040 and to more than double by 2065. That suggests (a) a proportionately smaller work force and (b) fewer people to carry the expanding burden of a nonworking, older population.[9] Immigration is not expected to turn this situation around, but it could slow the pace of this particular demographic shift to a 62 percent increase by 2040 and a 76 percent increase by 2065.

More generally, immigrant workers are responsible for expanding the quantitative size of the economy and its qualitative size (gross domestic product per capita). They constitute a significant proportion of the national workforce. Immigrants have also been critical to technological change. The most highly skilled immigrant can apply their scientific and engineering skills without too much concern about licensing and linguistic barriers. Moretti (2013: 242) notes that while foreign-born workers account for about 15 percent of the US workforce, they represent one-third of the engineers and half of the doctorates. He also observes that foreign-born scientists working in the United States are twice as likely to have won the Nobel Prize than native-born scientists.[10] Immigrants are also likely to be attracted to places that are distinguished by being unusually innovative, thereby supplying talent where it is in most demand. In addition, the patenting history suggests that immigrants (with a bachelor's degree) are twice as likely to apply for patents as native-born individuals (with bachelor's degrees).[11]

---

[8] Kaufmann (2019) also suggests that the shift in immigrant composition at the southern border from Mexican to Central American in 2014 may have served as something of a political trigger just in time for the 2016 election.

[9] Social security payments to retired workers are only partially funded by recipient deposits into the system. The rest is funded by currently employed workers.

[10] Moretti (2013: 242) goes on to say that immigrants are more than 30 percent more likely to start a business than native-born entrepreneurs and that they account for one-quarter of new high-tech firms with over $1 million dollars in annual sales.

[11] The caveat on this finding is that it depends on how one counts immigrants. The patenting edge is associated with people who have entered the United States with work or student visas. Immigrants who come primarily to join extended families do not patent any more frequently than do native-born individuals.

In terms of immigrant impact on more local economies, one evaluation problem is that they disproportionately cluster in the higher and lowest education levels. Those in the higher educated levels are more likely to have an immediate positive economic impact. Less skilled immigrants are an important source of labor supply for entry-level service jobs in child/elderly care, agriculture/gardening, house cleaning, and construction. They work at lower wages in these areas than native-born workers might—assuming native-born workers sought these jobs. In that respect, they lower the cost of some services to the rest of the population. Yet, in general and after an initial lag, immigrants are more likely to be employed than the native-born and immigrant wages do not seem to lower wages of native-born workers significantly except for those who left high school without a degree (about 9 percent of the US population).

Most of these generalizations do not differentiate between authorized and unauthorized immigrants except for the numbers involved. But one of the ironies is that the number of unauthorized immigrants has been decreasing since 2007, and especially in terms of the number of Mexicans involved thanks to the Great Recession discouraging employment opportunities (Krogstad, Passel, and Cohn, 2019). By 2017 the number of unauthorized immigrants working in the United States had declined to numbers associated with the 1990s. The second irony is that popular opinion on immigration in the United States has reversed itself in the past three decades. In 1994, 63 percent of respondents felt that immigrants were a burden, with 31 percent disagreeing. By 2019, 62 percent responded that immigrants were a strength, with 28 percent disagreeing (Radford, 2019).

The preceding analysis suggests that Trump and the Republican Party have benefited from a combination of racism and the displacement of economic woes (stagnant wages, inequality) on immigrants. Both processes are at work, but there may also be something even more basic at work. Inglehart (2018) argued that security breeds tolerance and insecurity leads to heightened xenophobia and a cultural backlash against eroding traditional norms. The several decades of postwar US prosperity encouraged the gestation of more liberal attitudes toward several social topics, ranging from abortion to the acceptance of sex before marriage, gay/lesbians, and women's rights in general. But these new attitudes do not emerge across the generational spectrum equally. Younger members of society are more likely to adopt more liberal attitudes if they have not experienced much insecurity. The attitudes of older members of society, on the other hand, were forged in earlier periods of economic insecurity and thus are less affected by the advent of a more secure environment.

Table 6.3 offers ample evidence for the nature of the problem. Older generations are much more conservative than they are liberal. The gap is 31 points in favor of conservatives. Younger generations are more liberal than they are conservative, although not by a great deal. Thus, as older generations leave the US

Table 6.3 The Balance of Conservatives and Liberals by Generation in American Society in 2015

Generation	Birth years	Conservative	Moderate	Liberal	Conservative-Liberal Gap
Millennials	1980–1996	28	40	30	−2
Generation X	1965–1979	35	39	23	+12
Baby Boomers	1946–1964	44	33	21	+23
Interwar	1900–1945	48	33	17	+31
All		38	36	24	+14

Source: based on Norris and Inglehart (2019: 101).

scene, the society becomes proportionately more liberal in attitude, but plenty of conservatives remain to feel threatened by the ongoing societal changes that they observe all around them. Throw in the diminishing white majority perceptions amid a long period of economic stagnation, and one has a toxic cocktail of resentment and resistance to ongoing change that is manifested in political preferences. The problem is even more aggravated if the threat perceptions are reinforced by people living in rural communities where there is less diversity in opinions/perceptions and if selective media attention provides further reinforcement. This type of political context, according to Inglehart, becomes increasingly receptive to authoritarian populism appeals along the lines of Perot, Buchanan, and Trump.[12]

Political Processes

Urban-Rural Cleavage

It has already been suggested that the lack of opinion diversity in rural environments can reinforce instinctive conservatism. Apparently, there is even more to rural-urban differences than merely the ease of conformity. Part of the contemporary political polarization is rooted deeply in political-economic history (Rodden, 2019). In the second industrial revolution that transpired in the last

---

[12] Part of this process and context is a shift away from strictly economic concerns toward cultural/identity issues, which helps to explain why blue-collar workers sometimes vote for overtly plutocratic billionaires. The appeal of cultural/identity issues override economic class concerns (Norris and Inglehart, 2019: 323).

third of the nineteenth century, industrialization in the United States was focused on a number of Northern cities that possessed accessible locations, labor pools, and proximity to the railroads. These cities expanded into important nodes in the national economic network of its era, attracting immigrants with jobs and affordable housing. That meant dense populations living near the industrial sites. It also meant large numbers of urban laborers with problems associated with their working conditions that political entrepreneurs could champion. Republicans sided with capital and large firms then as now. Urban workers tended to vote for Democratic candidates who were more friendly to labor's concerns.

Things changed in the next century. The late nineteenth-century industrial centers lost their production dynamism and jobs. Part of the problem was that traditional location had lost some of its attraction. Highways and trucking reduced the need for access to railroads. Cheaper land and workers in the suburbs and rural areas offered ways to cut production costs. Some of the urban workers left to be closer to the new sites, but many remained in the older, now increasingly de-industrialized towns. Yet they remained dense population centers with strong Democratic voting records. An urban-rural political cleavage was not created by these changes, but it has been strongly reinforced by the geographical history of American industrialization.[13]

Republican politicians found that they could connect to workers in the suburbs and places where unions were absent or weakening. Democratic politicians have continued to champion urban concerns and have also tended to support information technology producers that have selected certain urban areas for their activities. Thus, an urban-rural cleavage has been perpetuated despite a vastly changing political-economic landscape. Political stances have shifted with these changes. In the nineteenth century, industrialization needed protection from competition while agrarian producers preferred free trade to best sell their raw materials and food output. In the late twentieth and early twenty-first centuries, now suburban workers damaged by the loss of jobs due to globalization and rural farmers seek protection while IT producers promote free trade.

Other trends have aggravated the urban-rural cleavage. The African American migration from the South to the North seeking employment encouraged Black concentration in the older urban areas. As their votes became more important, so, too, did the political appreciation for civil rights. Moreover, the movement of job sites, the automobile, and white flight encouraged white concentration in the suburbs. Northern urban areas have tended to be more tolerant of societal changes in views on abortion and sexual identities. Suburban and rural areas have

---

[13] Rodden (2019) notes that the initial US political cleavage between Federalists and Democratic-Republicans divided commercial/urban interests and landed/rural elites.

been less tolerant of these changes.[14] Christian evangelicals who had first reacted against integration in Southern schools were easily mobilized for an anti-abortion crusade (Williams, 2010; Balmer, 2014; Dowland, 2015).[15] Geographical concentration was thus accentuated by attitudinal and issue concentration.

The Anglo-Saxon commitment to winner-take-all formulas for political victory means that Democrats can win handily in dense Northern urban areas but win or lose close elections in less dense areas. Old constitutional compromises give small states political advantages over large states in the Senate and the Electoral College. Both parties engage in gerrymandering to take advantage of opportunities to bias the boundaries of voting districts at local levels to favor their own chances of winning. But the Republicans have been more successful in this endeavor. Similarly, the Republicans have specialized in suppressing opportunities for probable antagonistic populations to vote in the first place, while Democrats have specialized in encouraging the expansion of voting rights in general with the underlying premise that more people voting should be good for their own causes. States, as a consequence, tend to be "blue" or "red" and stay that way unless their population bases change sufficiently by in- and out-migration.[16] Urban-rural cleavages are thereby institutionalized by political propensities but, of course, the main mechanism is that geography separates very different sub-populations with different life experiences, values, and preferences that politicians can exploit, or, if one prefers, that politicians must heed.

Although this long-term interpretation implies that the urban-rural cleavage is carved in stone, recent data suggest that there is some fluctuation, but it does not seem all that elastic on the urban end of the continuum. Democrats can lose some voters in urban areas while they have demonstrated that they can lose large shares of the rural vote—11 percent between 2008 and 2016 and less in the suburbs—5 percent over the same time period. If these are short-term swings depending on who is running in each race, the cleavage exists but should not be exaggerated. On the other hand, it may be that one party is simply discovering how to maximize its natural strength on the rural end of the cleavage. Another election or two may tell.[17]

[14] See Cramer (2016) on the "us versus them" attitudes of rural Wisconsin voters and Mason (2018) on the development of a Republican coalition embracing whites, Christians, males, and rural voters.

[15] On the Republican Party's development of campaigns to utilize racial issues, see, among others, Aistrup (1996), Fountain (2016), Heer (2016), Schikler (2016), Abramowitz (2018), and Haberman (2018).

[16] Conservatives leaving states perceived as too liberal means that the states that they leave are only likely to become more liberal. States that become more urbanized and less rural are also likely to become more liberal. But some states are less likely to be subject to population flux or urbanization for that matter and will remain red.

[17] On the other hand, perhaps the urban-rural-suburban conceptualization misses the true causal relationship. One recent finding (Wasserman, 2020) on vote growth finds that Democratic

Table 6.4 Urban-Rural Splits in 2008, 2012, and 2016

	Democrats			Republicans		
	2008	2012	2016	2008	2012	2016
Urban	63%	62%	59%	35%	36%	35%
Suburban	50	48	45	48	50	50
Rural	45	39	34	53	59	62

Source: based on data reported in Kurtzleben (2016). The numbers do not always add up to 100% because of third party candidates.

Another way of looking at this question is to focus on states as opposed to total votes cast. Given the significance of the Electoral College, total votes are not the ultimate criteria. In a recent FiveThirtyEight exercise (Rakich, 2020), an index of urbanization was constructed by calculating the average number of people that lived within a five-mile radius of every census tract. Each state's weighted census tract urbanization scores were then aggregated and averaged. The urbanization scale runs from a low of 8.26 to a high of 12.56. If half of the states are placed in upper and lower categories (10.37 is about the midpoint), the distribution of states according to whether it leaned Democratic or Republican in 2016 is reported in table 6.5.

The demonstrated correlation is again clearly strong if imperfect in the table. But the "errors" (less urbanized states that vote Democrat and more urbanized states that vote Republican) are very small states in the Democrat column and, for the most part, states that appear to be becoming or already are more purple (a mixture of Republican red and Democratic blue voting tendencies) in the Republican column—with Utah and Indiana constituting the two exceptions. Moreover, the correlation should be imperfect because no one promotes the urban-rural cleavage as the only explanation for voting behavior. Yet table 6.5 does underline one facet of this problem. It appears likely to be present for some time to come. Many of the rural states are unlikely to become denser. The densest states are unlikely to become less urbanized in the future.

vote growth in 2016 is correlated with people living less than five miles from a Whole Foods, Lululemon, Apple Store, or Urban Outfitters store. Republican vote growth was correlated with voters living less than ten miles from a Cracker Barrel, Tractor Supply, Bass Pro Shop, or Hobby Lobby store. Nonetheless, the locations of these stores are not exactly independent of urban-rural distinctions.

Table 6.5 Urbanization by State and Partisan Lean Tendency in 2016

Urbanization	Partisan lean Democrat	Partisan lean Republican
Upper half	New York, New Jersey, California, Massachusetts, Rhode Island, Maryland, Illinois, Connecticut, Colorado, Washington, Hawaii, Delaware, Virginia, Michigan, Oregon, Minnesota	Nevada, Florida, Arizona, Texas, Pennsylvania, Utah, Ohio, Georgia, Indiana
Lower half	New Mexico, Maine, Vermont	North Carolina, Missouri, Nebraska, Tennessee, Wisconsin, Louisiana, Kansas, South Carolina, Oklahoma, New Hampshire, Kentucky, Alabama, Idaho, Iowa, Arkansas, West Virginia, North Dakota, Mississippi, Alaska

Data Source: (Rakich, 2020).

Democrat-Republican Divergence and Party Coalition Differences

One view of contemporary party divisions is that the Democrats remain a "big tent" coalition with moderates contending with more extreme leftists, while the Republicans have become a homogenous conservative ideological movement. This interpretation is not without some support, but the more interesting story is the party dynamics that have led to the contemporary impasse on multiple issues. Nor is it clear that big tents and ideological movements need to constitute different political animals.

The Democratic Party evolved from Jeffersonian agrarian values and opposition to the Federalists. Espousing limited government in general and anti-federal government in particular, the early Democratic Party, especially in the Jackson era, resembled the contemporary Republican Party in many ways. A split between Northern and Southern factions in the run-up to the Civil War helped the Republicans win the presidency in 1860. In the second half of the nineteenth century, Democrats were well ensconced in the South thanks to the Republican links to post–Civil War Reconstruction. Nonetheless, Democrats had problems winning the presidency, putting aside Wilson's win thanks to a Republican split in 1912, until Roosevelt put together a coalition that united Northern liberals with more conservative Southerners. This New Deal coalition managed to win the presidency in the 1930s and 1940s, but the coalition foundation was never all that stable given its North-South axis or liberal-conservative merger.

African Americans had traditionally voted Republican after the Civil War but never received much in return for their votes. Reconstruction had run out of steam early, allowing Southern Democrats to greatly reduce the ability of African Americans to participate in Southern politics after the 1870s. Republicans paid little attention to this ethnic voting group in the North or the South. Schickler (2016: 45–47), however, gives credit to four changes for encouraging the inherent instability of the New Deal coalition: (1) African Americans were moving North in response to employment possibilities; (2) African Americans became a more significant voting bloc in Northern cities in the 1930s for New Deal politicians who responded with increased attention to civil rights issues; (3) some labor unions promoted civil rights as part of the New Deal; and (4) World War II highlighted military integration problems, which led to more federal government attention to civil rights issues. By the end of the war, civil rights had become an integral component of the liberal identity whereas it had been muted at the beginning of the New Deal in order to form the coalition. Southern Democrats were reacting negatively to the first three of these factors before the war began and became even more susceptible to Republican presidential candidates after the war ended.

The Republican Party of the mid-twentieth century had its own warring factions. Midwestern conservatives struggled with Northeastern moderates for control of the party. The latter group could control the party's presidential nomination process because it controlled enough of the large states in the 1940s and 1950s. But even Republican moderates were more attractive to Southern Democrats who were increasingly splitting their tickets—voting Republican at the presidential level and Democratic at lower levels. Republican campaigns to gain Southern votes started becoming more explicit in the Eisenhower era and escalated in the Goldwater campaign for the 1964 election, by which point Republican moderates were no longer in a powerful position within the party. By this time, the Democratic Party had become increasingly liberal in tone and policy, further encouraging Southern attraction to a conservative Goldwater strategy that, among other things, emphasized resistance to federal intervention in the South's way of life. Similar appeals were continued by Nixon's stress on states' rights and law and order as a thinly veiled appeal to white racism in the South and elsewhere. In this fashion, a new coalition wedding Midwestern conservatism with white Southern racism led to Democratic politicians crossing over to the Republican Party and an increasingly Republican Southern voting bloc no longer needing to split their voting tickets.

The Republican Party's Southern Strategy implied an explicit battle plan to increase the number of GOP votes gained in Southern states.[18] It was that, but it

---

[18] Republicans have not had a monopoly on Southern strategies. The New Deal was based in part on a Democratic Southern Strategy. So, too, was Biden's 2019 reversal of electoral losses in primary voting.

became something more. It involved a rebranding of the party, in part because the rebranding became nationalized in focus almost from the beginning. One might say that it southernized the Republican Party, except that it turned out that non-Southerners were attracted to the same party pitches—hence the rapid nationalization.

Franklin D. Roosevelt's odd New Deal coalition pairing Northern liberals and Southern segregationists was never destined to last forever. Truman's efforts to desegregate the military after World War II and an anti-discrimination plank in the 1948 Democratic Party platform were viewed as threatening to the Southern status quo. One response was the breakaway Dixiecrat movement, a third-party insurgency predicated on a states' rights platform, which captured several Southern states in the 1948 election. In 1960, the Democratic campaign led by presidential candidate John Kennedy devised its own Southern strategy by naming Lyndon B. Johnson of Texas as his running mate, ostensibly to ensure Southern votes in what was to be a close election.[19] In 1964, Republican presidential candidate Barry Goldwater had defeated the moderate wing of his party for the nomination. Part of his campaign against the Democratic nominee, Johnson, was opposition to the 1964 Civil Rights Act, which Goldwater argued should be a matter of states' rights to determine. In other words, if Southern states chose to remain segregated, so be it. Other than Arizona, the only states that were won by Goldwater were in the South.

The 1968 election, featuring the loser of the one in 1960, is usually portrayed as initiating the Republican Southern Strategy. Nixon promised to be fair to the South in terms of federal interventions in Southern practices. But this time Nixon made moderately disguised overtures to Southern voters by appealing to them on a law-and-order emphasis that camouflaged an appeal to whites worried about African American promotion of an expanded civil rights agenda as well as whites concerned about African American crime.[20] That might seem like an overly cynical observation, but Republican Party operatives freely admitted that this aspect of the Republican campaign employed coded terms to appeal to white fears.[21] Coded terms were needed to reduce the potential loss of votes outside the South.

[19] In the 1952 and 1956 elections, most of the states won by the Democrats against the Eisenhower campaigns ironically were in the South, despite having Adlai Stevenson of Illinois as the presidential candidate. In 1960, the popular vote difference between the winner and loser was less than 113,000 votes. Kennedy won in Texas, Louisiana, Arkansas, Georgia, South Carolina, and North Carolina. Alabama's and Mississippi's electoral votes went to a Southern senator.

[20] Strictly speaking, the 1968 Nixon campaign apparently chose to avoid a pan-Southern campaign and concentrated on Southern border states. To have competed with George Wallace in the Deep South might have been costly in Northern states (Guillory, 2019).

[21] See discussions involving Kevin Philips (see Boyd, 1970, for instance) and, for later campaigns, Lee Atwater (Perlstein, 2012). It is hard to do better than to quote one paragraph from a 40+ minute interview that Atwater gave in 1981: "You start out in 1954 by saying 'Nigger, nigger, nigger.' By 1968 you can't say 'nigger'—that hurts you, backfires. So you say stuff like, uh, forced busing, states' rights, and all that stuff, and you're getting so abstract. Now, you're talking about cutting taxes, and all these

In subsequent iterations, it is argued that this Southern Strategy added opposition to feminism and religious fundamentalism to the mix (Maxwell and Shields, 2019). The defense of traditional gender roles appealed to a number of Southern white women, so the Republican Party pushed family values after 1980.[22] As the Southern Baptist Convention became more conservative, the Republican Party opposed federal attacks on segregated Southern schools (including private, faith-based ones), endorsed anti-abortion movements, and kept their distance from the idea of LGBTQ civil rights. Gun rights were also a natural addition to the issue inventory.

But it soon became clear that what worked in the South could also get votes outside the South. Busing inner-city children to suburban schools, breaking down segregated white and Black communities in terms of housing, and affirmative action hiring created resentment outside of the South. Thinly disguised attacks on minorities via calls for enforcing law and order à la the Willie Horton campaign ploy in 1988, reducing entitlement payments, and shutting down immigration that involved non-whites made for attractive campaign appeals to people who worried about maintaining white and Christian majorities. The Republican Southern Strategy became nationalized. Republican voters gradually became white, Christian, male, and rural in the South and everywhere else (Mason, 2018). The Democratic coalition increasingly resembled the opposite. Still, the important point to make is that Trump's base can be described as white, Evangelical Christian, males without college degree, and rural. Trump did not invent his base; it was already there waiting for him. The evolving Southern Strategy set up an electoral situation highly conducive to this base more effectively than more conventional Republican politicians.[23]

Political Polarization

While it was noted earlier that there is an argument that only one of the two parties has become more ideological, the data on personal identification

things you're talking about are totally economic things and a byproduct of them is, blacks get hurt worse than whites. . . . 'We want to cut this' is much more abstract than even the busing thing, uh, and a hell of a lot more abstract than 'Nigger, nigger.' "

[22] As late as 2016, Hillary Clinton won the votes of a majority of white women, but not in the South.
[23] One more irony is that a good number of the alternative Republican candidates for the presidential nomination in 2016 were from the South, unlike the candidate who triumphed (although he has since moved his home residence to Florida). Nine of seventeen Republican candidates were based in Southern states (Ted Cruz, Texas; Marco Rubio, Florida; Jeb Bush, Florida; Rand Paul, Kentucky; Mike Huckabee, Arkansas; Jim Gilmore, Virginia; Rick Perry, Texas; Bobby Jindal, Louisiana; and Lindsey Graham, South Carolina). This is surely additional testimony to the nationalization of what had originally been a Southern Strategy.

suggest otherwise. Both party memberships have moved toward either the conservative (Republicans) or liberal (Democrats) ends of the political spectrum. There are, however, more conservatives in the Republican Party than there are liberals in the Democratic Party (see figure 6.9). In 1994, 58 percent of Republican respondents identified themselves as conservatives. By 2018, the proportion was up to 73 percent. In contrast, only 25 percent of Democrat respondents identified as liberal in 1994. The number had doubled (51 percent) by 2018. In both cases, the number of self-identified "moderates" declined (33 percent to 22 percent in the Republican Party and 48 percent to 34 percent in the Democratic Party). Thus, it seems fair to say that the two parties have moved farther apart, with perhaps the Republican Party being more homogenous in the direction it has moved.

Independents have stayed roughly similar in their ideological self-identifications over the 1994 to 2018 period even though they have increased in number. Although though fewer people are willing to acknowledge party membership, overall ideological tendencies in the population are not too different. The number of liberals (1992–2018) has increased from 17 percent to 26 percent of the population. The number of conservatives has fluctuated a bit but stayed the same (36 percent in 1993 and 35 percent in 2018). Moderates have declined from 43 percent to 38 percent over the same time period. So, there is still a middle, but it seems to be shrinking gradually.

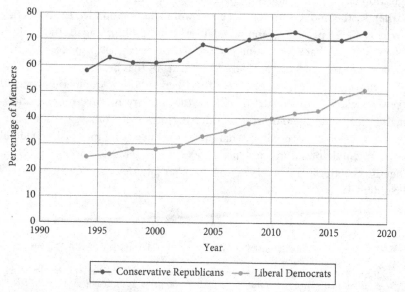

Figure 6.9 Party Membership Polarization, 1994–2018
Source: based on data reported in Saad (2019).

Another way of looking at this problem is to point out that the traditional Republican Party has virtually collapsed and been taken over by more extreme viewpoints that have long been present and growing in strength within the Republican-conservative ideational spectrum. Ziblatt (2017) argues that the success of conservative parties in controlling their extremists is critical to the survival of democracies. Failure of the center-right to manage its extremists either leads to, or represents, a prevailing sentiment that conservative-right politicians cannot win popular elections. Increasingly, non-democratic approaches become attractive for resisting what are viewed as inevitable or highly probable losses. If the center-right has surrendered to, or been overtaken by, the far right in the American case, the very open question is whether the center-right can regain control. Most answers to the question have to assume that there is a center-right left to reassert control.[24] If it can regain control, it might be forced to modify some of its positions to win more votes. As it stands, the far right appears to be entirely deaf to the need to improve its minority position by adopting less exclusive stances. Instead, it puts more emphasis on voter suppression tactics.

Be that as it may, the decline of moderates and moderation is compounded by the diminished number of people who trust the federal government "to do what is right most of the time" (Pew Research Center, 2019). In the late 1960s, people who were surveyed responded fairly favorably to the trust question at a high 75 percent rate. By the end of the next decades, the same question elicited only about 25 percent to respond as favorably as they had earlier. By the mid-1980s, trust in government had rebounded to encompass perhaps 40–45 percent of the population, only to plunge again in the mid-1990s. Battling back to around the 50 percent level just prior to 2003, the handling of the Iraq war and other problems of that decade drove the government trusting percentages down to 14 percent of the population by 2019 (Pew Research Center, 2019).[25] Given the honesty of governmental messaging and the ups and downs of policy performance in these decades, particularly in periods of crisis, it is hard to blame anyone for mistrusting federal governmental intentions and policy execution. This is another problem that preceded the record-breaking number of prevarications uttered by President Trump.[26]

---

[24] An optimistic take on this possibility can be found in Saldin and Teles (2020). However, figure 6.9 suggests moderate Republicans may be increasingly hard to find.

[25] In 2019, 3 percent of the population still trusted their government to always do the right thing.

[26] According to the *Washington Post* (Kessler, Rizzo, and Kelly, 2020), Trump made 16,241 false or misleading claims in his first three years in office.

Figure 6.10 Polarization in Congress
Source: Lewis, 2019.

Congress

These polarization numbers and the ones reported in figure 6.10 suggest that ideological polarization at the mass level is not quite at the levels currently exhibited by the Congress (Farina, 2015; Iyengar, 2019). Of course, the figure also demonstrates that the current legislative polarization is not unique. Similar levels were observed in the decades leading to the end of the nineteenth century (Brady and Han, 2006; Cambell, 2006). This may be another straw in the wind that political dysfunction and extreme levels of polarization become more likely as the economy undergoes radical change.

That legislative polarization has something to do with legislative productivity is underscored by the shifts in meaningful activity. One indicator is the change in the number of committee hearings pertaining to the construction of legislation (Willis and Kane, 2018). In 1989–1990, the House had 957 hearings and the Senate had 254. By 2015–2016, the number in the House had shrunk to 254 (about 27 percent of the 1989–1990 numbers) and the Senate was down to 69 hearings (also 27 percent of 1989–1990 activity). It is not that there is less to do or fewer problems to address. Majority parties control the quantity and pace of deliberation. Agendas are tightly regulated (Wallach and Wallner, 2018). Less policy deliberation and production are the outcome.

The real question with Congress is whether polarization is the root of all dysfunction or is it simply one feature among many that gets in the way of accomplishing much. Hawkings (2018) suggests five "M's" explain why Congress is "broken," and only some of the factors are linked to political polarization per se. One is that the costs of running for office have risen dramatically and legislators must spend much of their time raising *money*, especially in the House. Even so, fewer and fewer seats are contested thanks to gerrymandering of congressional districts (or *maps*). But legislators still need to demonstrate something to their base of voters, so instead of legislative product they emphasize their keeping the partisan faith. A third factor is that vanishing hometown newspapers mean that local *media* do not cover Washington, DC, activities very closely and the national media do not focus on individual legislators much unless they are quite powerful. Fourth, legislators no longer interact socially with their colleagues in both parties as they once did in more bipartisan days (*mingling*). The fifth factor is *masochism*. Legislators try to live up to their constituents' low expectations of Congress. More political support can be gained by legislators criticizing their own institutions than by reforming said institutions.

In contrast, Binder (2015) emphasizes that salient policy issues tend to be deadlocked in Congress. Only when one party controls both houses and the presidency is there some reduction of this tendency. The instinct of both parties is to attempt to block legislation or activity which they oppose and the other side favors. Given strong polarization, bipartisan coalitions for specific issues are simply hard to construct. Consequently, less gets done and problems are left to be addressed sometime in the future.

These views are not really in conflict. Congressional dysfunction can be a product of both political polarization and institutional characteristics. These features come together in organizations in which the primary directive is to keep one's job as long as possible. It also guarantees institutional dysfunction with few chances for genuine reform or revitalization short of radical electoral realignments (Alberta, 2019).

Yet even realignment may not suffice to turn things around. Yglesias (2007) captures a structural reality underlying Congressional bipartisanship that suggests realignment can make institutional functioning less likely but more realistic.

[I]t really is remarkable that for all of the bellyaching about the decline of bipartisan behavior there's very little attention paid to the fact that there are actual reasons this happened. . . . The Jim Crow South gave rise to an old structure of American political institutions whereby both of the parties contained substantial ideological diversity. This had the benefit of setting the stage for a wide array of cross-cutting alliances. It came, however, at the cost of consigning a substantial portion of the population to life under a brutal system of apartheid ruthlessly upheld through systematic violence.

After the system collapsed, there was a decade or so period during which the voters and parties were re-aligning themselves during which we had cross-cutting alliances but no apartheid. And now the aligning process is done, so we have two parties where essentially all Democrats are to the left of essentially all Republicans and so you can have relatively few genuine bipartisan coalitions.

Yglesias (2007) clearly gives the root cause award of dysfunction to polarizing changes in the political parties' make-ups. It seems unlikely that the present parties will revert to former ways of combining liberal and conservative views within the same party.

Presidents

Interestingly, most analysts focus exclusively on Congress in terms of its grid-lock, but there is a presidential role that is important as well. It is rare to see any discussion of relative decline that compares American presidents. One of the main exceptions is Genovese and Belt (2016) who have framed a presidential politics text around the tissue. Table 6.6 summarizes the categorization of the Nixon through Obama regimes, all of whom presided during a relative decline period. While presidents are loath to mention the decline word (Trump's Make America Great Again slogan is the obvious exception, although even there decline is left implicit), Genovese and Belt contend that post-1970 American presidents have been familiar with the problem and have responded in different ways.

It would be hard to disagree with the lack of entries in the "defeatist" column. It would also be difficult to imagine how such a presidency would function. Trump is easily added to the first column of "enforcers."[27] Our immediate question is whether we really need four different categories for the last eight presidents. The distinctions among the middle three categories—hang-on, adapters, and accepters—seem rather fuzzy. Why not simply contrast presidents who stress reversing decline and those who adapt to a declining situation? That would suggest that the three middle categories in table simply reflect different strategies. "Accepters" are cautious, "adapters" readjust commitments (as in finding

---

[27] The "enforcer" term seems awkward in this context. Something like "rise againers" would seem to be more appropriate.

Table 6.6 American Presidents and Relative Decline Strategies

Enforcers	Hang-on	Adapters	Accepters	Defeatists
Reverse and rise	Reassert power	Readjust and adapt	Controlled decline	Decline as doom
Ronald Reagan George W. Bush	George H. W. Bush	Richard Nixon	Jimmy Carter Bill Clinton Barack Obama	
Power can be reclaimed by increasing military spending and reasserting America's rise	Attempt to maintain hegemonic control within certain bounds and limits	Attempt to maintain hegemonic power by readjusting commitments to fit resources; exert creative leadership	Accept the inevitable but make it less painful, with clear recognition of limits	Since decline is inevitable, nonreversible, and determined, give in to it

Source: based on Genovese and Belt (2016: 34).

regional powers to take on some of their once hegemonic role), and "hang-oners" tend to sound like "accepters."

The immediate point in engaging in this side issue is that what policies American presidents choose to pursue can be helpful or non-helpful in terms of reversing decline. Those who adapt or accept tend to do little to change the trends toward further relative decline even if they talk about how they would like to bolster the future position of the United States. Those who stress reversing decline and re-rising like phoenixes believe that increasing military spending and talking tough will do the job. They are sadly mistaken. Unless they rebuild the economic foundation for systemic leadership, they are relying on coercion and bluster—which may work briefly but is unlikely to pan out over the longer term. In other words, the last eight presidents have done little to substantially reverse US relative decline. In that respect, they must be viewed as part of the problem.

We can probably push this conclusion a bit farther and note that the three occupants of the "enforcer" category (Reagan, Bush II, and Trump) have each pursued largely unilateral strategies as opposed to multilateral strategies. Moreover, each successive president within this category has pursued unilateral strategies in a more exaggerated way than their predecessors. Reagan attacked small Caribbean states directly and Central American states by proxy. Bush II undertook initiatives in Afghanistan and Iraq from which it proved extremely difficult to extract US forces. Trump flirted with going to war with North Korea and Iran, fixated on building a wall along the Southern border while completely alienating most American allies. The passage of time and the cumulation of relative decline encourages some chief executives to try harder with fewer and fewer resources. The problem is that they seem to believe in their strategies of relying on rebuilt military strength and fail to fully appreciate that systemic leadership does not depend exclusively on possessing a coercive advantage over the rest of the world. In trying to enhance national security their way, less national security is attained and opportunities to do things that might genuinely contribute to turning around relative decline are passed up.

Media

One of the clear contributors to growing political polarization and its maintenance has been the development of media designed to appeal to specific segments of the population. Once upon a time, citizens tuned into the relatively neutral and often bland news programs offered by the major television networks and some proportion of the population regularly read newspapers. As a source of political news, newspapers are a dying format outside of a few major outlets such as the *New York Times* and the *Washington Post*. The major television networks have lost viewers in the face of numerous competitors offered by cable news and streaming entertainment sources. They have not disappeared from the political news scene, but their influence has been largely pushed aside by other sources of news.

New sources of information are one thing. Selection biases are something else. Polarization increases and is sustained by the strong tendency to select sources that reflect biases congenial to the selectee. Left and right watch entirely different programs and hear vastly different narratives that reinforce the initial biases underlying the selective receptivity. Moreover, they distrust the sources preferred by the people who vote differently than they do.

Conservative Republicans rely heavily on Fox News. Republican moderates share this dependency but not to the same extent and are willing to trust the fare offered by the other networks. Liberal Democrats are focused almost to the same extent as conservatives but to a wider range of sources (CNN, *New York Times*, PBS, and NPR). More moderate Democrats resemble moderate Republicans in watching and trusting more networks, but they switch CNN for Fox News at the top of their most trusted list.

Figure 6.11, however, suggests that the information polarization is even greater than that suggested by table 6.7. When asked what sources were consulted in the past week for news on elections and politics, a continuum of sources calibrated to ideology emerged with even less overlap than is found in table 6.7. Rather than discuss the various sources, the main finding is that people farthest to the left rely on the sources listed above the upper dotted line (above Univision) and people farthest to the right relied exclusively on information sources listed

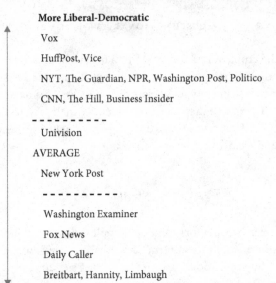

More Liberal-Democratic

Vox

HuffPost, Vice

NYT, The Guardian, NPR, Washington Post, Politico

CNN, The Hill, Business Insider

- - - - - - - - - -

Univision

AVERAGE

New York Post

- - - - - - - - - -

Washington Examiner

Fox News

Daily Caller

Breitbart, Hannity, Limbaugh

More Conservative-Republican

Figure 6.11 Party, Ideology, and News Source Preferences

Source: based on Jurkowitz et al (2020). The figure demonstrates respondent self-placement on party and ideology and identifies the sources of political and election news in the past week of the survey. Dotted lines demarcate liberal (20 percent of respondents) and conservative (18 percent of news respondents) news bubbles. Only the sources above or below the dotted lines were relied upon for election news.

Table 6.7 Top 5 Sources Trusted for Political and Election News by Political Preference

Democrat/Lean Democrat		Republican/Lean Republican	
Liberal	Moderate/ Conservative	Moderate/Liberal	Conservative
% who trust each source for political and election news			
CNN 70%	CNN 65%	Fox News 51%	Fox News 75%
NYT 66	ABC News 63	ABC News 47	Hannity (radio) 43
PBS 66	NBC News 61	CBS News 42	Limbaugh (radio) 38
NPR 63	CBS News 60	NBC News 41	ABC News 24
NBC News 61	PBS 48	CNN 36	CBS News 23
% who distrust each source for political and election news			
Fox News 77%	Fox News 48%	CNN 43%	CNN 67%
Limbaugh 55	Limbaugh 34	MSNBC 32	MSNBC 57
Breitbart 53	Hannity 28	Huffpost 30	NYT 50
Hannity 50	Breitbart 22	BuzzFeed 29	NBC News 50
NY Post 27	BuzzFeed 20	Fox News 29	CBS News 48

Source: Jurkowitz et al. (2020).

below the lower dotted line (below the *New York Post*). These left and right information bubbles captured 38 percent of the respondents almost equally divided
by ideology (20 percent for liberals and 18 percent for conservatives). Thus, the
people with the strongest-held or most extreme positions are both numerous
and relying on vastly different sources of information. To the extent that all the
sources listed are likely to reinforce where people fall on the ideological spectrum, the possibilities of convergence on what is going on in the real world remain nil. The likelihood of any changes in political position is equally low.[28]

The Catalyst

Since this chapter is not about Trump, there is less need to spend much time on
the catalytical events (see figure 6.1) that set up an extreme outcome. The Great
Recession of 2008 was an extreme economic shock almost on the order of a depression. Most population groups lost something, ranging from employment to
investments. Depression was headed off, despite strong Republican resistance,
by governmental Keynesian intervention in the economy. Whether the intervention should have been (or could have been) greater than it was continues to be
debated. The consequent recovery was slow and characterized by several features
that aroused antagonisms and reflected widely disparate opinions on what
should be done. Bailouts of failing industries and limited penalties for the financial firms whose high-risk behavior caused the recession were appreciated differently by different groups. The first African American president was also variably
received. Some thought it heralded a breakthrough in American racial relations,
while others saw it as an implicit threat to white privileges. An initiative to extend
a medical safety net to millions of uninsured ran into a buzz saw of people who
disliked the extension and the requirement that all members of the population
should demonstrate evidence of medical insurance or face a penalty.

Conclusion

Thus, Trump and his regime is something of an aberration; it is also an outcome
of longer-term processes. His approach to governance may reflect Trump's own
idiosyncrasies but it also reflects a time of transition from one economy to another. Relying on Atkinson (2004: 26–27) again:

> In each transition period there is a lag between the speed of technological trans-
> formation and the corresponding institutional, cultural, political, societal, and

---

[28] Highly politicized media bubbles are reinforced by think tanks that often can be identified as
leaning hard to the left or right.

individual transformation. Scientists, engineers, and entrepreneurs are often driven to change the world through rapid development of new technologies and development of new business models. The rest of society takes longer to catch up, being committed to old ways of doing things, old investments, old skills, old institutional arrangements, and old attitudes. As a result, during the periods when a new techno-economic system is emerging, organizations, institutions, laws, governments, the built environment, and attitudes and culture lag behind. But some do not just passively wait, many actively resist the change as it threatens entrenched ways of doing and established economic positions. Moreover, old economy stakeholders, whether in business and government or as consumers and workers, usually have more power than innovators. That is one reason.... Economic growth usually stagnates. That is also why these transitional periods bring forth strong debates and arguments about the future and what kind of society is desirable. Usually these debates are between those who view the new order with fear and trepidation and seek to hold onto an idyllic past, and those who embrace the changes and promote the future.

US political polarization is quite familiar with the fight between those who fear what they see as coming and those who embrace what they hope is coming. Polarization and dysfunction, presumably, will persist until one side of the debate wins out. Since it is hard to stop economic and other changes and transformation, probability favors "those who embrace the changes" over the ones who try to slow its full arrival. That is the optimistic take. The pessimistic aspect, however, is that we have no idea how long the transition period will persist or how hard the opponents to change will resist.

Nonetheless, the problem remains that domestic political dysfunction contributes to US relative decline in two ways. It blocks or at least hinders any concerted attempt to remedy the causes of relative decline—not that concerted attempts have been overt and frequent. Given the dysfunction, it is hard to even imagine a governmental policy of seriously accelerating the economic transformation that is underway. Instead what we get are serious federal attempts to increase gasoline consumption in automobiles—something short of committing to electrification of automobiles—followed not long after by deregulation of future gasoline consumption and the expansion of gasoline extraction efforts. Alternatively, preliminary attempts to reduce reliance on carbonized fuels in response to global warming (as in the Paris Agreement of 2015) are abandoned with a stroke of the pen and a nod to the alleged hoax of climate change. One step forward, two steps back is not a winning recipe for dealing with the problems of the twenty-first century. Nor does it help to maintain global leadership.

The other way domestic political dysfunction detracts from the maintenance of global leadership is that global leaders depend on domestic support for its provision of public goods. As the support becomes politicized and wanes, it is increasingly difficult to carry on at the global level. The United States' first and perhaps premature attempt to participate in global public good construction, Woodrow Wilson's effort to have the United States join the League of Nations, failed because Wilson could not elicit sufficient support. Waning domestic support for global leadership at the other end of the leadership life cycle can only accelerate its demise.

After reviewing external (chapter 5) and internal (this chapter) dimensions of relative decline, the next chapter looks at unipolarity. Less than three decades ago, it looked as if the United States was once more on top of the world and in a post–Cold War position even stronger than had been the case in the aftermath of World War II. Yet, as has been said by others (see Layne, 1993, 2006), it was something of a mirage.

7

The Unipolar Mirage

One of the reasons the world seems confusing to onlookers, especially in the United States, is that it was not very long ago that a very large number of people were convinced that the United States had won the Cold War, ideological history was dead, and a new era of US predominance in a unipolar world had emerged.[1] Then came 9/11, long wars in Afghanistan and Iraq, and an almost return to world depression on a scale not seen since the 1930s. How can these disparate impressions be reconciled? Is/was US triumphalism warranted, or was it a matter of misreading the structure of world politics? The argument here is that US triumphalism was not justified, and the world did not really turn unipolar over night with the collapse of the Soviet Union. What happened after the end of the Cold War, more accurately, was a temporary deviation from a longer sequence of protracted relative decline by the system's lead economy—the United States. Starting from a very high level of power concentration, the United States has a long way to go to fall out of first place in the global hierarchy. Yet that does not mitigate the gradually weakening foundation for power and influence with which the United States operates. Some of that relative decline is natural and inevitable; some of it is traceable to poor US decision-making that privileges the short term over long-term consideration.

Part of the misinterpretation of systemic structure can be traced to the way in which we study polarity or distributions of power. Our collective approach is characterized by six problems that lead to debatable conclusions about how world politics works. After a discussion of the problem set, some solutions are advanced utilizing the operationalization of global power discussed in chapter 2. These data are used to characterize polar distributions since 1816. In the end analysis, power concentration comes and goes. Whether it is associated with differential propensities to conflict remains an open question.

---

[1] An earlier version of this chapter appeared as William R. Thompson, "The Problems with Unipolarity," in *The Return of Geopolitics*, ed. Albert L. Bergesen and Christian Suter (Berlin: Lit Verlag, 2017).

American Global Pre-eminence. William R. Thompson, Oxford University Press. © Oxford University Press 2022.
DOI: 10.1093/oso/9780197534663.003.0007

Six Problems

The study of unipolarity is characterized by six problems—some of which are distinctive to the topic, while others are more generic to the study of international relations.[2] The two generic problems are a tendency to exaggerate the impact of any single variable, that is, a univariate explanation, and the absence of any consensus about how to go about measuring the distribution of power—something that is fundamental to arguments about what difference greater or lesser concentrations of power might make. The four non-generic problems are related to the generic ones. One is the absence for any threshold for the attainment of polar status. As a consequence, weaker and stronger candidates are lumped together. The second problem is the conflation of relative power and the presence or absence of challengers. People who study unipolarity assume that high relative power is accompanied by the absence of significant opposition when in fact that has not been the case. It may be that the presence or absence of challenges to leading states is more important than the actual distribution of power. But, it will be argued, it is difficult to talk about one without considering the other. Yet the third non-generic problem overlaps with the second one. Polarity is strongly static.[3] If a slice of time is coded as possessing the attributes on one type of polarity, it is assumed to be so characterized equally throughout the designated time period. Such stationarity seems highly unlikely, especially over a long period such as a century or even a half-century. The alternative is to focus more on dynamics. How the distribution of power is changing may be more important than identifying the category in which it falls roughly over some specific interval. Finally, the fourth non-generic problem is the tendency to view power distributions solely through a military lens. Military power is certainly important, but it hardly operates in a vacuum. The economic foundation that pays for military power is just as important. To examine one dimension while ignoring the other is simply distortional. Polarity needs to be examined in the context of its military-economic base.[4]

---

[2] For the unipolarity literature, see, among others, Krauthammer (1990/1991), Layne (1993), Owen (2003), Buzan (2004), Mowle and Sacko (2007), Brooks and Wohlforth (2008, 2015), Ikenberry, Mastanduno, and Wohlforth (2011), Monteiro (2011/2012, 2014), Hansen (2012), Kai He (2012), Fettweis (2017), Gowa and Ramsay (2017), and Lebovic (2018). It is a topic that seems to be fading in salience over the past decade.

[3] See, for instance, the older polarity literature: Deutsch and Singer (1964), Waltz (1964, 1979), Bueno de Mesquita (1975), Siverson and Sullivan (1983), Wayman (1984), Sabrosky (1985), Hopf (1991), and Kegley and Raymond (1994). Not all the analyses of this earlier era were static—see Thompson (1986), Spezio (1990), and Mansfield (1993).

[4] Lest one dismiss this perspective as overly materialistic, there is certainly more involved in establishing and maintaining a foundation for power. Cultural and ideational factors can play a role, but soft power does not lend itself readily to an empirical examination of power distribution.

Each of these problems deserves some elaboration and resolution if we are to figure out what to make of unipolarity claims. However, since the questions of power metrics, thresholds, and military-economic considerations are readily linked, it is most convenient to collapse these three problems under one heading, leaving us with four clusters to discuss.

Univariate Explanations

The entire history of polarity analysis has been plagued by the tendency to assume or to proceed as if the only thing that matters is the distribution of power. Waltz's (1979) structural realism framework is the leading example. Even if one wished to privilege structural factors over others, how, one might ask, is it possible to reduce structure to a single variable? The irony is even more complete since most students of international relations are quick to claim great complexity for their subject matter. Yet, even when we know better, we proceed to promote univariate explanations. Power distributions do this. Arms races or alliances make decision makers do things they might not have done otherwise. Living on islands encourages the development of navies, while surrounding mountains make people more insular. Democratic regime types do a great deal of that. The presence or absence of groupthink makes all the difference in crisis outcomes. Without Hitler, there would not have been World War II. If Archduke Ferdinand had not been assassinated, no World War I would have occurred.

While we need to advance generalizations linking variables, we should be cautious in taking any two-variable generalization too seriously. If one variable could explain a great deal of variance, would we not have stumbled on this magic elixir by now? Of course, many analysts think we have found powerful univariate explanations. The only problem is that if one holds one's breath long enough, significant objections are usually forthcoming. The reason is simple. International relations is more complex than many other fields of inquiry. Even Albert Einstein knew that. The problem is that we tend to overlook complexity when assembling our explanations. Maybe we must do this lest the sheer complexity of world politics paralyze us from advancing any explanations. But in doing so, we need to keep in mind just how limited is the probability that any one variable is going to account for a considerable amount of variance in whatever it is that we are trying to explain.[5]

[5] One of the ultimate ironies in the polarity literature is that Waltz (1979) devoted some space to criticizing reductionist theories and then proceeded to develop a univariate, structural realist explanation based on polarity.

Polarity, in general, is usually relied upon to explain system stability and levels of conflict. The distribution of power should possess some link to these topics. It does not seem implausible that a system in which power is highly concentrated might be more stable and less conflictual than one in which power is widely dispersed. What happens in between the two ends of the concentration continuum may be less easily predicted. Even within the polarity literature, there is some recognition of complexity in the occasional tendency to differentiate between polarity and polarization (Rapkin, Thompson, with Christopherson, 1979). A bipolar world, for instance, need not be highly bipolarized with all or most of the population adhering to one pole versus the other. It follows that a bipolar system that is also highly bipolarized could very well be more conflictual than a bipolar system that is not particularly bipolarized. We do not have to very far back in international history to find an example in the waning years of the Cold War.

That some analysts persist in assuming that polarity and polarization mean the same thing is unfortunate and perhaps part of the more general analytical problem. Here, however, it is only invoked to suggest that one does not have to go very far to find qualifications to the power of information about power distributions.

Static versus Dynamic Interpretations

The sixteenth through much of the first half of the twentieth centuries are often described as multipolar in structure. Is it conceivable that 445 some years were equally multipolar? At various points in time, Spain, France, and Germany held predominant positions within Western Europe. Did that not alter the way in which a multipolar distribution of power might be expected to work? Alternatively, the following bipolar era in the second half of the twentieth century was characterized by a long period in which the United States held a monopoly on the capability to deliver nuclear bombs/missiles over sufficient distances to reach its main opponent. At some point in the 1960s this began to change, and by the 1970s the United States was according nuclear parity with the Soviet Union. Should we expect bipolarity to have the same impact in the 1950s as in the 1980s? Of course, other processes such as learning to avoid full-fledged confrontations may have intervened as well. But the initial bipolarity was at the very least highly asymmetrical at the global level in the early years of the Cold War. It became less asymmetrical in terms of relative capabilities after the 1970s but remained lopsided in favor of the United States nonetheless.

Kirshner (2015) attributes the emphasis on static structure to the development of Waltz's (1979) structural realism, but static polarity arguments were of course quite common in the 1960s. Structural realism may have further reinforced static

structural arguments but it certainly did not invent them. Yet Kirshner is correct to stress that classical realists such as Gilpin have argued for looking at how
power distributions change as a more important factor than how we might code
structure at any given point in time. The question, of course, remains an empirical one but the dynamic interpretation certainly sounds more plausible if we
must make a choice.

Power Metrics, Thresholds, and Military-Economic Foundations

International relations analysts have never done well at measuring one of our
most central variables. To be sure, measuring power is not simple. Ideally, we
would like to be able to assess who influences whom to do what, but we usually have to settle for identifying who possesses varying shares of resources that
are thought to provide foundations for influencing other people and states.
Unfortunately, we do not agree precisely on which resources are thought to
be most important. Waltz (1979: 131) suggested a long list of possible resources: population size, territorial size, resource endowment, economic capability, military strength, political stability and competence. The Correlates of War
power concentration index (CINC) enthrones six indicators as something akin
to an industry standard: iron and steel production, military expenditures, military personnel, energy consumption, total population, and urban population.[6]
Other scholars, especially those working in the power transition research program, emphasize gross domestic product as the best single indicator of national
strength.

The multiple indicator indices represent the most prevalent approach to
measuring power distributions. When in doubt, hedge your bet by combining
a number of different indices and hope that something works.[7] Of course, this
interpretation is more than a bit cynical. An argument can be made for focusing
on each one of the indicators found in the Waltz and COW menus. The question, however, is whether an argument can be made to look at all the indicators
at the same time with equal weight given to each one. This type of argument, in
fact, is usually missing altogether. Once one lists the factors that observers have
thought to be relevant, it is just assumed that we can throw them together and

---

[6] Despite the widespread and professed dissatisfaction with the index, it is used repeatedly if for
no other reason that it is readily available and intermittently updated. It is fair to say that some of the
components are quite attractive indicators—the real question is whether they should all be combined
and combined in an unweighted fashion.

[7] It is not clear that anyone has ever followed Waltz's advice in operationalizing his list of power
indicators.

see what happens. Yet what tends to happen is that bulk is privileged over quality. Large populations, economies, and armies can be useful resources. Their utility can also be exaggerated if the population is undereducated and impoverished or if the economy or army lacks cutting edge technology. By and large, bulk resources are more useful in local or regional defensive situations in the sense that large countries are hard to occupy and control. Alternatively, large countries can overwhelm small neighbors. Historically, states that have dominated their home regions (think India in South Asia, China in East Asia, Russia in Eastern Europe, or France in early modern Western Europe) have often depended on bulk predominance. Other things being equal, the bulk resources are less useful in global contexts because they are hard to mobilize for power projection purposes. Large populations can provide ample cannon fodder but not necessarily much else. Large underdeveloped economies generate little surplus that can pay for complex weapons platforms. This liability has long been a problem and was certainly manifested when India and China's gross domestic products were the largest in the world prior to the Industrial Revolution. Their large economies did not prevent their defeats by relatively small forces with advanced cohesion and technology. For large armies to be effective they need appropriate firepower and relatively scarce (historically) naval and aerospace capabilities to be transported over long distances.

When one looks only at bulk resource indicators, the outcome can be misleading. When one combines bulk resources with non-bulk resources (for instance, energy consumption, gross domestic product per capita, or naval size), either they cancel one another if they are equal in number or the bulk resources trump the non-bulk factors because bulk indicators tend to lead to concentrated outcomes. States with large economies also tend to have large populations and armies. Thus, our indices of power give too much weight to bulk considerations and not enough to qualitative considerations.

Some of this problem is intertwined with problems in interpreting "great powers." Since most international relations analysts assume that the history of international relations should be equated with regional international relations in Western Europe, we begin with a checkered understanding of which states have been major powers—and thus potential poles. If eighteenth-century Prussia or nineteenth-century Italy can be counted as great powers, it becomes clear that the standards for major power status have not been uniform historically. This practice has been maintained by the Correlates of War codification of post-1816 major power status, which ignores the non-European world prior to the mid- to late nineteenth century and awards status promotions to the United States and Japan after they defeat other states not viewed as major powers. France and Britain retain their major power status after World War II dubiously. Germany and Japan regain their major power status after 1990 for reasons that are not altogether clear. In general, we simply lack consensual understanding of what counts for power purposes or where the threshold for promotion might lie even though we have proceeded as if we have agreed to something when we adopt COW standards.

A more defensible position is to suggest that there are three classes of states in international relations. Most states are minor powers with restricted military and/or economic capabilities. They may be stronger in one sphere than in the other, but they do not rank highly in both spheres. There are states that do rank relatively highly in military and economic capabilities, but their ability to project economic and military power are restricted for the most part to their home region. Then there are the few states that have the capability to project power beyond the home region to other regions. These states are global powers.

While we cannot assume that this alternative framework will find widespread appeal, it does have clear implications for how one goes about measuring the distribution of power. If the tripartite classification is adopted, measurement of power distributions must be careful about mixing regional and global powers or, alternatively, bulk and non-bulk resource capabilities. If we are addressing the global distribution of power, global powers should take precedence over regional powers. To make this distinction, some threshold distinguishing regional from global powers is necessary.

But there is another way in which the absence of thresholds becomes problematic. Let us assume for the sake of argument that we can count the number of global powers accurately. If there is only one, must the system be unipolar? Yet what about bipolar, tripolar, and multipolar situations? Where do we draw the lines between and among these categorizations? Too often, polarity discussions proceed as if there is no problem in moving back and forth among these designations when that is simply not the case. Take the following example: what should we make of a system with two global powers, one of which claims 75 percent of the total capabilities that count, and the other state possesses only 25 percent? Is the system unipolar or bipolar? If it is bipolar, is it bipolar in the same sense that a system with a 50:50 split in capabilities could be said to be bipolar?

Another illustration of the problem is to imagine two systems with three or more global powers. In one system, the capability distribution of the three leading states is 50 percent, 25 percent, and 25 percent. In the other, it is 36 percent, 34 percent, and 30%. How should we code system 1 or system 2? System 1 might be unipolar, or maybe it is tripolar/multipolar but certainly not tripolar/multipolar in the same sense that system 2 is. Putting aside for the moment the categorization problem, how should we view a system in which the leading state has declined in relative position from a 25 percent lead over its nearest rival (as in 50 percent versus 25 percent) to a 2 percent lead (as in 36 percent versus 34 percent)? Most polarity discussions have no answer for these questions because they choose to ignore precise thresholds. A state that leads by 2 percent is still considered the leader even if such a lead amounts to rough equivalence with other leading states. Yet no matter how these situations are construed, there can be little question that a lopsided edge over rivals is different from not much of an edge.[8]

An alternative approach is to talk about algebraic qualifications of unipolarity. Buzan (2004) and Brooks and Wohlforth (2015) have talked about a single superpower (i.e., unipolarity) but accompanied by one or more relatively weak challengers—as in $1 + X$ or $1 + X + Y$. The X and Y qualifiers suggest that the predominance of the single leading state is somehow qualified or in the process of becoming qualified. X and/or Y are significant actors but not yet in the "superpower" category. The problem here is that not much more information is conveyed beyond the caveat that unipolar leaders are confronted by challengers. At what point do these challengers rise to high enough status to change one into two or more great or superpowers?[9] In the absence of any explicit thresholds, the X and Y will remain nominal qualifiers for some time to come. But what if X and Y are allied or act in concert? Do we aggregate their combined resistance? It is good to highlight the presence of challengers. Yet leaving them as X or Y remains awkward for operationalizing the distribution of power, just as forgoing the application of explicit thresholds leaves us in a subjective limbo when it comes time to estimate degrees of change.

The third problematic dimension of this cluster is the proclivity to differentiate between military and economic capabilities. For most polarity analysts (but not all), only military capabilities count. This tendency may reflect disciplinary preferences for analysts to specialize in one domain or the other. Thus, many international relations scholars have chosen to do security or international political economy (IPE) exclusively. Not surprisingly, it is the people who have taken the security path who are most likely to stress the significance of military capabilities alone. Similarly, IPE analysts are the ones who are most likely to argue that it is difficult to focus on one sphere and to ignore the other.

Yet it seems hard to deny that some states have economic clout but little military technology. Others have military technology but weak economies. Both types of states are handicapped in what they can do in world politics. In extreme cases, former superpowers cannot afford to send their submarines to sea for fear

---

[8] Compare the situation with voting observations. A candidate with a 10 percent lead close to voting time is considered a sure thing to win. A candidate with a 1 or 2 percent lead is not a sure thing. Her lead in polling may not even be statistically significant.

[9] This approach is reminiscent of the older, Cold War tendency to refer to the Asian balance of power as a 2.5 power configuration. The Soviet Union and the United States were counted as 2 powers. China was the 0.5 power. Yet at least this approach had the merit of implying two states were roughly equal and the third was not equal to the first two. What was left open-ended was whether China's relative position was closer to 0.25 or 0.75 the weight of the other two states? Or, perhaps it would have been more accurate to say that the capability distance between China and the Soviet Union was less than the distance between China and the United States?

that they will never return. Major economies with limited military capability must rely on allies to defend them from military attack. States moving up the hierarchy must make choices between expanding military capabilities or economic investments. They also must decide what kind of military platforms they can afford or figure out how to build. Even singular superpowers have significant problems financing their military activities abroad. It seems unlikely, therefore, that we can divorce discussions of military capabilities from the context of economic limitations. Nor should we overlook the economic motivations for improved military capabilities. Moving up the economic hierarchy puts pressure on decision makers to expand their military arsenal to better advance and protect their expanding interests. Polarity needs to be measured in both military and economic terms.

Conflating Power Concentration and the Presence or Absence of Challengers

The aforementioned 1 + X+Y practice raises an additional problem. In unipolarity discussions it is only natural to stress the dominance of the single leading state. But we need to combine the absence of thresholds and the temporary vicissitudes of world politics in order to generate a cautionary note. The absence of explicit thresholds means that if the challengers are temporarily absent from the picture, the state left standing, almost regardless of its relative capability position, can be said to qualify as the unipole. In the interval most celebrated as a unipolar era—from the end of the Cold War to some indefinite time thereafter—the United States was said to be at the apex of a unipolar hierarchy in large part because the Soviet Union had disintegrated and China had adopted a strategy stressing domestic development over foreign adventures. If the United States was catapulted to the top of the heap by default—that is, by the temporary absence of strong competition—it is not surprising that that situation did not last long or that the unipole did not manage to get much accomplished. The question remains, however, just how predominant the United States was in that unipolar interlude. Was it a genuinely unipolar interval or just a passing fluke of world politics? Must a unipolar state have no real competition to be able to claim unipolarity? However unlikely that may be, the moral of the story is not to ignore what else is going on besides the perceived predominance of the leading state. Thresholds or no thresholds, the systemic situation is apt to be different when the unipole is very strong and uncontested than when it is moderately strong and challenged. Thus, we need to know not only how high up the hierarchy the leading state is but also just how far ahead the leading state is from the competition.

The Regional-Global Problem

Finally, there is the question of perspective. What level of analysis should we focus upon for determining polarity structures? The reflexive answer is the "international system." Yet there is something of a trap in this answer depending on how one answers the auxiliary question of how many systems are encompassed by "the international system"—one?, several?, more than a dozen? Is the international system like a Russian doll? Open it up and one finds many smaller dolls in descending size order? As long as the answer to the initial question—how many systems are encompassed by the international system term—is more than one, there is a problem of how many of these systems, or which ones, should we measure for distribution of power purposes.

For some time, analysts have recognized that there are a number of regional subsystems that have different polarity structures from the one that most people think of as the international system. So, whether we refer to the "master" system as an international or global one, there could be multiple mini-international systems that possess independent structures worthy of examination. But one of the reasons we do not usually do this procedure for multiple systems is the assumption that the regional subsystems are subordinate to the more general global or international structure. So, one might have a global system that is bipolar and a regional subsystem that is multipolar, apolar, or even unipolar and it might not make a whole lot of difference to political outcomes outside of the region or within it.

But what if the regional distribution of power is more important than the global distribution? This is a novel question that does not surface very often. It comes up in a very telling manner in a recent study by Tunsjø (2018). Tunsjø starts by suggesting that we do not compare within category polarity structures. Instead, we assume that all uni-/bi-/multipolar structures are similar. But what if they are not? The illuminating Tunsjø comparison involves the Cold War focus in Europe with the emerging Sino-American standoff in East Asia. He argues that both regional theaters were (or are becoming in the Asian case) bipolar. In the European case, political geography pitted a large Eurasian land power against a powerful North American sea power. Few physical obstacles stood in the way of the land power moving its tanks toward the Atlantic Ocean. To deter expansionary movements into Western Europe by the Eurasian land power, it was necessary to threaten nuclear obliteration because even with a large coalition of NATO states, it was improbable that sufficient land power could have been built up to serve as an alternative deterrent.

In the East Asian case, a different political geographical configuration exists. The region is divided into continental and maritime segments. China naturally dominates the continental portion but, as a traditional land power, its access to the maritime portion is restricted by water.[10] The leading sea power, the United States, is unlikely to make much headway militarily in the continent, but it can exploit the water barrier in conjunction with its sea power to protect the maritime chain extending from the Korean peninsula through Japan and Taiwan around to Australia, New Zealand, the Philippines, Singapore, and Indonesia. India complicates this interpretation but, for the present, it can be ignored as not part of East Asia.

The payoff of this perspective is that there is less reason to anticipate a reliance on nuclear obliteration because the geography is different. Mother Nature stands in the way of full regional hegemony in continental and maritime East Asia whereas it does not/did not in Europe after World War II. That might mean better chances of a limited clash or war at sea in the Asian case, in comparison to the European case, but the threat of nuclear war costs should work to keep such a clash limited in lethality and objectives.

Tunsjø comes up with an innovative argument by introducing comparison to polarity analysis and by bringing in the second variable of political geography to differentiate two conflict zones or regions. The combination of all three (comparison, political geography, and regions) delivers a new way to look at the relationship between power distributions and conflict behavior. The obvious question in this respect is whether his regional polarity assessments are more powerful than global ones. In these cases, US, Soviet, and Chinese behavior seems more influenced by local or regional considerations than they are by global issues. If that observation holds, the regional polarity assessment appears to have the most utility.

Problems That Deserve Resolution and Attempts to Do So

Polarity discussions continue to be too subjective—who counts, what counts, and how much counts? Explicit criteria for delineating different types of, and changes in, power distributions should be desirable. Explicit thresholds for rank are also necessary. Otherwise, we will continue to talk around each other with varying but ambiguously defined notions of what we are talking about. We probably also need to consider different databases than those that are conventionally relied upon. It is not clear that the "industry standards" have served us well. Moreover, we need to integrate military and economic capabilities in assessing how power is distributed in the international system.

---

[10] The term "naturally" is used cautiously because the historical irony is that China has not always dominated East Asia. When Han Chinese control the territory that we now think of as China, predominance in East China comes naturally. Earlier versions of China were sometimes much smaller in territory or controlled by non-Chinese groups.

A possible solution for explicit polarity criteria (Modelski, 1974; Rapkin, Thompson, with Christopherson, 1979) has been around for some time but has never caught on. Whether this reflects a resistance to explicit criteria, disapproval of the specific criteria, or some combination thereof, is not clear. One criticism that has been broached (Brookes and Wohlforth, 2015), that the threshold for unipolarity is too high because no state has ever exceeded it, is simply wrong as long as one calculates the threshold in terms of the pooled capabilities of the most likely elite culprits, as opposed to using world capabilities as the denominator.[11] It also depends, of course, on what specific capabilities are examined—an issue we will examine shortly.

The polarity rules or criteria are simple and can be expressed in one complex sentence:[12]

In a unipolar system, one state holds more than 50 percent of available power;
  in a bipolar system, two states combined hold at least 50 percent of available power, and each holds at least 25 percent;
  in multipolar systems, power is concentrated in three or more states with each possessing at least 5 percent of available power but no two states holding more than 25 percent.

The logic is that a state that can match the capabilities of any combination of elite opponents (more than 50 percent) is a highly concentrated power configuration that can qualify as unipolar. This type of logic harks back to the original nineteenth-century interpretation of great powers qualifying for their elite status by being perceived as capable of defeating another great power. In this case, however, the configuration allows for the possibility that one state could defeat a coalition of all the other elite powers in the system. Bipolarity needs power to be concentrated in the capabilities of the leading two states, and some semblance of symmetry between the two is most desirable. Consider an extreme alternative. Two states control 60 percent of the capabilities, but one state claims 45 percent and the other 15 percent, giving one state a 3:1 advantage. Highly asymmetrical bipolarity is unlikely to work exactly as whatever effects are attributed to symmetrical bipolarity. For multipolar systems, some asymmetry is tolerable but not too much lest the system move toward a genuinely non-multipolar system in which a number of states are equal in their relative capability positions.

Nonetheless, there are a few possible holes in the schedule. One that was encountered earlier is that it is conceivable that one state could possess an

---

[11] Interestingly, the criticism did not move the critics to suggest a threshold that they thought was more realistic.
[12] These rules have been slightly modified at the multipolar level from the original specifications.

impressive lead that still fell short of the 50 percent threshold. If one state controlled a capability share in the 40s (40–49 percent) and no other state controlled as much as 25 percent (otherwise the system might be unevenly bipolar), it is not clear what to designate such a configuration. "Near unipolarity" was the category used earlier, and it seems useful to retain this in between structural situation. It is also possible to imagine an exceptional multipolar system in which there are only three states with one or more states exceeding a 25 percent share. The question would then be whether such a clearly tripolar system would be expected to function differently than a typical multipolar (or bipolar) system.[13] That seems to be a question that can be put off until it is actually encountered or becomes a theoretical puzzle.

The polarity schedule provides concise instructions on how to tell the difference among various polarity types. It does not tell us how to construct the percentage shares that are needed for data in hand. Nor does it tell us when to rely on regional as opposed to global polarity assessments. The first question can be dealt with easily. The second one probably does not have a definitive answer. It will depend on the question. In chapter 9, for instance, we will return to the Tunsjø approach when the query focuses on likely US-Chinese rivalry interactions.

Coding for Polarity

Table 7.1 lists relative power capability shares for selected years. The reader is reminded that this approach focuses on the global distribution of relative power projection shares. If we were only interested in the European or East Asian regions, a different calculus with different indicators would need to be made. As hinted earlier in chapter 2, regional power projection has tended to revolve around tanks, jet fighter aircraft, and the ability to move large numbers of infantry. Global reach is more focused on naval vessels, strategic bombers, and ballistic missiles. The point, however, is that we have been conflating the global system and the European region for too long. Some distinction needs to be maintained even if it runs afoul of our Eurocentric versions of world history.

Table 7.1 shows the 1816–1945 period beginning in unipolarity, continuing as unipolar for two decades, then followed by three decades of unipolarity and near unipolarity.[14] The rest of this period comes across as multipolarity, with a very strong relative British position through the nineteenth century. In the twentieth century, Britain's power projection position was weakening and in the

---

[13] Schweller (1998) once thought tripolarity was or could be distinctive.

[14] Near unipolarity equals situations when one power controls at least a 45 percent share but less than a 50 percent share.

Table 7.1 Major Power Global Power Projection Shares, 1816–2018

	Britain	Russia	France	United States	Austro-Hungary	Germany	Italy	Japan	China
1816	.647	.128	.172	.030	.022				
1825	.548	.165	.228	.047	.011				
1835	.488	.214	.216	.067	.015				
1845	.469	.222	.229	.073	.007				
1855	.547	.147	.237	.062	.005	.002			
1865	.343	.100	.233	.191	.010	.041	.081		
1875	.411	.144	.194	.069	.017	.090	.075		
1885	.417	.068	.306	.042	.012	.037	.102	.016	
1895	.403	.093	.196	.090	.010	.082	.111	.015	
1905	.386	.091	.116	.175	.013	.148	.040	.031	
1915	.384	.061	.061	.101	.040	.232	.051	.071	
1925	.310	.012	.166	.322		.011	.113	.065	
1935	.232	.262	.065	.165		.145	.044	.086	
1945	.254	.067	.025	.630		.010		.013	
1955	.070	0	.010	.920					–
1965	.042	.171	.07	.770					–
1975	.054	.272	.023	.649					.001
1985	.031	.375	.024	.568					.002
1995	.032	.330	.031	.602					.004
2005	.048	.259	.033	.650					.009
2018	.021	.275	.035	.577					.091

Note: Entries are provided for states before they attain major power status if there is something to report but not after they have lost their status.

1920s and 1940s was either roughly matched or eclipsed by the US position. The post–World War II era began in military unipolarity and, in many respects, has yet to move away from it.[15] The US share did benefit from the collapse of the Soviet Union but not all that much. Despite the discernible similarity in the two

[15] The term to be emphasized here is "military unipolarity." Systemic leadership is not defined by its military arsenal alone, of course, but there is an unfortunate tendency to restrict polarity categorizations to the distribution of military resources.

movements over time of the respective global leaders (Britain and the United States), the outcome will not seem very familiar to most analysts.

The relative positions of both global leaders declined overall, with some deviations from decade to decade (figure 7.1). Interestingly, both departures from the negative slopes of the trend lines are due to Russian behavior. In the British case, one of the causes for the bump up in the fifth decade was mobilization for the Crimean War. In the US case, the reversal in trend was primarily due to the collapse of the Soviet Union. Britain lasted only two decades before dipping below the unipolar threshold. The United States has stayed above the threshold for seven to eight decades but has resumed a downward movement in the eighth decade since the second world war. Whether the US trajectory will continue to resemble the British trajectory remains to be seen. Both the Chinese and Russians are working hard to see that the negative trend continues. Other states are acquiring aircraft carriers and nuclear submarines as well. But, as noted in earlier chapters, there is no reason to assume that the United States will decline beyond some relatively high floor—unlike Britain's ultimate fate.

A case for asymmetrical bipolarity emerges in the 1970s according to table 7.1. Yet one could also argue for persistent unipolarity. Should that caution a rethink about the measurement apparatus? Perhaps, but not necessarily so. One thing that is missing in the global power projection index is any reflection of nuclear warhead "overkill." In other words, once one possesses a second-strike capability, does it matter how many more warheads or projection capabilities are available? The index simply counts the distribution of nuclear warheads in

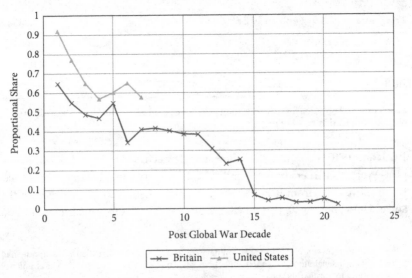

Figure 7.1 British and US Decline in Global Reach Power Projection Share

terms of lethality and accuracy (and, of course, other types of capabilities). Yet at some point the utility of more warheads is limited. Thus, the way the index is constructed ignores the substantive nuclear parity that was achieved in the late 1960s or early 1970s in the Cold War. Giving more credence to this element would make a stronger case for global military bipolarity after the late 1960s and through as far as the table goes for that matters—but not before when the Soviet Union had major problems developing accuracy and acquiring the ability to deliver their missiles to the desired targets in North America. But even so, few analysts would argue that Cold War bipolarity was ever symmetrical in terms of overall capability. It was primarily efforts to overcome the asymmetry that led to the unintended demise of the Soviet Union.

Once the Soviet Union did collapse, the United States was left standing as the sole surviving "superpower" but without the major lead in its economic/energy foundation that it had possessed earlier. It had the military capability to project power in several directions, but it was less able to pay for it. As it turned out, the temptation to use that military capability, in a brief interval that was unconstrained by rival opposition, did not necessarily lead to the military capability being used prudently.[16] Nor did the military expenditure outlay lead to much in the way of upgrading the power projection military capability—as opposed to spending money on ground activities in Afghanistan and Iraq.

What is often described as the "unipolar moment" did not quite measure up to a full-scale unipolar episode. Moreover, it was due almost solely to the temporary absence of Soviet/Russian activities and the lower-profile strategy adopted by the Chinese in the late twentieth century that prioritized economic development over international adventures. Both developments seem to have run their course. The Russians have become more active in an attempt to regain some of their lost status. It did not have to work out that way, but there was probably some probability that it would. The Chinese are now more prepared to engage in military operations in the East and South China Seas, and perhaps elsewhere.[17] Whatever the appropriate adjective for the moment, it seems to have passed. None of this means that the United States does not remain the most powerful state in the system. That is not the issue about which we are arguing. Rather, the question is how strong the US relative position was in the two decades after the end of the Cold War. The argument here is that it was not as strong as decision makers thought in the heady triumphalism of winning/surviving the Cold War. It was not genuinely unipolar because the military edge component considerably outweighed the economic-energy component of the foundation.

---

[16] It is hard to imagine two wars with Iraq, let alone a long occupation, during the Cold War years given the Soviet links to the Hussein regime.

[17] A new Chinese naval base in northeast Africa, for instance, suggests some commitment to patrolling western Indian Ocean waters.

Unipolarity conditions have existed, at least as specified by the standards employed in this chapter, but they are not recognized widely as such. The periods immediately after the Napoleonic Wars and World War II qualified as unipolar from a global perspective. We do not tend to recognize those years as unipolar for several reasons. We do not think globally and instead blur the distinctions between regional and global activities. The Soviet Union could threaten to do various things in Eurasian sub-regions that were close at hand. Even so, often, the perceived and asserted threats did not correspond to actual Soviet capabilities. US observers tended to give Soviet capabilities too much credit—as demonstrated by alleged bomber and missile gaps that tended to emerge around electoral times.

Another reason for overlooking these periods of high concentration is that unipolarity has come early when global war winners are in a rush to demobilize and often before they have fully absorbed their newly leading roles. As lead economies and sea powers, the emphasis has been placed on reviving markets and prosperity, not dictating terms to other states and taking over their territory (Levy and Thompson, 2011). Unipolar powers tend to be reluctant or unable to take full advantage of their strong positions. For instance, the US monopoly on atomic weapons was explicitly used to persuade Japan to surrender, but it was not used to force concessions from the Soviet Union. Alternatively, one could argue that Britain's gold and sea power in 1815 was of limited relevance to postwar negotiations over what to do about the French problem in Western Europe. Even during the Napoleonic Wars, it had had serious problems maintaining its coalitions designed to defeat the French armies. Thus, it is easy to exaggerate even very strong powers ability to influence other actors. These observations remind us that it is easy to exaggerate the power and influence of even unipolar powers.

Conclusions

Power distributions are not meaningless, but their interpretation requires caution and does not appear to be as straightforward as is often assumed. Static characterizations can be treacherous if they suppress different dynamics at play. The past two centuries have been characterized by global power concentrations that were initially quite high in the aftermath of the Napoleonic Wars and World War II, respectively. The leading global power controlled a disproportionate share of economic power, as manifested in new technology and energy sources. Each state also virtually monopolized power projection capabilities with global reach. These high concentrations of power capabilities were not infinite in duration. The high concentrations peak and then decay rather slowly. Power projection shares tend to decay more slowly than technology/energy shares do.

Just where unipolarity fits within these long and slow deconcentration propensities will no doubt continue to be debated. However, the argument advanced here is that the much-acclaimed post–Cold War unipolar phase was less than it seemed. It passes muster as a unipolar phase according to a polarity operationalization template, but it did so more on power projection capabilities than it did on technology/energy capabilities. Its behavioral manifestations seem less linked to the development of a novel power foundation and more attuned to an exaggerated sense of triumphalism on the part of elites affiliated with the global leader and the very temporary absence of major power challenges. At the same time, ironically, we tend to ignore the strong evidence for unipolarity in earlier, postwar circumstances or, alternatively, the very strong position of the United States throughout the ostensibly bipolar Cold War period.

In sum, unipolarity has played some role in contemporary world politics. However, it may not be the role(s) usually ascribed to it. Global unipolarity may very well also be less potent an explanatory variable than we have thought. At the very least, polarity coding requires a fair amount of qualifications and caveats. Nonetheless, the main purpose of this chapter has been to explain how the United States moved from unipolarity to relative decline in a handful of years. The answer is that it did not. Thinking that it did is a mirage. Something had changed but we misidentified what it was. Relative decline had been ongoing all along. If that had been recognized, we might have avoided a great deal of unpleasantness in the first decade of the twenty-first century.

Chapters 5 through 7 complete the present examination of US relative decline. The next question is what should we expect given the significant decline of the global system leader. The last three chapters take on this question in different ways. Chapter 8 centers on whether we have reason to anticipate the concentration process continuing as before. The answer is no. Technological innovation will be much more difficult to monopolize even for brief periods of time. Global war seems to be defunct as an institution for changing global leadership.

8

The End of Systemic Leadership
as We Have Come to Know It?

In the development of theoretically guided, future scenarios for a hypo-
thetical US-China system leader transition, five possibilities are sketched in
Rapkin and Thompson (2013): global war ("Transition War"), peaceful transition to Chinese leadership ("Pax Sinica"), re-emergence of US systemic leadership ("Pax Americana"), no transition in a world governed by liberal peace
institutions ("Liberal Peace"), and "more of the same" (slow Chinese ascent
and protracted US decline). All these possible futures are not equally probable,
but none are totally implausible. Of the five, the most likely future appears to be
more of the same. Why this might be the case is the subject of this chapter but
the reasons for thinking that this scenario is the most probable one are predicated on significant changes in the operating parameters associated with the
historical evolution of system leadership. Given these changes, the emergence
of new leadership seems less likely and it may mean that the nature of traditional systemic leadership or hegemony has come to an end. That would mean
that Pax Sinica and a revived Pax Americana would be unlikely. Although US-
Chinese conflict of some sort cannot be ruled out, global war is made less likely
by nuclear deterrence and the extreme costs of a future major power war, if
for no other reasons. The liberal peace hinges on whether its conflict reduction mechanisms can encompass actors not interested in upholding the status
quo. Presumably, the future demise of systemic leadership could make political space for the expansion of Kantian instruments, but that is only one possibility. Other observers have arrived at a similar conclusion, albeit for different
reasons. After first briefly reviewing two earlier perspectives on this question,
the focus shifts to delineating the changes in systemic leadership parameters
that seem most critical.

Other Interpretations

Conservative commentators like to point out that discussions of systemic leadership decline are even more cyclical than systemic leadership. Their point is
meant to undermine the discourse by implying that people seem to be prone

American Global Pre-eminence. William R. Thompson, Oxford University Press. © Oxford University Press 2022.
DOI: 10.1093/oso/9780197534663.003.0008

to warning about imminent decline and worse without much cause. Therefore, there is no real need to take these Chicken Little Cassandras seriously. Dismiss it as yet another round of the geopolitical sky is falling. Or should we take these warnings seriously as a clue to things genuinely changing? The usual questions include how far has the United States declined as system leader and who is the most likely successor? Chase-Dunn et al. (2011), Buzan (2011), and Grinin and Korotayev (2014), separately and differently, have added a novel twist to this set by introducing a third question: assuming the United States is in decline, why should we assume that there will be a successor? They contend that hegemonic cycles are disappearing. As the US systemic leadership gradually fades, no one state is likely to emerge as its replacement. We are in for a radical transformation of systemic structure and one in which a singular hierarchy is absent. They may be right but not necessarily for the reasons that they have put forward. There are other reasons to think that systemic leadership may not only be eroding but also disappearing as a structural feature of contemporary world politics.

How one views this issue depends very much on how one conceptualizes systemic leadership. While Chase-Dunn et al. view hegemonic decline as a world-system regularity, Buzan sees it as the demise of a relatively short-lived superpower thanks to a changing environment no longer conducive to fostering such concentration of power. Grinin and Korotayev see disappearing systemic leadership as an inadvertent byproduct of globalization processes. An alternative perspective, the one that is advanced here, views it as a consequence of changes in the technological dynamics that have been most responsible for generating systemic leadership in the first place. Whereas Chase-Dunn et al. and Grinin and Korotayev largely perceive exogenous factors at work, Buzan thinks it is a combination of endogenous and exogenous factors.[1] Of course, it may turn out that none of these explanations will hold up. Or some integration of the multiple culprits put forward could provide the best answer. After all, the argument advanced in this chapter is not mutually exclusive with the interpretations advanced by Chase-Dunn et al., Buzan, and Grinin and Korotayev. We may have to wait a generation or two to find out which processes are most critical. In the interim, we should keep an open mind about the interaction of processes that are still unfolding.

The present argument for the demise of systemic leadership as we have come to know it hinges on a combination of changes in the likelihoods of innovation concentration, energy transition, and the onset of global warfare. If

---

[1] In marked contrast, most discussions of hegemonic transitions take the factors that generated hegemony for granted. It is also assumed that whatever worked in the past will work the same way in the future.

economic innovation is no longer as concentrated as it has been in the past millennium, if sources of relatively inexpensive energy are no longer available, and if global warfare is no longer very probable, it is less likely that the future world economy will be dominated by a singular lead economy. In the absence of a singular and dominating lead economy, traditional systemic leadership will disappear. Whether what replaces it will be a more sophisticated form of global governance remains to be seen, but since the traditional format is quite primitive—a form of "might makes right"—there is at least some reason for holding out hope for an improved level of global governance. Certainly, the problems that need managing at the global level demand and deserve much more concerted attention than they receive now.

To make the case, the Chase-Dunn et al. (2011), Buzan (2011), and Grinin and Korotayev (2014) interpretations are first introduced briefly as baseline approaches. Some reservations are expressed about the applicability of some parts of the arguments, but none of the arguments can be rejected completely. Yet since their conclusions appear to have a great deal of merit, it is worthwhile developing an alternative argument that gets us to the same place—a future and radical transformation of how political-economic power is structured in world politics.[2]

The Chase-Dunn et al. Interpretation

From the world-system perspective, the incumbent hegemon, the United States, had worked through its leads in commerce and industrial innovation by the 1970s and is now attempting to maintain its affluence on the basis of widespread investment and financial power. The possibility that some semblance of a technological lead might be resurrected in, say, biotechnology, cannot be dismissed. Yet, the prospects for a concentrated technological resurgence seem dim. One reason involves energy. The United States had been able to supplant a coal-based Britain with inexpensive petroleum, much of which was generated at home. Any future economic transition is facing rising energy costs, not declining prices. Thus, energy access considerations suggest that decentralization and deglobalization, along with resource wars, is more likely than another round of global hegemony. At some point, as costs continue to rise, global trade and investment volumes should be expected to decline. Long-distance

---

[2] There are, of course, other arguments such as the conflict deterrence of economic interdependence or nuclear weapons that might well influence the likelihood of conflict in the future, but these alternative arguments do not explicitly lead to an expectation of changing the very foundations of systemic leadership successions.

transportation should become prohibitive. Activities should become more localized.[3] Moreover, the strong potential for environmental catastrophes should add additional pressure on destabilizing deglobalization tendencies. Hegemonic cycles, in short, will be replaced by a retreat from global activities on several fronts.

In the interim, the incumbent hegemon is experiencing slow decline. Chase-Dunn et al. note that the current US share of the world economy is twice as large as Britain's peak share. The US peak share at the end of World War II had been 3.5 times as large as Britain's peak. Therefore, it has a higher point from which to fall. Rising economic challengers, as noted, are far from closing in on the US technological lead and even farther away from catching up militarily. But, at the same time, the United States' legitimacy as a source of global governance has been squandered in a decade or more of unilateral use of coercion. The governance institutions created after 1945 are similarly weak on legitimacy concerns but more so on effectiveness grounds. There is little in the way of global governance to head off the coming conflicts over resources, coping with environmental distress, and combating the deglobalization propensities.

The Chase-Dunn et al. perspective is most useful in comparing differences in the nature of British and US decline. The United States started far ahead of the British position and, hence, has farther and longer to decay. Rivals seem way behind on anything resembling military parity and both factors work against the possibility of global warfare recurring in the immediate future as it did in the period 1914–1945. These observations are quite useful, but they can be amplified by additional considerations along similar lines.

The future roles of energy costs and environmental catastrophe are more speculative. They assume that we are essentially stuck with employing ultimately declining supplies of coal and petroleum. Energy costs will rise inexorably, and the environmental problems will be all the worse for the continued reliance on hydrocarbons. Regrettably, they may be right, but we will not know how bad the future will be just yet. Some kind of moderate Mad Max scenario may be lurking down the road.[4] So, too, could major innovations in energy use and perhaps even innovations to deal with environmental deterioration. Whichever type of future we are facing, it is possible to develop an argument about the likely demise of systemic leadership cycles without a crystal ball.

---

[3] Here Chase-Dunn et al. lean heavily on Tainter's (1988) argument based on the long history of rising and falling societies.

[4] A Mad Max scenario, borrowing from the dystopian movie of the same name, mixes extreme environmental deterioration, highly limited energy supplies, and virtually no governance independent of organized criminal predation.

The Buzan Interpretation

Buzan first differentiates between great powers and superpowers. Superpowers are states with a reach (political, military, economic, and cultural) that extends across the entire global system. Great powers are the next rank down—states that can extend their reach to more than one region. It is superpowers that he thinks will go extinct, not great powers. As in the case of dinosaurs, the once sustaining environment is changing so radically that a superpower cannot be sustained.

Five reasons for superpower extinction are advanced. It is not clear how many superpowers have existed according to Buzan, but he thinks the United States is the current solitary example. Its superpower status is contingent on "peculiar historical circumstances" that in the nineteenth century pushed Western states far ahead of the rest of the world and were artificially amplified by the destructiveness of World War II. The United States was the primary beneficiary of these circumstances, but the effects are not something that can be experienced infinitely. First, destruction related to the second world war has been repaired. Two, rising powers are restoring the state of affairs prior to the nineteenth century in which China and India had to be listed as major powers. Third, the United States is in a slowly emerging, moderate decline in which the US population is increasingly balking at paying for expensive involvement in the outside world. At the same time, other states are weary of abuses carried out by the United States in the name of systemic leadership. Four, that pre-nineteenth-century distribution of power prevailed in a world in which states were not all that interdependent. In the twenty-first century, they will be tightly bound, interdependent, and post-colonial in attitude. Most states will no longer support the leadership pretensions of the lone superpower. Fifth, and finally, there are no new superpower candidates on the horizon. China is the only real possibility.[5] Yet it still lacks the material foundation, a domestic leadership unified in playing an ambitiously expansive role in world politics, and legitimacy for systemic leadership from other actors.[6] Once the United States retreats to its regional base in North America, no state is likely to seek to replace it.

In the absence of a superpower, the world will be divided into some yet-to-be determined number of regions subject to the varying management styles of resident great powers. While such a world might see increased inter-regional conflict, Buzan suspects that this world will prove to more pacific than the present one. De-centered globalism will be a more benign structure because it will be characterized by a more equitable distribution of power, nuclear weapons,

---

[5] The European Union is ruled out as an improbable candidate because it lacks enough integration and the will to play a major power role.

[6] China's reigning communist ideology is not viewed as a model by most of the rest of the world, and it lacks a set of allies that might form a supporting coalition for its global activities.

anti-hegemony sentiments, and collective problems to resolve at the global level like climate change. A more "live and let live" attitude should reign supreme.

Buzan's approach is distinctive in a variety of ways. Perhaps most significant for our purposes, his interpretation does not revolve around the relative decline of the United States' materials position, as do most decline models. Instead, he argues that people inside the superpower will reject leadership ambitions and people outside the superpower will reject US claims to systemic leadership. Yet it is not clear that systemic leadership depends solely on ideational grounds. External legitimacy and internal support are certainly useful, but neither is likely to be forthcoming without considerable material changes. When the United States' relative position was strongest at the end of World War II, American decision makers felt that they had to inflate the Soviet threat to gain domestic support. The maneuver worked but would it work as well when the US relative position is less than dominant? Similarly, external legitimacy is most useful and probably vital to sustaining a supportive international coalition. But it alone would certainly not suffice to encourage US claims to global leadership. Nor would its absence preclude those same claims from being used to mask US activities outside its home region.

The likelihood is that some significant relative decline in material capability must interact with domestic and external attitude change to attain a fully transformed world. Just how that works is hard to say. Despite US abuses of leadership, decision makers abroad still seem to cling to the hope of renewed US leadership. Domestic public opinion on the United States' appropriate role in world politics moves up and down. More relative capability decline seems probable. We may not have to hold our breaths for several decades to find out if Buzan is right. Neither external dismay about the course of US foreign policy or internal leadership weariness are absent from the current landscape of world politics. A second term for Trump or somebody like him might be the last straw.[7]

The Grinin and Korotayev Interpretation

The Grinin and Korotayev argument begins by acknowledging declinist discussions in the 1970s and 1980s. They see this discourse as premature. The development of new IT technology in the 1990s and the collapse of the communist bloc propelled the United States into a short-lived era of absolute hegemony. Perceptions of omnipotence tempted US decision makers into a number of strategic errors that led, in turn, to weakened capabilities, increasing public debt,

---

[7] Buzan was reacting to George W. Bush's regime. If had written his paper a decade later, he might have been convinced that the demise of superpower age was already upon us.

and, ultimately, the financial meltdown of 2008. Despite these handicaps, US systemic leadership survives in a weaker form than has been manifested earlier in the post–World War II era. It will probably persist for a few more decades in a gradually weakening format before succumbing entirely. But no new system leader is likely to supplant it or replace it because no state will be able to generate the many leadership qualities (military, economic, financial, cultural) that the United States has been able to bring together since 1945.

Yet it is not simply the absence of a suitable candidate that spells the end of the hegemonic cycle. Grinin and Korotayev attribute the main cause of this development to globalization. Core powers, predominated by the United States, have increasingly specialized in producing new technology while they pushed older technologies to the periphery due primarily to its cheaper labor costs. In the process of doing so, they made the periphery economically stronger and hollowed out their own industrial infrastructure, abetted by aging populations, a reluctance to engage in hard work, and a commitment to free trade. This last element is representative of a "globalization trap." The West, led by the United States, had promoted the wisdom of free trade when it favored the West. Now that it favors a rising periphery, the West finds it difficult to retreat from its own rhetoric into some type of protectionism.

In any event, the outcome is a movement toward economic convergence between the Western core and the faster growing, former periphery. In a flatter landscape, the relative economic power of the United States and the West in general become more ordinary and less exceptional. US systemic leadership should gradually decline as its lead on the rest of the world erodes—thanks to the rest of the world catching up to its former lead.

Naturally, there are some caveats to this interpretation. Grinin and Korotayev are careful to distinguish middle-ranking states from the bottom billion within the periphery. The former are currently demonstrating more convergence with the West than the latter but they think this bifurcation is only temporary and that, ultimately, all the rest will experience economic convergence. This forecast is made despite also acknowledging that the income disparity between the West and the rest remains substantial (five to one). They also see a new era of major economic innovations coming that could be centered, as in the past, on the West. But should this new technology be monopolized initially by the West, its effects on economic divergence will only be temporary because of the gains made by the periphery in the transfer of capital and production facilities. As a consequence, a respectable proportion of the once Third World will be prepared to adopt and adapt the new technology (primarily health and biotechnology)—as opposed to being forced to wait for it to become old technology that needs to be outsourced. Moreover, as noted previously, the United States' systemic leadership role will linger for a while longer in a primus inter pares form because the United States will retain some of its capability advantages, albeit less so than in the past, and because there will be some continuing demand for its global services.

There are at least two (perhaps 2.5) possible problems with this interpretation. One involves the nature of US decline. Their explanation focuses on the ancient Greek approach to explaining decline as a result of hubris (discussed in Rasler and Thompson, 1994). Actors, believing too much in their own competencies, are struck down by the gods for not knowing their limitations and place. If the United States could dissipate its absolute hegemony in less than a decade of errors, one must wonder just how fragile its foundation was in the first place.

A second area of concern has to do with the perception of converging economic capabilities. In Grinin and Korotayev, the evidence for this convergence is expressed in terms of relative shares of gross domestic product (GDP). There is no question that some convergence in GDP is taking place. From a long-term perspective, the GDP divergence brought about by Western innovations will be something of a blip in time. India and China, for a long time, led in GDP shares given their large populations, if for no other reason. We are returning to something approximating a natural order in this respect. Whether the same can be said for GDP per capita disparities or income divergence is another question. There is no denying that some portion of the world's population is improving their income status. Still, convergence in income levels will be a much slower process. If or when a new round of technological innovation occurs, it is conceivable that some of the gains made in terms of both income and economic size convergence will be lost or seriously set back. Whether that happens probably depends on how many and how quickly former peripheral economies can overcome what is called the middle-income trap. Few states outside of the global North have been able to overcome this trap and make the transition to high-income economies via becoming able to adapt or even generate themselves the latest technological innovations.

Grinin and Korotayev may well be right about the low probability of China rising to the system leader occasion. But their rejection of this possibility is based on a linear projection from the US position. It assumes that a successor to the United States must be as powerful on as many fronts, or more so, than its predecessor. While this has been the case since at least 1494, if not earlier, it need not work that way in the future.

Still, forecasts about income convergence and succession are a matter of speculation for now, and one can adopt optimistic or pessimistic stances. As it happens, however, there are other reasons for anticipating a somewhat flatter economic and political-military landscape in the future. They are linked closely to the foundation for systemic leadership and, consequently, seem capable of undermining its perpetuation as a primitive governance format.

A Different Approach to the Predicted Erosion and Demise of Traditional Systemic Leadership

There are three future possibilities. One is that the United States could succeed itself, just as the British did earlier. However, the chances of this happening do not seem great from a 2021 perspective. There are few indicators that might suggest something like this taking place anytime soon. On the other hand, observers might have said something similar about Britain in the 1760s and 1770s. We may not be in a good position to see radical changes ahead. Therefore, the safest position is to leave the option open even if it does not seem all that probable. Something similar could be said about the second possibility—that a new system leader will emerge in the twenty-first century and supplant the United States. Somehow, that outcome seems not much more probable than the first. It is difficult to envision either China or the European Union mustering the technological and global capabilities necessary to emerge as the next global leader. Neither outcome is completely far-fetched, however, so, again, this second possibility cannot be ruled out completely.

The third possibility is that the irregular cyclicality of systemic leadership might disappear altogether. If one traces the lineage back in time, it is hard to find much evidence of the pattern before Song China (tenth and eleventh centuries CE). At least after Song China, it is possible to track sequential leadership, albeit highly transitional in the pre-1800s manifestations, that becomes more impressive in capabilities and more global in scope over time. Immediately prior to, and overlapping with, Song China, there was a significant outburst of Arab-Persian maritime commerce connecting the Gulf to China. Yet before this activity, we have only intermittent agrarian empires and the equally intermittent if more rare operations of small trading states (Dilmun, Phoenicians, Carthage, Athens).

About 1,000 years ago, a pattern of systemic leadership began to emerge. It took another 500 years for the pattern to begin to take on a more global scale. Even the US version of the story has had areas to which its influence does not quite reach at anything resembling full strength. Systemic leadership, therefore, has always operated less than fully planetary-wide even if its "writ" has been extended further with each passing century. None of this means that the trends must continue forever into the future. Moreover, there are strong reasons to think that the trends and cycles may not continue.

An alternative argument for anticipating no new systemic leader in the future has five components. Four pertain to the nature of technological waves and one involves the probability of global war. In brief, if the concentration, pace, timing, or impact of technological waves changes significantly and/or if the crystallizing effect of global war disappears, a new round of systemic leadership would seem less likely.

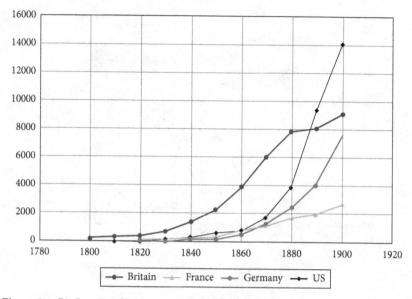

Figure 8.1 Pig Iron Production in the Nineteenth Century

Lead economies and systemic leadership are predicated on economic production advantages due to a disproportionate share of economic innovations. In the industrial phase of the sequence, both Britain and the United States enjoyed long advantages. Figures 8.1–8.3 depict the British edge in pig iron production (figure 8.1) and coal consumption (figure 8.2) and the US edge in automobile production (figure 8.3). Britain held a lead in the nineteenth century that only grew greater until other states began to close the gap. The US lead in automobile production was almost as long. Japan's challenge in automobiles was not threatening before the 1970s.

These examples are not chosen randomly. The indicators capture production edges that were quite central to the British and US economic leads.[8] Ironically, the British lead in iron production finally surpassed the record set in Song China days, some 800 years earlier. Still, the point is that these production advantages were maintained for at least seven or eight decades before some other state finally caught up and surpassed the leader. Assuming a wave of new technology (most likely having to do with information technology, nanotechnology, or biotechnology), is it likely that its pioneer will enjoy a lead over everyone else for seven or eight decades? The pattern has been for one state to monopolize commercial/

[8] The data are taken from U.S. Department of Commerce (1975) and Mitchell (2003a, 2003b, and 2003c).

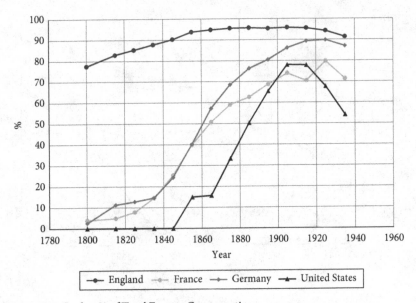

Figure 8.2 Coal as % of Total Energy Consumption

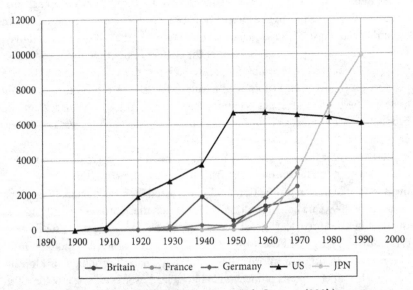

Figure 8.3 Automobile Production in the Twentieth Century (000's)

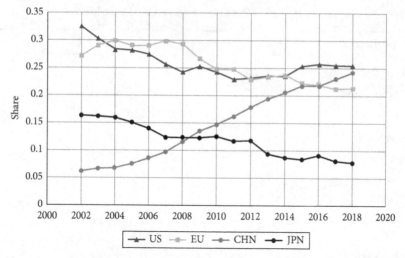

Figure 8.4 Share of Value-Added Knowledge and Technology-Intensive Industries
Source: based on information reported in National Science Foundation (2020).

technological innovation at a time. As its lead erodes, a few other states eventually catch up and pass the onetime leader. The new technology gradually diffuses,
albeit selectively to other Northern economies. This once glacial process evi-
dently has accelerated and is no longer restricted exclusively to the traditional
North. Technological diffusion, especially since 1945, has meant that a number
of economies are capable of technological innovation and/or absorbing other
people's technological innovations quickly. In sum, the competitive field has
widened considerably.

This part of the argument might seem to overlap with Grinin and Korotayev's.
Catch-up and economic convergence are central to their argument as well.
But the convergence that is ongoing seems more selective than what Grinin
and Korotayev suggest. Figure 8.4 and table 8.1 illustrate this point in different
ways. Figure 8.4 plots relative shares of high-tech manufacturing and knowledge intensive services as an indicator of advanced economies (National Science
Foundation, 2020). The US and European shares have become increasingly similar in the past decade. Japan is falling behind, while China is moving to surpass Japan's share even though China's current share remains considerably
behind the US and European shares. If figure 8.4 was more like figures 8.2 and
8.3, however, the US share would be at the top of the figure and the rest would
have much lower shares, with no state or region higher than, say, 15 percent.

Table 8.1 Top 36 Technological Start-up Centers Ranked by Valuation

United States	Canada	Europe	Asia	Other
1–10				
Silicon Valley (1)		London (2.5)	Beijing (4)	Tel Aviv (6.5)
New York City (2.5)		Stockholm (10)	Shanghai (8)	
Boston (5)				
Los Angeles (6.5)				
Seattle (9)				
11–20				
Washington, DC (11)	Toronto-Waterloo (18)	Amsterdam (12)	Tokyo (15)	
Chicago (14)		Paris (13)	Singapore (17)	
Austin (19)		Berlin (16)	Seoul (20)	
21–36				
San Diego (21)	Vancouver (25)		Shenzhen (22)	
Atlanta (23)			Bangalore (26)	
Denver-Boulder (24)			Sydney (27)	
Miami (29)			Hangzhou (28)	
Dallas (31.5) Miami (31.5) Salt Lake–Provo (31.5)		Bern-Geneva (31.5) Munich (31.5)	Hong Kong (29)	
		Copenhagen (36.5) Dublin (36.5)	Delhi (36.5)	São Paulo (30)

Source: Startup Genome (2020).

Instead, the European share (aggregated as a region which some might argue is unfair) roughly approximates the US share, signifying some degree of technological convergence. China could eventually move into this high-tech zone, which, of course, would only expand the amount of convergence that will have taken place. Still, when it comes to high-tech industries, the number of competitors is expanded but finite.

Table 8.1, on the other hand, shows a somewhat different picture. If we focus on where the development of new technological innovation is occurring, a bit less than half are located in North America and more than one-third are in the

United States.[9] Asia has the next largest number (eleven, or slightly more than one-fourth of the pool). Europe is close behind, with nine start-up cities (slightly less than one-fourth) The remainder are limited to one in the Middle East (Israel) and one in South America (Brazil).[10] . Two-thirds of the world's technological start-up centers are in North American and European cities. The West retains a clear advantage but, at the same time, two-thirds of the total pool of start-up centers are located outside of the United States. Yet five of the top ten start-up cities are in the United States. Selective convergence characterizes the current world economy. It remains unclear how a pioneering technological lead in IT could be monopolized for very long in the twenty-first century (as opposed to what happened in earlier centuries). Innovation does not appear to be as concentrated as it was earlier.

The Global Innovation Index, developed by researchers at Cornell University, INSEAD, and the World Intellectual Property Organization, offers an alternative approach to this same question. This index is more comprehensive than the start-up centers identification. It seeks to quantify innovation as expressed in institutions, human capital, infrastructure, market/business sophistication, knowledge/technological outputs, and creative outputs. All but 5 percent of the world's population is covered, more than thirty sources are consulted, and some eighty-four indicators are used to create a global rank order.

Table 8.2 reveals few surprises. The most innovative economies are also the most developed ones. There are no genuinely peripheral countries in the top group, although Singapore and South Korea could be said to have been recently peripheral. The countries are listed in rank order determined by their total scores. As one moves from one country to the next, the scores do not change all that much. This would seem to suggest some amount of convergence again, but almost entirely within the global North.[11] One has to lower the threshold to the top 50 states to begin picking up an odd collection of more peripheral states: Malaysia (#32), China (#35), Costa Rica (#39), Chile (#46), and Barbados (#47) are all in the top 50; as are four petro-states—UAE (#38), Saudi Arabia (#42), Qatar (#43), and Kuwait (#50).

In sum, perusing the Global Innovation Index provides more evidence for selective convergence among the more affluent states and not much concentration of innovation. The United States does well in table 8.2 but not as well as in table 8.1. It is judged to have a relatively innovative economy, but so do several

---

[9] Covid-19, no doubt, will do extensive damage to start-ups but at this point we have no reason to assume that financial problems will cause more havoc in some parts of the world than in others.

[10] Australia and New Zealand could become part of a super-Asia at some future point.

[11] If GDP per capita is used as an index to identify the global North, all the top twenty-five are Northern. On this topic, see Thompson and Reuveny (2010).

Table 8.2 Top 25 Innovative Economies, 2019, According to the Global Innovation Index.

Rank	Score	Country	Rank	Score	Country
1	67.24	Switzerland	14	54.82	China
2	63.6	Sweden	15	54.68	Japan
3	61.73	United States	16	54.25	France
4	61.44	Netherlands	17	53.88	Canada
5	61.30	United Kingdom	18	53.47	Luxembourg
6	59.83	Finland	19	51.87	Norway
7	58.4	Denmark	20	51.53	Iceland
8	58/37	Singapore	21	50.94	Austria
9	58.19	Germany	22	50.34	Australia
10	57.4	Israel	23	50.18	Belgium
11	56.5	South Korea	24	49.97	Estonia
12	56.10	Ireland	25	49.55	New Zealand
13	55.54	Hong Kong			

Source: based on information found in Dutta, Lanvin and Wunsch-Vincent (2019).

other economies. At the same time, most of the similarly innovative economies are smaller in size.

Changing levels of analysis, table 8.3 examines the location of innovative firms. *Forbes* now generates a list of the 100 most innovative firms in the world.[12] The 2019 outcome is not all that much different from the information reported in tables 8.1 and 8.2. The United States dominates with 40 percent of the entries. No other state possesses more than 8 percent. Yet the other 60 percent of the world's most innovative firms are scattered around the globe. Twenty-eight firms are in Europe. Another twenty-five are found in Asia. Five are in Latin America, with one in Africa. Thus, we have more evidence for the persistence of the US lead but also for several other economies supporting innovative corporations. The real question is whether we should anticipate the US lead persisting or diffusing further? If forced to choose, further diffusion seems more likely.

[12] The methodology used is complex and involves the application of a proprietary algorithm, subject to several assumptions designed to make comparing firms more homogeneous, to a comparison of historical and future business performance. The greater the difference, the greater is the presumed innovativeness of the firm.

Table 8.3 Top 100 Innovative Firms in the World in 2018, According to Forbes

Number of Firms	Countries
51	United States
7	China, Japan
5	Britain, India, France
4	South Korea
3	Netherlands
2	Ireland
1	Belgium, Brazil, Canada, Chile, Finland, Indonesia, Italy, Russia, Spain, Sweden, Thailand

Source: based on data reported in forbes.com/innovative-compa-nies/list/3/#tab:rank.

Another slant on this issue is provided by looking at Alderson, Beckfield, and Sprague-Jones's (2010) analysis of the world city system. The premise is that the backbone of the world economy is structured around a network of cities in which production and decisions about how to produce are focused. Alderson et al. have coded the location of the 500 largest multinational corporations and their subsidiaries. By looking at which cities are the key nodes of the system (which cities have more headquarters with links to branches), the hierarchy that characterizes inter-city relations can be identified and compared over time. Table 8.4 lists the outcome for the top fifteen cities in the network at three points in time: 1981, 2000, and 2007. The bottom row of the table adds some additional information on the US share of the top fifteen sample.

Table 8.4 lists a number of fairly familiar cities. The top entries tend to be New York, London, Paris, and Tokyo. The other cities are a mixture of recognizable European, North American, and Asian cities. Several things can be said about the outcome. One is that the hierarchy is not identical at each time point even though there are strong elements of continuity, especially at the top. New York is number 1 or 2 in all three observations. London, Paris, and Tokyo tend to be found somewhere in the top six ranks.

The number of US cities declines, albeit non-linearly over time. Two-thirds of the 1981 top fifteen are American. In 2000 or 2007, only half as many US cities are found as in 1981 at the apex of the hierarchy. That outcome would suggest that US cities have declined in their command and control of the world economy. Other cities have displaced them at the upper end of the hierarchy.

Table 8.4 Intercity Power Relations, 1981–2007

Rank	1981	2000	2007
1	New York (2359)	Tokyo (3639)	New York (3072)
2	London (1065)	New York (2601)	Paris (2347)
3	Los Angeles (623)	Paris (2535)	Tokyo (2298)
4	Chicago (619)	London (1955)	London (1109)
5	San Francisco (442)	Dusseldorf (1278)	Munich (666)
6	Paris (435)	Amsterdam (897)	Amsterdam (638)
7	Detroit (429)	Zurich (893)	San Francisco (601)
8	Tokyo (403)	Munich (881)	Zurich (547)
9	Minneapolis (361)	Osaka (787)	Dusseldorf (463)
10	Cleveland (305)	San Francisco (755)	Toronto (415)
11	Philadelphia (293)	Frankfurt (515)	Chicago (413)
12	Saint Louis (279)	Vevey (491)	Philadelphia (394)
13	Pittsburgh (258)	Chicago (455)	Osaka (393)
14	Basel (256)	Stockholm (427)	Houston (359)
15	Stockholm (189)	Dallas (413)	Stockholm (346)
US Share	5968/8316=.718	4224/18522=.228	4445/14061=.316

Source: based on Alderson, Beckfield, and Sprague-Jones (2010: 1905).

However, there is also more concentration of command and control taking place.[13] If one calculates the share controlled by the top five entries in each column, the share increases in each successive time period (1981 = .614, 2000 = .648, and 2007 = .675). This outcome was predicted by Sassen (2001: 30). Globalization leads to a dispersal of production, but centralization of command and control need not follow. On the contrary, globalization has led to a greater concentration of central functions in a small number of global cities. While the top five have also become less US-oriented over the past more than thirty years, New York has retained and even enhanced its central role in the world city system. This finding would seem to support the generalization that the US role

[13] Thanks to Art Alderson for discussing how best to interpret the findings in table 8.4. That does not mean I listened closely.

Table 8.5 Cities in the American Hegemonic Cycle Ranked by Growth in Size

1800–1850	1850–1900	1900–1950	1970–2005
NEW YORK	CHICAGO	LOS ANGELES	Beijing
BALTIMORE	Buenos Aires	HOUSTON	Shanghai
PHILADELPHIA	Leipzig	DALLAS	WASHINGTON
BOSTON	PITTSBURGH	Hong Kong	Osaka
Liverpool	NEW YORK	DETROIT	Seoul
Manchester	Berlin	São Paulo	Singapore
Birmingham	Newcastle	Shanghai	Budapest
Glasgow	Dresden	Seoul	Madrid
Bombay	BOSTON	SEATTLE	Vienna
Rio de Janeiro	Budapest	Buenos Aires	Berlin
Brussels	Hamburg	ATLANTA	Tokyo
Newcastle	Rio de Janeiro	Toronto	Hamburg

Note: In the 1850–1900 interval, Philadelphia and Baltimore were ranked numbers 22 and 25 in the top 39 cities; in the 1900–1950 interval, Washington, San Francisco, New York, Boston, and Philadelphia ranked 14, 16, 24, 32, and 33 in the top 39 respectively; in the 1970–2005 interval, Los Angeles, Miami, and Chicago were ranked 15, 20, and 28 of the top 35 cities.

Source: based on Taylor, Hoyler, and Smith (2012: 28).

in world production is becoming less central. Yet its significance is not eroding away completely if it can continue to capture one or more of the highest-ranking places in the hierarchy. Thus the US prominence in the world economy is not likely to disappear quickly.

However, compare the outcome reported in table 8.4 with the one sketched in table 8.5. Table 8.5 lists cities according to their rank based on their growth in size and segmented by hegemonic cycle. In table 8.5's case, only the top twelve cities are listed by Taylor, Hoyler, and Smith (2012). In the hegemonic cycle table, the premise is that the production leadership demonstrated by successive hegemons will be reflected in urban growth. Yet it is not all cities within the hegemon that are expected to grow quickly. Production tends to be concentrated regionally. So, too then should urban growth be concentrated in the parts of the lead state that are leading new forms of economic growth.

Table 8.5 suggests that economic leadership in the world economy is linked to urban growth. Economic leadership may also be preceded by urban growth

Table 8.6 Fifty Greatest Breakthroughs since the Wheel

Years	Breakthroughs	Number of Breakthroughs
1700s	#8 vaccination, #10 steam engine, #23 sextant, #30 moldboard plow, #32 cotton gin	5
1800–1850	#12 sanitation systems, #26 telegraph, #29 photography, #46 anesthesia	4
1851–1899	#2 electricity, #7 internal combustion engine, #13 refrigeration, #18 automobile, #19 industrial steelmaking, #24 telephone, #33 pasteurization, #35 oil refining, #36 steam turbine, #39 oil drilling	10
1900–1950	#3 penicillin, #11 nitrogen fixation, #15 airplane, #21 nuclear fission, #28 radio, #38 scientific plant breeding, #41 rocketry, #44 air conditioning, #45 television, #49 assembly line	10
1951–1999	#4 semiconductor electronics, #9 internet, #16 personal computer, #20 the pill, #22 green revolution, #50 combine harvester	6

Source: based on information found in Fallows (2013).

(note the 1800–1850 outcome).[14] But as hegemony erodes, urban growth within the declining hegemon becomes less evident. Of course, the growth of other cities is not always due solely to the diffusion of production leadership, but it does suggest that the hegemon's lead position is slipping and giving way to a less centralized outcome vis-à-vis national economic growth.

If the introduction and development of new technology tends to cluster, there is no reason to assume that the impact of each cluster is likely to be equal. On the contrary, the clustering of new technology seems to have uneven impacts. Put another way, each cluster is not necessarily as powerful as the one that preceded it or the one that is likely to follow it. An informal way to illustrate this unevenness in new technology is provided by table 8.6. The *Atlantic Monthly* (Fallows, 2013) brought together a small panel of scientists, engineers, and technology historians and asked each participant to nominate and rank order twenty-five technological breakthroughs since the invention of the wheel. Some 30 percent of the nominations involved older technologies not shown in table 8.6. Seventy percent of the breakthroughs were thought to have occurred in the past 300 years. One problem with the dating of these innovations is that they focus

---

[14] Similar tables are constructed for the Netherlands and Britain in earlier centuries in Taylor, Hoyler, and Smith (2012) with similar outcomes but, of course, with different cities emphasized. The same pattern emerges in the two other instances. Urban growth precedes the advent of economic hegemony in the Dutch and British cases as well.

on their inventions more than their actual innovation. Nonetheless, if we differentiate them by half-century, the 1851–1899 and 1900–1949 contributions are quite impressive in fundamentally changing how people live their daily lives.[15] Whether one of the two half-centuries was more impactful than the other is something we could debate. Yet assembly lines, air conditioning, electricity, and the internal combustion engine/automobile presumably trump semiconductors and combine harvesters (1950–1999) and photography and anesthesia (1800–1850)—without wishing to denigrate the importance of any one of these perceived technological breakthroughs.

Table 8.6 hardly does justice to the British industrial revolution. Spinning jennies and railroads are both absent from the list and, no doubt, would have appeared on the list if the nominations had come much earlier in time or perhaps if the panel had been less US-centric in composition. It may also be that the internet and the personal computer will prove to be the foundations for very radical IT changes in the future in which large proportions of the population simply cease laboring. But that has not happened yet. The main point, nevertheless, is that the United States, as did Britain before it (even if it does not show in table 8.6), ascended to system leader status on very powerful waves. We acknowledge the strengths of these waves by referring to them as the first and second industrial revolutions, respectively. It follows that one of the reasons Britain and the United States were able to maintain their leads as they did is the very power of the waves they rode. The increases in mechanical power and speed that they introduced literally dwarfed what had prevailed in earlier times.

Another industrial revolution is coming, if it is not already underway, and will be ushered in by information technology's application to manufacturing and medicine. Its radical impact, when viewed from hindsight, may prove to be truly staggering. But if it is underway, its impact seems arguably less revolutionary than the first and second industrial revolutions must have seemed at the time. A whole generation was even devoted to trying to find some discernible productivity impact for IT technology.[16] In part this is due to becoming somewhat jaded to new technology. If you are accustomed to walking, an engine that propels you from place to place is astounding. If you are accustomed to engine propulsion, changing the source of propulsion from steam to petroleum or electricity is less amazing even though the shifts remain quite radical in implications.

---

[15] Smil (2005) made this point some time ago.

[16] However, see the productivity figures reported in Bailey and Bosworth (2014). Examining productivity in US manufacturing, they find almost all US productivity centered on the computers and electronic products category, with 1987–2000 the peak period, albeit continuing into 2000–2011 at a lesser pace. It may be that the next industrial revolution will only be fully manifested when all or most sectors of the economy have been thoroughly transformed by IT innovations. Radical innovations are most important, not so much in their own right, but more in terms of how they diffuse throughout the economy and alter it in a revolutionary way.

Another dimension of contemporary technology is that so many of the applications of IT seem to end up in trivial pursuits. The latest improvements in social media cannot compete with the advent of air conditioning in very humid places or the development of the internal combustion engine. As IT becomes increasingly important to saving lives and radically changing how we live our lives, as opposed to gossiping about life, its perceived impact will become more impressive.

At the same time, we should keep in mind that it is easy to underestimate the ultimate significance of new technology when it is still relatively new. An illustration is offered by the perspective of an economist writing critically about the wastefulness of petroleum in the 1920s. In particular, he was scornful about the use of crude oil for such unimportant purposes as making automobiles run. Automobiles were a

> mindless extravagance being used by fat-bellied bankers and bourgeoisie . . . by gay boys and girls in questionable joy rides . . . by smart alecks who find here an exceptionally flashy and effective way of flaunting their wealth before those not so fortunate as themselves.[17]

Sometimes, given time, the mindless extravagances turn out to be less mindless and extravagant. Questionable joy rides can become routine ways of daily life. Horses completely disappear as means of transportation and are replaced by motor vehicles.

None of these considerations lead to the conclusion that IT changes are somehow less significant than earlier waves of technological change. Rather, they only seem less revolutionary because they build upon the earlier waves and may be or seem more gradual in their penetration of everyday life. Even the social media applications ultimately will have more serious implications for how things work as they are put to different uses. But if we combine the subtlety and gradual spread of current new technology with the earlier discussed expanded competitive field for introducing new technology, it may well be that no single economy can expect to become as predominant as the economies that first introduced steam engines or became the primary innovator of internal combustion engines. More economies have become more sophisticated and, consequently, the threshold for establishing economic predominance has been raised.

A third possibility that is not yet fully clear is that the pace of technological clustering may also have changed. One model (Modelski and Thompson, 1996) developed on the historical pattern had each new system leader first establishing their lead economy status in one period, followed by a thirty-year

---

[17]   Quoted in Black (2012: 179).

period of intense conflict that established the system leader's lead in global affairs, which was then followed by a second technological clustering that reinforced the leader's lead economy status for another interval. This pattern worked fairly well for the past five hundred years (more precisely the late fifteenth century through about 1973). The late twentieth century should have been a gradual period of system leader decline with no full-fledged technological clustering. The period 1973–2000 was initially predicted to be a start-up period for information technology.[18] Instead, we experienced a confusing combination of US relative decline most evident in some areas, what may have been the first IT wave, mixed with a period of proclaimed geopolitical unipolarity. The last two developments tended to overwhelm the first of the three features, at least perceptually. Only now are the relative decline perceptions re-emerging.

One way to reconstruct what happened is to blame the excesses of the unipolar period for the latest perceptions of system leader relative decline. There is no question that the perceived omnipotence linked to unipolarity led to strategic hubris and considerable wasted efforts. But another approach is to suggest that the relative decline apparent in the 1970s and 1980s persisted slowly through to the current period in economic matters even while unipolarity appeared evident in military matters (see chapter 7). Yet the economic decline was clearly offset by a relatively weak technological cluster that appeared earlier than it might have in view of the older pattern of cluster timing. The IT nature of this new cluster encouraged quicker catch-up than usual as opposed to reinforcing the economic edge enjoyed by the lead economy. It is not Friedman's (2005) flat world in which everyone with a laptop is an equal player in the world economy, but IT technology is definitely more difficult to monopolize when huge global firms can be created from humble start-ups in home garages. One can do this almost as easily in Bangalore or Tel Aviv as in Silicon Valley (see table 8.1).

If this version is correct, the political-economic landscape has changed rather greatly. The timing of technological clustering may have picked up its pace and become less discontinuous, as in the immediate past. The most obvious manifestation is that computers, unlike jet air travel, continue to become faster, cheaper, have more memory, and can accomplish more tasks, ranging from mathematical computations to driving automobiles. If so, the traditional circumstances promoting systemic leadership and lead economies are apt to be undermined. However, it is also possible that 1973–2015 was indeed only a start-up phase and that 2015–2050 will encompass the main IT thrust. As usual, we must wait to see.

---

[18] Attina (2019) has suggested changing this dating (for the delegitimization phase) by moving the end of the period another fifteen years later—a suggestion that we have adopted because it seems to fit the pace of development. It may also signify that this start-up period was longer than earlier ones. We will have to wait to see what happens in the next three decades to see whether a genuine surge takes place.

In marked contrast, there appears to be much less immediate change forth-coming in the energy source landscape. New system leaders have benefited greatly from access to relatively inexpensive energy resources. The Dutch had peat and wind (both maritime and for windmills), the British had coal, and the United States also had coal but trumped coal with petroleum. Inexpensive energy is important for several reasons, but being able to turn out new types of manufactures cheaply and certainly more cheaply than their commercial rivals is one of the more important ones. New and radical technology does not always require new types of fuel, but large-scale production and marketing of new technology does depend on access to relatively inexpensive energy, which, in turn, has been associated with the advent of new energy regimes. Nonetheless, the argument is not that system leadership hinges on the development of new energy sources but that the more significant periods of system leadership did depend on new energy regimes. There is a reason why more analysts converge on the Dutch in the seventeenth century, Britain in the nineteenth century, and the United States in the twentieth century when discussion turns to "hegemony" in world politics. There are other candidates, but their credentials are less impressive. Moreover, each successive candidate of this trio engineered an increasingly more substantial energy transition and, consequently, was able to create stronger systemic leads.

It is not clear at all that anyone will have enough access to inexpensive energy sources in coming years (say, the next half century at least) to be able to orient their economies to maximally exploiting the cheap fuels. Petroleum will become more difficult to access and, therefore, more expensive. Eventually, it could well price itself out of the market for energy resources. A lot of things might happen eventually, but there appears to be some considerable correspondence between oil prices and the supply and demand for petroleum. As we approach a peak oil milestone perhaps around mid-century, if not earlier, high prices and severe shortages that are not temporary, as in the earlier oil shocks of the late twentieth century, presumably could undermine economic productivity. Unless the next system leader has access to some mystery energy fuel, a new system leader seems less probable.[19]

It is always risky to try predicting a century ahead, but that seems to be what most forecasters are suggesting for the emergence of a new energy regime built

[19] China is expected to rely heavily on coal through at least 2050, while the United States seems content with the seductive promise of fracked oil and gas. Natural gas would be better than oil from an environmental/global warming vantage point but it remains a fossil fuel and therefore will contribute to global warming problems. Renewable sources of energy seem set to replace more traditional sources only slowly. Of course, these expectations could be overtaken by vigorous attempts to accelerate the movement away from hydrocarbons. So far, such efforts remain largely verbal in China and the United States.

around renewables.[20] Interestingly, it is roughly the 2080s or later that is projected as a point at which dependence on renewables might transit past dependence on carbon sources. One difference, however, is that China will be increasingly importing all its carbon sources, while the United States will be able to generate most of its own carbon fuels. If these forecasts prove to be accurate, any future system leader will encounter major problems in creating a conducive energy foundation for technological innovation and industrial production. The problems may be sufficiently severe to postpone, at the very least, the likelihood of any near future (next seventy years) power transition. On the other hand, renewable energy growth has astonished most onlookers and perhaps these forecasts will need to be updated. Theoretically, it is conceivable that renewable energy (including nuclear power) could be dominant by 2050 in leading economies. But this breakthrough would require some considerable commitment that so far seems absent.

Yet one more factor critically undermining the traditional landscape for promoting lead economies and systemic leadership involves the probability of global war. Historically, lead economy status has not been sufficient to warrant systemic leadership. The crystallizing effect of global war has been needed first to resolve disputes about relative top dog status and to re-enforce the top dog status of the leader of the winning coalition. Global war has served as a primitive trial by fire for establishing leadership credentials. We have moved away from relying on trials by fire for other types of adjudication. We also appear to be moving away from global warfare. One argument developed in more detail elsewhere is that warfare between industrial powers has become too costly to contemplate. The potential gains of warfare in pre-industrial eras could outweigh the costs of combat, but the increasing lethality of industrialized warfare in the twentieth century became too great to match any conceivable gains.[21]

Such an argument does not rule out warfare between industrialized states, but it does limit its probability.[22] If global war is no longer an option, what functional equivalents might work to facilitate the crystallization of lead economy status into full-fledged systemic leadership? It depends on the gap between the lead economy and other economies. The greater is the gap, presumably, the less crystallization that is needed. Thus, if some lead economy emerged later in the century with so great a lead over everyone else that "resistance is futile," it might be possible to forgo the side effects of waging a global war. But if the gap is not so great, the options are few. Some automatic rotation among the most powerful

---

[20] Oliveira Matias and Devezas's (2011) analysis is based in part on surveying 180 international energy experts. Their "alternatives" category includes nuclear energy. See, as well, Li's (2014) forecast for China.

[21] Various schools of thought support this conclusion. See, among others, Levy and Thompson (2011).

[22] It also does not limit warfare between industrial and non-industrial states and groups.

candidates could be entertained. Or states aspiring to systemic leadership might have to compete to demonstrate their qualifications in some type of electoral situation. More likely, however, is that systemic leadership would become more partial in geographical scope than it has been in the past. Multiple system leaders functioning at the regional level is not difficult to imagine (as in Buzan's perspective). None of these three possibilities is mutually exclusive. Any two or all three could be attempted simultaneously. Whatever the case, it would spell the end of traditional systemic leadership in which one state loomed over the others in terms of its global technological and coercive capabilities. But this is a tradition long in the making and has only been manifested most definitively by the incumbent system leader. One could argue that the next phase will be a reversion to earlier patterns of weaker systemic leadership, but with greater potential for more institutionalized practices in governance given the nature of the existing problems, the long experience with very incremental improvements in problem management, and the existence of a number of intergovernmental organizations that are hardly problem-free.

The U.S. National Intelligence Council (2012) forecast for 2030 suggests a primus inter pares or first among equals status for the United States in a world in which no state is hegemonic:[23]

> The US most likely will remain "first among equals" among the other great powers in 2030 because of its preeminence across a range of power dimensions and legacies of its leadership role. More important than just its economic weight, the United States' dominant role in international politics has derived from its preponderance across the board in both hard and soft power. Nevertheless, with the rapid rise of other countries, the unipolar moment" is over and Pax Americana—the era of American ascendancy in international politics that began in 1945 is fast winding down. (U.S. National Intelligence Council, 2012: x)

The "primus inter pares" model suggests a likely interim strategy. The nature of the model literally suggests the selection of a leader who is not all that much different in capabilities from the actors doing the selection. It assumes a continuing need and desire for something resembling systemic leadership. It could reflect the traditional asymmetry as well in global reach capabilities. Historically, only one state, and sometimes an adversary or two, possesses the lion's share of coercive capabilities that can be applied over long distances. This asymmetry is not divorced from economic capability but often outlives the erosion of lead

---

[23] These forecasts appear every five years and go through extensive screening and feedback reviews before being published.

economy status. In situations in which global reach capabilities are highly valued, it guarantees at least a seat at the table, and often more, for any state that possesses them, if they are also prepared to put them at risk. Thus, we should expect primus inter pares leadership, overt or covert, in circumstances like the intervention in the Libyan civil war or organizing resistance to Chinese hegemony in the South China Sea. Systemic leadership in other venues in which a coercive edge is not much help would seem to be less likely overall. Climate change and liberalizing the world economy, for instance, are less likely with primus inter pares leadership.[24]

Finally, it should be noted that in the abstract there is much less disagreement between the position taken here and the arguments put forward by Chase-Dunn et al. and Grinin and Korotayev. Their position is that no other state in the system is likely to assemble the necessary attributes to claim systemic leadership.[25] We only disagree about why this might be the case. From the perspective advanced in this chapter, the main criterion is developing a world-class lead economy. It is too soon to dismiss China's ability to corner the market on economic innovation, but so far that quality has been largely lacking in Chinese production. China will surely become the largest economy in the world but that is a far cry from the most innovative economy in the world. Even if the Chinese economy does become the innovative center of the world economy, a second missing link—the absence of global war—could also work against the emergence of a new system leader. The point here is that the absence of worthy successors would also contribute to the maintenance of a primus inter pares situation.[26] However, it may very well be that there will be more than one state that enjoys that status.

Conclusion

Most of the discussion on the possibility of systemic leadership transition focuses on whether (or when) China will move past the United States and become the predominant state in the world system. But there are other possibilities. We should not assume that the cycle of successive leaders must continue forever or continue in the same way. Chase-Dunn et al. (2011) contend that the

[24] However, Mokyr (2009: 11) points out that Britain still led its continental neighbors in 1850 but that by 1914 it had been "demoted from 'leader' to 'one of many.'" The implication is that "one of many" status does not lend itself necessarily to leadership—something that was demonstrated clearly in 1914.

[25] This position is more implicit in Chase-Dunn et al. and quite explicit in Grinin and Korotayev.

[26] Beardson (2013) makes a strong case against Chinese attempts to develop an innovative economy working out soon but does not rule out a radical makeover eventually. Technological innovation, of course, is not the only problem China has to overcome in order to reach the pinnacle of the world economy.

hegemonic cycle will give way to less concentrated technology, rising energy costs, and environmental catastrophe. Buzan (2011) sees a decentered globalism leading to a heightened emphasis on regions that remain interdependent and participants in global trade. Grinin and Korotayev (2014) argue that the hegemonic cycle will end because of the impressive rise of previously peripheral actors. They may be right but there are other avenues to arrive at a similar conclusion. There are also reasons to be skeptical about either a dismal future or the ultimate rise of the "rest."

It is quite conceivable that the succession of system leaders could come to an end with or without a major change in international inequality. The systemic leadership role is predicated on a decisive edge in technological innovation and, increasingly, energy transformation that makes its economy the world's lead economy. A corollary of possessing the lead economy is a commitment to developing a lead in global reach capabilities. The erosion or loss of these leads entails relative decline and, historically, the replacement of one system leader with another after an intensive period of global conflict. But there is no guarantee that such a system must go on forever. If the parameters of the process are changed fundamentally, a different outcome can be anticipated.

Several parameters do appear to be changing. No state currently has an uncontestable claim to be the center of innovation for the world economy. The United States, arguably, retains some lead in this area, but economic innovation is no longer as concentrated as it once was. It may be, given the nature of IT, that it no longer can be as concentrated as it has been in the past. Then, too, technological leads once gained are harder to hold on to than they once were. The timing of technological clustering may have accelerated, although the jury is still out on this issue. Another possibility is that the differential impact of technological waves may be clouding our ability to read the present. The technological waves that brought Britain and the United States to their respective ascendancies were quite strong. We may be waiting for a wave that is equally strong. If it comes and is concentrated again in one economy, we should expect a lead economy outcome that resembles the past several hundred years. If it is not concentrated in one economy, we will have shifted to a different type of playing field. If it does not come at all as a new tsunami and technological innovation is less clustered or less impactful than in the past, we will also have shifted to a new political-economic landscape. At the same time, a very slow transition to a post-carbon-based energy regime may get in the way of optimizing the emergence of a new lead economy prior to sometime late in this century. Finally, global warfare became essential, increasingly so, to the rise of the last five leaders. If that coercive institution is much less likely than it once was, another important ingredient for the now traditional form of systemic leadership has left the scene.

Changes in some of the basic parameters facilitating the emergence of systemic leadership seem to point toward a primus inter pares model in which the incumbent system leader's advantages gradually erode until it no longer has a commanding edge on all other players. Normally, we would expect such eroded leadership to be supplanted by a successor. But if conditions are not likely to produce a successor, the primus inter pares model should be expected to give way to either some more complex form of governance or even less governance than has been seen in the past. Greater governance complexity may involve greater institutionalization, multiple system leaders (perhaps differentiated by region or function), or some combination of the two. The stark alternative would appear to be something along the deglobalization tendencies emphasized by Chase-Dunn et al. or some heterogeneous mix of circumscribed global governance for some types of activity and more regional governance for others.

The bottom line, however, is that power concentration remains a rather primitive foundation for global governance. A system that is more complex and less hierarchical should be expected to reconstitute the nature of systemic leadership. Exactly what shape the next leadership manifestation might take, assuming quite safely that the need for governance will persist, remains to be seen. Moreover, it seems unlikely to be seen anytime soon.

All of that still leaves the question of Sino-American interactions open-ended. Whether or not a future systemic leadership is in the cards, the two most obvious contenders—one an incumbent and the other a challenger—are engaged in a competition for systemic leadership. How should we expect this rivalry to play out? Chapter 9 takes a stab at answering this question by reviewing eight possibly relevant models/theories and their applicability to the ongoing rivalry.

9

The Second Sino-American Rivalry

For much of the last 500 years, Western Europe was emerging as the center of the world system until the wars of 1914–1945 exhausted that region's claim to centrality. Now East Asia appears to be becoming the or at least a center of world focus of similar prominence. World system centrality always comes with a price because the prize is so strongly desired and beneficial to its holders. Not surprisingly, observers have opined on the likelihood of East Asia turning into a pre-1945 West European doppelganger replete with multiple and warring rivalries despite an apparent record of moving away from high levels of conflict prior to the 1980s.[1]

In this chapter, the "Asian Ripeness for Rivalry" argument is briefly examined, and no evidence is found that the region is demonstrating any regional tendencies for increasing rivalry. What is sometimes overlooked by the regional emphasis, however, is the increasing prominence of the second Sino-American rivalry.[2] Pairing the two main contenders for technological centrality in the world system and a struggle over regional hegemony in East, or perhaps better described as eastern Asia, the parameters and outcome of this rivalry may prove to be more significant than any adversarial propensities for the region as a whole. Accordingly, the bulk of the present chapter focuses on what theoretical guidelines we might have for anticipating what is to come in the Sino-American duel. Eight theories/models are examined critically. Most seem to have problems that limit their utility for crystal ball purposes. One, based on a newly developed geostructural realism, is most promising but may prove to have a finite shelf life. On the other hand, if it works for several decades, that may be all that we can ask of a theoretical construction.

Asian Ripeness for Rivalry

The literature on Asian ripeness for rivalry is interesting and periodic. That is, it first appeared in the early 1990s and has resurfaced in the 2000s and 2010s.

---

[1] There is of course a contradictory and simultaneous movement to explain the Asian peace.
[2] The first Sino-American rivalry ended in 1972. The second iteration began in 1996 (Thompson and Dreyer, 2011).

American Global Pre-eminence. William R. Thompson, Oxford University Press. © Oxford University Press 2022.
DOI: 10.1093/oso/9780197534663.003.0009

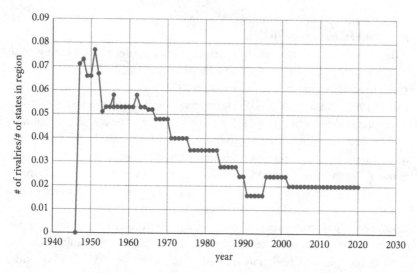

Figure 9.1 The Number of Asian Rivalries, Controlling for the Number of Asian States, 1946–2020

No doubt, it will be discussed again in the 2020s.[3] In most cases, it is clear that authors prefer to discuss the endogenous and exogenous causes of ripeness more than they are interested in clarifying what rivalry ripeness might mean. For some, rivalry ripeness is probably a synonym for increased conflict. Yet if we take the concept at face value, it should address either the likelihood of more rivalries emerging or existing rivalries escalating. By and large, neither of these alternatives seems to be happening.

Figure 9.1 gives us a quick and reasonably definitive answer to the first possibility: have the number of rivalries been expanding in Asia? Clearly, they have not. Conflict and rivalry in the region escalated very quickly immediately after the end of World War II. In 1947, there were two rivalries ongoing. A year later, there were four sets of states engaged in rivalry and by 1949, the number was up to six. That number had almost doubled again by 1962, with eleven rivalries active. Yet the number of states in the region had expanded even more quickly, with six in 1946 and as many as twenty by 1957. Regional system membership has continued to expand through 2002, reaching twenty-nine states while the absolute number of active rivalries has diminished to eight. If the number of

---

[3] See, for example, Friedberg (1993–1994, 2011), Berger (2000), Kang (2003), Acharya (2003–2004, 2014), He (2008), Cha (2012), Chan (2013), Alagappa (2014), Chan and Hu (2015), and Tunsjø (2018). Since this chapter was written in 2020, the prediction about the 2020s is self-fulfilling.

rivalries is the appropriate criterion, this figure suggests that the region has become steadily less ripe for rivalry.

The alternative meaning of rivalry ripeness, the tendency for existing rivalries to escalate, has been handled well by Alagappa (2014). He notes that Asia experienced fifteen interstate wars between 1945 and 2014.[4] Thirteen took place prior to 1980, and only two relatively weak manifestations of interstate warfare have broken out since that year. He goes so far as to describe the last four decades as a long peace, which he expects to persist at least through the next decade or two. He also notes that the main internal disputes have either ended (China-Vietnam, North Vietnam–South Vietnam, Laos-Vietnam, Cambodia-Vietnam) or stalemated (China-Taiwan, India-Pakistan, China-India, North Korea–South Korea).[5] Of course, a stalemate is not exactly the same thing as a termination. Presumably, a stalemate occurs when both sides of a conflict are unable to figure out how to advance their interests without incurring unacceptable costs. The problem, though, is that not only are cost calculations subjective, but both sides tend to keep pushing for ways to break the stalemate. Therefore, stalemates may be only temporary phases in ongoing rivalries. Nevertheless, it is a useful addition to the conceptualizations for describing some ongoing rivalries. It also implies that no strong tendencies for existing rivalries to escalate their levels of hostility are currently apparent.

We may conclude that the Asian region, at least as a regional sub-system, does not seem to be particularly ripe for rivalry. However, there is one major caveat to this statement. Alagappa focuses on intra-regional disputes. So, too, do many of the published articles on Asian rivalry ripeness. What is not always discussed at the same time are rivalries between Asian and non-Asian major powers. The first rivalry between China and the United States ended in the 1970s. The termination of the Sino-Soviet rivalry followed at the end of the 1980s. However, a second China-US rivalry began in the 1990s and may prove to be the defining rivalry of the twenty-first century—just as the US-Soviet Cold War defined much of the second half of the twentieth century. Asia will hardly be immune to what takes place in this rivalry. Nor, probably, will the rest of the world. And, most important, it is hardly clear that the ongoing China-US rivalry can or should be described as stalemated. That may prove to be the outcome, but the rivalry is still

---

[4] Alagappa follows the prevailing Correlates of War orthodoxy based primarily on satisfying a minimum of battle deaths and counts the following wars: India-Pakistan (1947–1949), Korea (1950–1953), Sino-Tibetan (1950–1951), China-Taiwan (1954–1955 and 1958), Sino-Indian (1962), second Indo-Pakistan (1965), second Indochina (1965–1975), second Laotian (1968–1973), Vietnam-Cambodia (1970–1971), third Indochina (1977–1979), Sino-Vietnam (1979 and 1987), and Kargil (1999).

[5] Alagappa's stalemate references are restricted to the post-1945 warring dyads, but the categorization could be extended to the Asian rivalries that have not gone to war in the past seventy years such as China-Japan.

in its infancy and we should leave the outcome categorization open-ended for some time to come. Both sides are making moves to alter the outcome in their own favor. China is attempting to break free of possessing an economy that only produces conventional manufacturing, stopping short of becoming the world's technological innovation center. The United States is seeking to prevent China's rise as the world's technological innovation center, among other goals. It is too soon to tell how these efforts will play out.

In the interim, the question is what to expect in terms of China-US strategies and interactions? Was strategic rivalry practically inevitable? Probably yes because (a) both states cannot occupy the position of the leading state in the Asian region and both states desire the position and (b) historically, the world economy has not been characterized by multiple leading technological innovation centers (Heath and Thompson, 2017). While that seems to be changing, the two economies will compete vigorously to occupy the lead innovation position until or unless they come to terms with the implications of multiple technological centers. Does either reason (a and/or b) make war inevitable? The answer is no. Yet that leaves a range of possible behaviors. We also have a range of social science arguments that seek to address circumstances such as this, but their application is not without problems. Eight theories will be examined critically: the Thucydides Trap, Power Transition, System Leader Retrenchment, Risk Assessment–Based Response to Rising Challengers, Time Horizon Assessment–Based Response to Rising Challengers, the Interactions between Rising and Declining States, Status Immobility, and Geostructural Realism.[6] Of the eight, it is the last one that appears to be the most useful one in the China-US rivalry case.

I am assuming that both actors will continue to be rivals through at least 2050. That is, neither China nor the United States will win their mutual competition within the next thirty years. While some observers grant a probable win to China because of its huge size, that outcome does not seem preordained. Scobell et al. (2020) put forward what seems the most reasonable bet. China's goals include strong governance, societal stability, economic prosperity, technological

---

[6] There are at least two others that might have been examined. Kliman (2014) and Goddard (2018) put forward models that emphasize the regime types of rising and responding states and how rising states legitimate their rise, respectively. Democracies distrust autocracies, and rising states need to frame their ascents within international norms to deflect the suspicions of status-quo-oriented states. Both arguments are plausible but do not seem to take us too far in the China case. Kliman's perspective seems more useful in differentiating between the responses to rising democratic and autocratic states (on this score, see also Thompson, 1997), as opposed to focusing on a particular autocratic case. The problem with Goddard's argument is that it is difficult to differentiate between instances of smart rhetoric/deceit and a relatively genuine willingness to abide by status-quo restrictions on behavior. Deng's advice to China to develop peacefully made a great deal of strategic sense in the late twentieth century. If less of this rhetoric is heard coming from China in the second decade of the twenty-first century, does that reflect a deliberate change in framing or perceptions that China's relative position has changed considerably from the 1980s?

leadership, and military predominance (at least regionally). The likelihood of attaining all five goals successfully by 2050 are not great, but neither is the probability that China will implode in the attempt to achieve what Scobell et al. describe as "national rejuvenation." More likely is that China will succeed in moving toward some goals but not others by 2050. Of course, the same analysis needs to be conducted for US grand strategy.[7] Presumably, a similar verdict or bet would be forthcoming for the United States. If that proves to be the case, the China-US rivalry will become the central conflict axis of the twenty-first century. How it plays out will have a strong influence on the world's future.

No assumption is made here that the Sino-American rivalry is the only major power relationship that is critical to global stability. There is also a Russian-American strategic rivalry to consider, but it is not really in the same class. The Chinese challenge to the American-centric order has both economic and military connotations: China has the potential to ultimately replace the United States as global system leader, whereas the Russian challenge is predicated solely on military competition. Russia can do great damage but is an unlikely candidate to ascend to the top of the global hierarchy. There are of course other, less global confrontations in the Middle East and Northeast Asia, involving Iran and North Korea, that possess implications for global stability as well. A third arena of "known unknowns" is how the world will cope with global warming in coming decades. Nonetheless, the Sino-American strategic rivalry seems likely to be the or a central focus for global security issues in coming decades.

The Thucydides Trap: Apples, Oranges, and Kumquats

The Thucydides Trap is a structural situation in which a rising power makes demands for changes in the prevailing status quo that are resisted by the incumbent leading power.[8] International relations scholars have examined these situations, often called power transitions, since the late 1950s without ever invoking Thucydides. Graham Allison (2017), however, is taking advantage of a rising

---

[7] However, Scobell et al. (2020) also forecast that China will be the pre-eminent military and economic actor in Asia by 2050 but still lagging somewhat behind the US global position in technological innovation and global reach. In their future scenario, the Korean problem is resolved peacefully in the next thirty years but the Taiwan issue remains unsettled. Japan and Australia remain allied with the United States but try to keep this connection low key. Scobell et al. (2020) do not say so explicitly, but they imply strongly that military conflict between China and the United States will remain less likely as long as Chinese decision makers perceive that they have not yet fully caught up to or passed the American position. Equally by implication, they assume that the United States will continue to improve its technological innovation and global reach capabilities and maintain its lead in these areas.

[8] Thucydides is given credit for first writing about the trap in terms of explaining Peloponnesian warfare by Sparta's reaction to Athenian gains some 2500 years ago.

China and a relatively declining United States situation to reinvent the threat associated with structural destabilization.[9] War between these central rivals, we are told, is not inevitable. The historical odds are 3:1 or 75 percent in favor of it happening. Since most people seem unaware of the implications of the collision course on which the two leading powers are on, the hazard of war is all the greater. It is the structural change that makes crises that ordinarily would be relatively easy to manage (think the assassination of the Archduke in 1914) transform into an escalating cascade of hostilities in which decision makers lose control of events and become more vulnerable to committing themselves to going to war. If the structural change can be likened to a pile of dry wood, any spark could conceivably ignite the pile into a flaming bonfire (Thompson, 2003).

Yet how do we, or more appropriately, Allison know what the historical odds are? The numbers are based on sixteen similar instances found in the history of world politics over the past 500 years. Twelve of the events that are listed in table 9.1 led to the onset of war. Only four situations managed to escape intense conflict.

Some people like to believe that every event is unique and ultimately incomparable. Others find enough similarities to treat multiple cases as members of a category. Allison obviously believes that his sixteen cases are comparable because they represent some general category of "rising" states clashing with "ruling" states. But if we are to take heed of the high odds associated with the historical lethality of such situations, we must first come to terms with the comparability of the sixteen episodes in world history. It is not clear how to define "rising" and "ruling," but we can assume that the events encompass situations in which a new major power's capability position approaches the relative capability position of the predominant state in a given structure. We are told that the rapidity with which this structural passage occurs makes things more dangerous but not how close the challenger's position has to be to begin invoking feelings of fear and insecurity.

Still, there are several other problematic aspects of the group of sixteen cases. If one wanted to know what the chances are of being attacked by a rabid rabbit while playing golf, the first thing an analyst would do is to eliminate information on situations where there were no rabbits and golf courses. Places with both rabbits and golf courses could then be examined to determine how often rabbits became rabid and then attacked golfers. Put another way, it is possible to compare apples and oranges if one knows that the comparative focus is on fruit and not on apples or oranges per se. But table 9.1 has ten kinds of "fruit" listed in the domain column: four cases of global empire, two or three cases of land/sea Europe, two

---

[9] See Chan (2020) for what is probably the most comprehensive critique of the Thucydides Trap argument.

Table 9.1 Allison's Sixteen Case Database

Timing	Ruling state(s)	Rising state	War	Domain
Late 15th century	Portugal	Spain	No war	Global empire
1st half of 16th century	France	Habsburgs	War	Land—Western Europe
16th–17th centuries	Habsburgs	Ottoman Empire	War	Land—Central/East European/sea—Mediterranean
1st half of 17th century	Habsburgs	Sweden	War	Land/sea—Northern Europe
Mid-late 17th century	Dutch Republic	England	War	Global empire
Late 17th–mid-18th centuries	France	Britain	War	Global empire/land—Europe
Late 18th–early 19th centuries	Britain	France	War	Land/sea—Europe
Mid-19th century	France (land)/ Britain (sea)	Russia	War	Global empire
Mid-19th century	France	Germany	War	Land—Europe
Late 19th–early 20th centuries	China-Russia	Japan	War	Land/sea—East Asia
Early 20th century	Britain	United States	No war	Global/sea—Western Hemisphere
Early 20th century	Britain	Germany	War	Land—Europe/global
Mid-20th century	USSR/France/Britain	Germany	War	Land/sea—Europe
Mid-20th century	United States	Japan	War	Land/sea—Europe*
1940s–1980s	United States	USSR	No war	Global
1990s–present	Britain-France	Germany	No war	Europe

*Presumably, the entry should read East Asia.

cases each of land Europe and global empire/land Europe, and one case each of land Western Europe, land Central/Eastern Europe/Mediterranean Sea, land/sea Western Europe, land/sea East Asia, and global/Western Hemisphere. So, apparently it makes no difference if two rivals are contesting global predominance, regional predominance, or some combination of sea (global) and land (regional) contestation. The problem here is that if there is some reason to treat these types of cases as not all belonging to the same category, an analyst should be most hesitant in aggregating them for the purpose of assessing probabilities. Two land powers fighting for predominance in a single region is one thing. States fighting over regional hegemony and global predominance are quite another.

Applied to the contemporary world, the question is what kind of rivalry is the current China-US adversarial relationship? Is it a contest between a global power and a regional power over predominance in Asia, or is it a case of two global powers competing for optimizing their influence over the entire planet? The China-US rivalry may become the latter but, so far, it seems to resemble the former situation. It makes a difference because each type of rivalry presumably has a different probability of going to war. What is most evident is that the rivalry is not a case of two land powers vying for regional supremacy—perhaps the most war-prone type of rivalry context.

One problem, then, is that the cases do not readily aggregate unless one assumes that structural context makes no difference. If they do not aggregate readily, it is difficult to assess the historical probability of the China-US rivalry going to war. A second problem is found in the "ruling" and "rising" columns. Several of the categorizations are quite debatable. Portugal was most "established" as an imperial power in places such as West Africa or the western Indian Ocean—that is, in areas in which the Portuguese and Spanish did not compete. In other areas, the Portuguese arrival did not precede the arrival of the Spanish by all that much. The Spanish and Portuguese, for that matter, fought wars early (1470s) and late (1580s). How does that translate into no war?

Something similar can be said about the France-Habsburgs case. France had a larger population than the Habsburg territories, but France did not predominate in Western Europe when it moved into Italy, where it was soon opposed by Spanish resistance. That is, it is not clear who should be designated as ruling or rising in the first half of the sixteenth century. The Ottomans and Swedes moved into Habsburg territories in the sixteenth and seventeenth centuries, but the Ottomans had been around for a while by the time they marched on central Europe. The Dutch-English confrontation of the seventeenth century showed up in various parts of the globe but it was primarily oriented to the control of European and Atlantic trade. The Anglo-French rivalry in the late seventeenth through the early nineteenth centuries was much older and could be traced back to William the Conqueror in 1066. It also was characterized by conflict in the

Caribbean, North America, and India, but the two states were not contesting which state predominated in Western Europe so much as Britain sought to ensure that France did not rule there. Allison makes two different rivalries of this long feud in which one state rules and the other is rising and then switches which one rules and rises later in their rivalry. Somewhat similarly, Allison has Germany as a rising state in the nineteenth century and three times in the twentieth century. One wonders how often a state can rise. Alternatively, in what sense was Russia a rising state in the mid-nineteenth century? Britain and Russia had been Eurasian rivals since at least the eighteenth century and Russia was certainly an important part of the coalition that had suppressed the Napoleonic French challenge and kept France contained in the first half of the nineteenth century.

In five cases, there is more than one "ruler" identified. Does that suggest more than one rivalry case in each instance? Instead of sixteen cases, are there twenty-two? But then, one must take into consideration how many cases seem to be missing. England and the Netherlands fought Spain in the sixteenth and seventeenth centuries, Japan took on China for East Asian predominance in the late sixteenth century, France re-emerged in the seventeenth century to compete with Spanish predominance, rising Russia defeated Sweden in the Baltic region, France then re-emerged to compete with the Dutch about the same time as the English were, rising Prussia took on Austria in the eighteenth century, and Japan continued to compete with the Soviet Union in the early twentieth century (perhaps neither was a ruling or rising state?). These suggestions could add another seven or eight cases, thereby making thirty cases in all or almost double Allison's sixteen. The problem here is that one needs to first establish the time periods in which some state "ruled" and other states "rose" within rivalry contexts to compute how often they fought (and when? early, late, or constantly?), as opposed to loosely suggesting cases of interest for rough periods of time. It is not enough to say that rivalries have a high probability of going to war.

Most rivalries, depending on how one defines a rivalry, do not go to war. What we really want to know is how long does it take for two states in a rivalry to escalate their hostility to warfare? For instance, in the China-US case, if the rivals manage to avoid warfare until the second half of the twenty-first century or until close to the end of the twenty-first century, is Allison still right that they have a high probability of going to war? Of course, this ties back to the early question of what kind of rivalry is the China-US case and how might their rivalry change later in the century. Contesting Asian predominance is one thing—global hegemony may prove to be a much different question.

Finally, if one constructs a historical sample, it is incumbent upon the analyst to also assess how other variables have evolved over time in ways that might alter the probability of intense conflict in some form. Economic interdependence in the twenty-first century is much different and far more complex than in it was in the sixteenth century. So is the lethality of weaponry available to the major powers. In the sixteenth century, armies of 20,000 or so fought with pikes, swords, and primitive guns. In the twenty-first century, it is possible to eliminate all life on the planet in a full-bore nuclear exchange. Do none of these changes matter for calculating contemporary warfare probabilities?

Social science rules and best practice do not preclude the construction of historical data bases. On the contrary, the need for historically sensitive analysis demands it. Those same rules do, however, suggest caution in not confusing a kumquat for an apple or an orange. Misperceptions and strategic accidents can lead to war-level, conflict escalation. It may well be that that mistakes are more likely in periods of adjustment in relative power configurations. Rising states do have problems of negotiating status-quo changes with states that have staked out their predominance earlier. Even so, just what the probability of war might be for China and the United States in their current rivalry remains unclear. All things considered; it is probably much less than 75 percent. Yet just how we should go about assessing the probability in a persuasive manner remains to be demonstrated. Otherwise, the research design trap tends to trump warnings about the Thucydides Trap.

There is an entirely different way to approach the question. Leadership long-cycle theory (Modelski and Thompson, 1996; Thompson and Zakhirova, 2018, 2019) posits a lineage of eight global system leaders, each constituting the most innovative economy for a finite period over the past 1,000 years.[10] If we ask the question of how often the new system leader defeated an incumbent system leader in battle in order to become the new leader, the answer is only 25 percent of the time—exactly the converse of Allison's 75 percent prediction. Song China was defeated by the Mongols, but it is hard to describe the Mongols as seeking to become a new technological leader. As technological leadership drifted west, Genoa supplanted Venice as the initial carrier of Chinese goods and ideas to the Mediterranean. But it did so only because Venice backed the losing side in a Byzantine civil war and lost its Black Sea positioning on the overland Silk Roads. Venice did later defeat Genoa after a series of wars and with some help from the Black Death. Portugal was critical in moving the European political economy beyond its Mediterranean and Atlantic foci. Venice aided Ottoman and Mamluk opposition to Portuguese movement into the Indian Ocean but stopped short of

---

[10] This lineage involves assumptions about the initial divergences between eastern and western Eurasia and the subsequent development of a global system that operates somewhat independently of various regions such as Europe or Asia. There is also no equivalence given to various holders of the status of global system leader over time. A sequence in technological innovation began in China in the first millennium CE and was imported west after the Mongol conquests by Italian city states and Portugal as transitional carriers. The modern end of the sequence features the increasing reliance on fossil fuels in the Dutch, British, and American leaderships. But the respective power of the last three leaders has increased tremendously as well.

engaging in direct conflict. Portugal's centrality was brief in the early sixteenth century. Toward the end of that same century, it was absorbed temporarily by Spain in a succession struggle and Portuguese capabilities were used against Dutch rebels and their ally, England. Toward the end of the seventeenth century, the Dutch intervened coercively in supporting William's claims for the English crown against the Stuarts but the Netherlands' seventeenth-century centrality was already waning (thus prompting the Dutch intervention) and was exhausted in the French wars (1688–1713). The first British lead was thus achieved without having to defeat their now junior Dutch ally. Britain II succeeded itself after its coalition defeated Napoleon in the second round of French wars (1792–1815). The United States, although it fought early wars with Britain (1776–1783 and 1812–1815), emerged as the current global system after the British exhausted themselves in the German wars (1914–1945).

So, the Venetians defeated the Genoese and one could argue that the Dutch defeated the Portuguese after it was absorbed by Spain. That is, two cases involved the new leader defeating the old leader, although interpretation of the Dutch-Portuguese confrontation could be viewed several ways. In the other six cases, the new system leader did not have to defeat an incumbent. Clearly, there was a great deal of violence associated with these transitions, but it encompassed suppressing challengers, some of whom represented potentially rival centers of technological innovation and some of which did not. As always, it depends on how you ask and proceed to answer the question at stake.

Power Transition

The power transition model has been around since the late 1950s. Developed initially by A. F. K. Organski (1958) in an introductory textbook, it eventually became a research program jointly led with Jacek Kugler and others (Organski and Kugler, 1980; Tammen et al., 2000). As a research program, the analytical focus has shifted away from structural power shifts to encompass a variety of other topics, but our interest remains centered on the initial systemic concern. The international system's power structure is viewed as a triangle. At the peak is the dominant power. Immediately below the dominant power is a belt of great powers, some of whom are in league with the dominant power while others that are dissatisfied with the prevailing distribution of power and privileges are opposed. Below this major power belt is the rest of the world's state actors, which also have allegiances either with the dominant power or with its opposition.

The fundamental dynamic is the rate at which one or more of the dissatisfied great powers catches up to the relatively declining position of the dominant power. This is the power transition situation in which conflict between the two states is highly probable after a rising great power challenger achieves a position approximating 80 percent of the declining leader's position as measured in terms of GDP. Power transitions are inherently inevitable because as states increasingly industrialize (after 1750), demographically larger states are likely to catch up with and surpass demographically smaller states, other things being equal. Conflict is equally probable because the declining dominant power is likely to be non-accommodating to the rising challenger's preferences for a new distribution of power and privilege reflecting the changed systemic circumstances and consequent dissatisfaction with the status quo. A war to resolve the positional disputes has been the most likely outcome.

One of the problems with the power transition argument has been how to assess the level of dissatisfaction of the rising challenger.[11] The outbreak of war signifies considerable dissatisfaction, but how should one assess the level of disgruntlement prior to the onset of war?

In the case of contemporary China, there is clearly a desire for changing systemic rules—China has started an alternative IMF after attempting to improve its decision-making role in the existing IMF, wished to expand control of movement through the South China Sea, and appears to be developing an expanded politico-economic role throughout Afro-Eurasia with its Belt and Road Initiative program operating in a large number of states that could substantially reorient the shape of globalization, and with its cultivation of access to the Indian Ocean via South and Southeast Asian ports and bases. Building multiple aircraft carriers, perhaps as many as six, is another indicator of at least wider-reaching ambitions, if not dissatisfaction per se.

The United States, bogged down in Afghanistan and the Middle East, initially seemed somewhat accommodating of China, but that approach was also configured on a peculiar expectation that China would evolve into a supporter of the status quo as it became more affluent. China also enjoyed lobbying support from firms hoping to make a killing in the expanding Chinese market. Those expectations have withered in the face of Chinese attempts to acquire Western technology by any way possible, including requiring foreign firms to surrender technology in return for participation in the Chinese marketplace and engaging in intensive espionage. The Trump administration reversed previous US administrations' approaches to dealing with China by seeking to persuade China to abandon its high-technology ambitions and by penalizing China with an ever-increasing array of protective tariffs. Not surprisingly, the tariffs do as much if not more harm to US consumers and manufacturers than to Chinese exporters (Flaaen and Pierce, 2019). Why Chinese decision makers would abandon efforts to make its economic production more cutting-edge

---

[11] DiCicco and Levy (1999) is a comprehensive critique of the power transition model.

because the United States says it should be also less than clear. But then these extreme moves by the United States may or may not survive into a post-Trump era. So far, the tariffs are being maintained but one no longer hears as much about demands that the Chinese desist from challenging the US lead. There may or may not be greater emphasis on technological self-sufficiency but there also seem to be new concerns about Chinese military gains. In sum, American rhetoric is less confrontational to date but it is less clear whether the underlying American policy is any less hard line.[12]

Observing US bullying and Chinese intransigence (or vice versa) month by month is one thing. There seem some grounds for perceiving expanding Chinese dissatisfaction and US non-accommodation. Moreover, if we adopt the power transition research program's insistence on measuring transition in terms of GDP, a Chinese transition is at least in the offing, if not already upon us. Yet there is a big difference between catching up in terms of GDP and catching up in the leadership of technological innovation.[13] In addition, nuclear deterrence and/or military asymmetry seem to be operative in suppressing the likelihood of military conflict between the United States and China in the foreseeable future. This could be viewed as reflecting a temporary stalemate in Aligappa terms that might persist only if the absence of innovation leadership or the presence of nuclear deterrence and/or military asymmetry acted as suppressing factors. The problem is that we have moved outside of the power transition argument once we begin juggling the possible interactions of economic catch-up, however interpreted, and military deterrence/asymmetry.

Another problem is that the power transition research program awards demographic advantages a major underlying role. In other words, the state with the bigger population is expected to win. But what if that emphasis is not as critical as some would portray it? If nothing else, it will take some time to fully transform China's population into a post-agrarian political economy. Then, too, if the emphasis on high-technology production is germane, population is not the main driver that it is for the enlargement of GDP. It is conceivable that China could greatly improve its standing in technology innovation without usurping the American position. Assuming China will enhance its high-tech position, we are probably in for some extended period of dual technological leadership. If so, that would probably also mean an indefinite postponement of a definitive power transition—something we really have not experienced before. Should the "indefinite postponement" persist, the application of a power transition model would seem premature at best and possibly just not all that relevant.

---

[12] It could also be that policy hawks and doves are still wrestling over which viewpoint should have the upper hand in making China policy while coping with Covid-19 takes precedence.

[13] China's catch-up in terms of GDP depends on how that measure is calculated and whether one takes into consideration cost of living qualifiers.

System Leader Retrenchment

If transition does not appear to be on the near horizon, what about incumbent retrenchment? Figure 9.2 sketches an outline of MacDonald and Parent's (2018) argument that retrenchment is the most likely outcome given great power relative decline. One problem in applying this perspective is that it has a major qualifier. "Decline" is defined as a decrease in the ordinal rank of a great power. Presumably, they mean that a state that is third in the rankings at time x and slips to fifth place by time x + 1 has declined. There is no inherent problem with this restriction except that for our purposes: (1) it is not restricted to the leading power and (2) the current leading power is still the current leading power. The United States has not yet become the system's second-ranked power and it is possible that it will not fall farther than sharing the first-place position with another state in the foreseeable future. Technically, then, the MacDonald-Parent retrenchment theory does not really apply to the problem being discussed here.

Yet rank orders can be awkward metrics. Imagine, for instance, that one state is number 1 in the system with a 35 percent share of relative power. It slips to a 28 percent share as another state moves up from a 20 percent share to a 27 percent share. One still has a 1–2 ranking that has not formally changed, but now the two leading states have power share positions that are quite similar. Or another situation might start with a leader that claims 50 percent of relative power and its closest rivals can muster only 20 percent between them. But let us say that rival X moves up from a 10 percent position to a 25 percent position while rival Y moves from 10 percent to 15 percent of relative power. If there are only three states in the system's elite, these changes imply that the leader has dropped to a 30 percent share of relative power—again without altering the rank orders associated

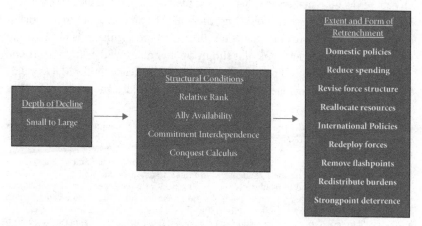

Figure 9.2 The Retrenchment Imperative

with the original and altered scenarios. In both cases (the 35 to 28 and the 50 to 30 movements of the leading power), one rival is very close to having caught up fully with the leader. Presumably, we would not care to dismiss these scenarios as situations not involving relative leadership decline. And, moreover, one might think that any retrenchment urges associated with an ordinal loss of rank would translate to major interval losses of relative rank as well. After all, the figure explicitly states that the argument should work for all decline situations, from small to large. Therefore, there could be something in the retrenchment propensity to consider even if the fit is not exactly perfect.

MacDonald and Parent (2018) say that, given some amount of decline, four variables determine whether and to what extent retrenchment is pursued. Two variables make retrenchment less likely. The higher the initial rank, the harder it is to contemplate retrenchment. Habit is also well-entrenched and there may be too many powerful vested interests in maintaining a lead to overcome readily. Second, the extent to which commitments are interdependent also makes retrenchment more difficult because reductions in one area will tend to cascade into other areas and decision makers will prefer to exercise more control over the steps they take. The best way to control the adjustment process may be to avoid it altogether.

On the other hand, two other variables facilitate the likelihood of retrenchment. The more allies one has, the more they can pick up some of the former responsibilities of the leading state. A conquest calculus that favors defense over offense can also be facilitative in the sense that a state can reduce its offensive capabilities and fall back on defensive capabilities that may be cheaper to maintain in any event.

If retrenchment emerges from this four-variable mix as probable, rational decision makers can cut costs at home or abroad through a variety of measures.[14] Of course, decision makers may behave less than rationally. But the real problems with this perspective are twofold. One, there may be no choice but to retrench if commitments overwhelm available resources. Yet retrenchment is not likely to revive or turn around lost rank. It is simply a better match with what can be done given fewer resources to expend on doing something. Relatedly, the MacDonald-Parent scheme omits altogether the process that precedes and leads to decline.

[14] A process not specified in the figure is that MacDonald and Parent assume that decision makers will act to restore some correspondence between commitments and declining resources lest they be removed from office by domestic constituents who prefer not being overcommitted given a diminished resource base. Thus, it is being assumed that both decision makers and domestic populations will act rationally in reading their changing environments. Yet, as Brexit implies, irrationalities in assessing how to respond to relative decline can linger on for quite a few years. Many decision makers and a respectable proportion of the population seem to believe that Britain can return to some semblance of its previous status by withdrawing from a European Union that is holding it back and forcing it to accept unwanted migration and regulation. From an outsider's perspective, such an outcome seems most unlikely.

Perhaps, ultimately, it does not matter. In the systemic leadership case, however, saving money and resources on diminished activities means an acceptance of diminished status only if one assumes that overspending or overcommitment were not the main drivers of relative decline in the first place.

What if the declining system leader is not prepared to accept its waning condition? It may still retrench tactically to deal with immediate threats, as in the classic British response to Germany's catching-up prior to World War I, but, as in the British case, tactical success will not necessarily improve its relative positional problem. So, some sort of retrenchment is indeed probable, but it is at best a delaying tactic that puts off the decline problem to another decade or two. More to the present point, however, it is not clear what possible retrenchment might tell us about the ongoing Sino-American rivalry. At best, it might suggest that the United States should back away from engaging in the rivalry either fully or at all while it improved its capability foundation for competing with the Chinese. To date, calls to intensify technological innovation in the United States with governmental support have fallen on deaf ears. Instead, the emphasis has been to stress negotiation, impose penalties for the weaker side attempting to catch up, and variable efforts to organize a resisting coalition.

A Risk Assessment Response to Rising Challengers

Facing intense competition, great power retrenchment or retreat is one possible course of action. Another is to attack or oppose a rising challenger before it can catch up. Montgomery (2016) offers a theory for that type of strategy. Figure 9.3 delineates some of the more probable situations in an argument that has a leading state first assess how the regional outcome will affect its own interests, what it prefers in the region from which the threat is emanating, and then determine the nature of the regional power shift underway. Has it been completed or is it still in progress? Does it have clear implications for the leading power's hegemony? Depending on how these questions are answered, the outcome is binary—to either oppose or accommodate.

The second line of interconnecting boxes in figure 9.3 demonstrates what is expected if the leading state perceives that a regional challenger is unlikely to block its own access to the region. Whether it prefers regional parity or primacy, the second main consideration is whether a new regional order has been constructed. If so, the leading power should accommodate the regional challenger in order to preserve its own privileges. If the regional order remains unsettled, the leading power should attempt to thwart the challenger on the presumption that it should be easier to return to an earlier form of regional stability than to construct a new order.

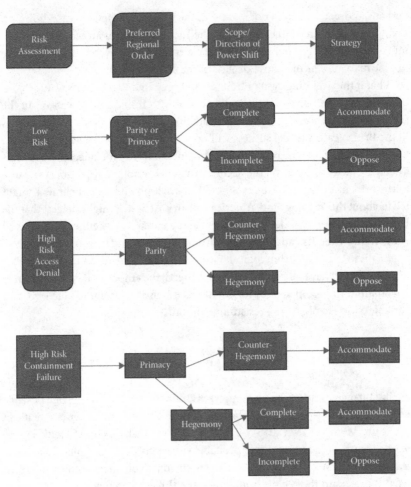

Figure 9.3 Risk Assessment and Strategic Outcomes

The second row beneath the four categorical foci assumes the opposite—that a regional challenger will seek to restrict the leading state's ability to extract resources from the region in question. In this case, the leading state would prefer to avoid circumstances granting regional primacy to the challenger. Regional parity is better for the leading state's continued access to the region. However, if regional primacy would help block another state's hegemonic ambitions at the global level, the leading state should accommodate a situation that contributes to its own security. If the rising challenger acquisition of primacy in the region would serve its own wider hegemonic plans, it should be opposed.

The Risk Assessment schema tells us that the United States is likely to oppose China's bid for regional hegemony. That is certainly worthwhile in differentiating among a variety of cases, but it does not tell us much about how the United States might oppose China's ambitions. Nor does it say anything about what the Chinese might do in response.

A Time Horizon Assessment of the Response to Rising Challengers

Edelstein (2017) has developed an alternative argument about how declining powers are likely to respond to rising powers that is remarkably parsimonious. He argues that the response depends on the time horizons that the two parties are working on or within. Decision makers think they know their environment reasonably well in the short term. How things might change in the more distant future is less well known. Thus, actors will behave differently depending on whether they are thinking about now or some time ahead.

If they are both operating with a long-term perspective, hegemonic war is most likely unless the declining power thinks/hopes that the rising power's intentions will become less malign over time. At some point down the road both sides know they are likely to come to blows. The rising power need only wait until the declining power has declined sufficiently to be defeated readily. The leading power has incentive to put off the inevitable but knows that it will have to defend its privileges eventually.

If the declining power wishes to retain its advantages into the near future, it could contemplate some sort of preventive strike to weaken the threat posed by the rising power before it becomes too strong—and assuming that the rising power is provoking the leading power prematurely. If both parties are mired in short-term perspectives, intermittent clashes with occasional episodes of cooperation are more likely. Only when the leading but declining power takes a long-term perspective and the challenger avoids provocations in the short term is cooperation probable. Otherwise (see figure 9.4), some type of conflict is most probable. One side or the other is likely to attack the other.

Three of four combinations predict some sort of conflict in the simplest version of the theory. But it turns out that there are a couple of ways to complicate the issue. One is that decision makers rarely operate solely in one temporal dimension. Rather, factions are likely to adopt either short- or long-time perspectives simultaneously. Declining power hawks will push to see some coercive policy applied against the rising challenger now while declining power doves will argue that an attack in the short term will only serve to make more malign intentions on the part of the rising power all the more likely. It is better to wait until

		Perspectives		
		Declining	Rising	
		Power	Power	Conducive to
Other short-term threats		long	short	cooperation
Opportunities for short-term gains		long	long	hegemonic war
Level of concern about long-term		short	long	preventive war
Intentions of rising power		short	short	cooperation/

Skirmishes mix

where: Short-term perspectives are focused on the immediate future in a static context and long-term perspectives are focused on a future that will emerge after some predictable but necessary transformations of the structure in which they operate.

Figure 9.4 The Time Horizon Framework
Where: Short-term perspectives are focused on the immediate future in a static context, and long-term perspectives are focused on a future that will emerge after some predictable but necessary transformations of the structure in which they operate.

convergence processes have had some time to develop. Should that happen, there will be less to fight about. We have seen something along these lines play out in the Obama administration with liberals gaining the upper hand until the advent of the Trump administration's China hawks. Yet as this last statement suggests, it is possible for decision makers to argue about a rising challenger's intentions and for one point of view to prevail sufficiently to influence subsequent policy so that we can say which perspective seems to be winning in the short term.

Another complication, though, is that short- and long-term perspectives per se need not be benign. That is, short-term perspectives could be either malign or benign. So, too, could long term perspectives. So, we have four short- and long-term perspectives rather than two (short and benign, long and benign, short and malign, and long and malign). Parsimony quickly becomes a casualty. Edelstein does not build this into the argument displayed in figure 9.4, but he does acknowledge it implicitly when he talks about challengers avoiding provocations in the short term. Either a short-term perspective is provocation-prone or it is not. Otherwise, it becomes two different variables.

A third complication is supplied by Edelstein explicitly when he "front loads" his theory by noting that different things can lead to short- or long-term perspectives being adopted in the first place. As noted in figure 9.4, they include short-term threats emanating from other sources than the challenger, opportunities for short-term gains via cooperation, and the extent to which the declining power is paying attention to the rising challenger's threat potential. So, a declining power may choose to deal with a proximate threat and ignore more distant threats. The declining power's behavior would not then be predicted by Edelstein's argument but by other considerations.

Opportunities for short-term gains intervening in the decision calculus seems already inherent in the possibility that short-term perspectives might be either malign or benign in different circumstances. The third influence on which perspective might be adopted suggests that the declining power might or might not recognize a rising state's threat potential but might also be too busy elsewhere to do anything about it. For instance, a heavy involvement in the Middle East meant that power projection capabilities were committed to one or more places far from where they might be needed to oppose a rising challenger in East Asia. In the contemporary US case, it has proven difficult to extract troops and weapons from the Middle Eastern tar baby in order to redeploy them to the Indo-Pacific theaters.

One question that is left unsettled is whether the three variables that predict to the short and long temporal perspectives tend to be more or less powerful than the temporal perspectives themselves. Alternatively put, were US decision makers more apt to hope that Chinese decision makers would become more liberal over time if they knew the US Middle Eastern involvement precluded giving the rise of China much attention in the first decade of the twenty-first century— or if it was difficult to imagine interrupting the strong economic interactions associated with US consumption of commodities manufactured in China? It is hard to say, but one gets the impression that it is easier to find evidence for the first three variables in Edelstein's argument than it is for the prevalence of short- and long-term perspectives among decision makers. What is least heartening is to contemplate how few decision makers seem to demonstrate anything approximating a long-term perspective in the first place.

The Interaction of Rising and Declining States

Itzkowitz Shifrinson (2018) looks at the interaction between a declining great power and a rising state from the perspective of the rising state, not the more customary declining state's viewpoint. His two variable theory asks whether the declining great power has (a) strategic value for the rising state and (b) what is the military posture of the declining great power. In marked contrast to the power transition position, if the declining power has high strategic value (as an ally, for instance), the rising state should be expected to be supportive—as indicated in figure 9.5. A weak declining state needs strengthening. A still-strong declining state requires bolstering. However, if the declining great power has little strategic value, the rising state is likely to hasten the decline trajectory either slowly (if the

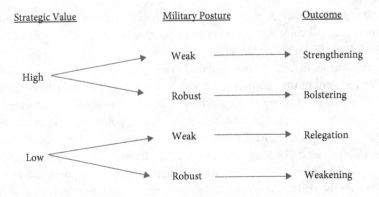

Where:

Strengthening = taking steps to sustain or improve a declining state's position

Bolstering = taking low cost measure to prevent a declining state from further positional slippage

Relegation = predatory and intense challenge of a declining state

Weakening = allow gradual shift in power distribution utilizing limited measures

Figure 9.5 Declining and Rising State Interactions
Where:
Strengthening = taking steps to sustain or improve a declining state's position
Bolstering = taking low-cost measure to prevent a declining state from further positional slippage
Relegation = predatory and intense challenge of a declining state
Weakening = allow gradual shift in power distribution utilizing limited measures

declining state retains considerable capability) or quickly (if the declining state is relatively weak).

Note that Itzkowitz Shifrinson is not addressing what to expect necessarily in the case of the decline of the leading great power and its main challenger per se. His argument speaks to generic great power decline and rising great powers. Yet a declining system leader remains a declining great power and its main challenger is a rising great power as well. Presumably, the more generalized argument should apply to a specific dyad.

The main problem with this argument is when does the rising state make its assessment of the declining great power's strategic value? Britain turned out to have strategic value for the United States in the twentieth century but not so much in the nineteenth century. In the nineteenth century, Britain's low strategic value and strong naval position should have encouraged the United States to sit back and wait for further decline. It is not clear that that is what US decision makers did, but the gradual weakening outcome seems to fit by default. In the twentieth century, Britain's strategic value increased in US eyes and the United States strengthened Britain's ability to survive two world wars. At the same time, though, Britain's vast empire was anything but strengthened by US actions.

What about the Anglo-German relationship in the late nineteenth and early twentieth centuries? Germany was almost never quite sure what Britain's strategic value might be prior to the outbreak of World War I because Britain evaded Germany's attempts to ally with Britain. In the run-up to World War II, Germany had fewer illusions about Britain's utility. Relegation or an intense predatory challenge seems to be what the theory in figure 9.5 would predict. Challenges did occur and one could certainly label them as predatory (initially in Czechoslovakia and then in Poland). But one thing the Itzkowitz Shifrinson schema leaves out is the relative strength of the rising state.

Germany in 1939 was largely bluffing. It was not robust but a relatively weak challenger at first that gained strength as its opposition crumbled. Germany also chose to focus more on the Soviet Union than on conquering Britain. In retrospect, it would have made more sense to take British opposition out of the equation before taking on the vast and seasonally cold plains of the USSR. That is not what happened. That it did not probably tells us something about the limitations of a theory that is constrained to assume and focus on dyadic structures, albeit great power ones. The relationship between two great powers can become very hostile, but the nature of their interactions may depend on what great powers outside the dyad choose to do.

In any event, the US strategic value for China is presumably low even if its military posture remains robust. Itzkowitz Shifrinson would therefore predict that China would or should adopt a weakening strategy and wait for US relative decline to accomplish Chinese objectives without needing to resort to violence. That could end up being the Chinese grand strategy. The problem is that Chinese decision makers could grow impatient and move to a more vigorous adversarial strategy. Alternatively, the United States' relative decline is not only slow-moving, it is also likely to stabilize at a high floor. The Dutch and now the British have moved to relatively weak positions after their incumbencies at the top of the global system. It is unlikely that the United States will ever sink as low in the global hierarchy. If a weakening strategy seemed to be producing no further results, we may be back to adversarial impatience, but considerably down the road.

Rising Power Status Immobility

Rising powers face a structure that is already constructed. The two questions are whether their preferences can be accommodated and are they powerful enough to cause major problems when their goals are perceived as not likely to

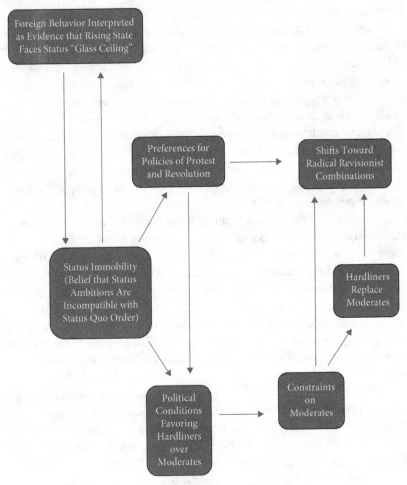

Figure 9.6 Ward's Status Immobility Model

be realized. The German and Japanese cases prior to the two world wars of the twentieth century are well-known instances of the non-accommodation of two states that became antagonistic revisionist opponents of the more status-quo-oriented powers. Figure 9.6 captures Ward's (2017) simple model of how this process works within the rising power's elite decision-making circles. If elites feel that the prevailing order will not accommodate their demands and hard-liners come to power, the probability that the rising power's foreign policy will become seriously revisionist is vastly increased.

Ward's model is straightforward and helps to balance the literature's emphasis on how the older powers will respond to the new powers. But it is a model that focuses on a dynamic that largely takes place (or does not) after the arrival of the rising power to elite status. It does not tell us much about how we get to the glass ceiling perception. Perhaps some of the other models reviewed in this chapter can be utilized for that purpose.

In the case of China, the model would suggest to watch and see what happens in coming decades. Will Chinese decision makers be frustrated by an international order that refuses to make way for the ascent of China? The answer is probably yes—based on the history of accommodating the arrival of new powers—but we do not know to what extent this will occur. The prevailing systemic order could also disintegrate in view of the declining strength of its adherents in which case there would be fewer structures and glass ceilings to rebel against. Will hard-liners crowd out moderates? That, too, will presumably hinge on how burden-some the "glass ceiling" is perceived. But will revisionist powers be as prone to going to war as past revisionists have been? The costs of such behavior have risen substantially. A decoupling from the old order may prove to be more attractive.

Geostructural Realism

Of the eight theories examined, geostructural realism is one of two (the other being Thucydides' Trap) that were developed explicitly to account for Sino-American rivalry behavior. Geostructural realism, as the name implies, adds a geographical variable to structural realism's emphasis on the distribution of power. Where structural realism of the Waltzian persuasion focused on com-paring bipolar versus multipolar structures, Tunsjø (2018) prefers to argue that all bipolar structures are not equal. Different geographical configurations lead to varying outcomes and, therefore, geography is more important than the distri-bution of power per se.

Tunsjø (2018) spends some time demonstrating that the United States and China are the system's two superpowers because of their strong capabilities and because no other great power comes close to matching their capability. Thus, their rivalry is configured by a bipolar matrix. We have experienced a bipolar matrix before in the US-Soviet Cold War, but the way it played out in the twen-tieth century is not a good guide to what we might expect in the twenty-first century because the geographical configurations are much different. The Cold War centered on a US-led coalition balancing against a Soviet bid for regional hegemony in Europe. The adjacent Soviet Union possessed military superi-ority in a region in which there were no major obstacles to a Soviet push to-ward the Atlantic. Geography offered no natural obstacles to a land army. The exhaustion of the European great powers at the end of World War II presented no natural base for resistance to a hegemonic takeover. American sea power alone could not provide a credible defense of Western Europe. Therefore, the response involved strong balancing in the form of a military alliance and an emphasis on arms racing and technological reliance on nuclear weapons. War, once it commenced, would quickly become total and therefore too costly to contemplate. Nuclear deterrence in the form of massive retaliation, once the Soviet side acquired a second-strike capability, meant that war in Europe was increasingly unlikely. Stability in the center, however, encouraged instability and proxy combat in the periphery.

In the twenty-first-century East Asian region, the balancing goal is once again to prevent a large land power ascending to regional hegemony. However, the geography is different in the sense that the region is divided into a continental land mass and a maritime flank stretching from the Korean peninsula to Singapore and Indonesia. Chinese land power is superior on the continent but is confronted with the "stopping power of water" and the superiority of American sea power in the Pacific. If this standoff pertains, one should anticipate at best moderate balancing (no strong military alliance), an avoidance of arms racing, and, by and large, an emphasis on conventional military power at sea. While the possibility of limited warfare is greater than in the earlier Cold War situation, a major war remains unlikely thanks to a less intense rivalry and a variety of factors not highlighted by the theory that had characterized the Cold War (zero-sum ideological hostility, economic independence, and nuclear weapon costs). Whereas the nuclear costs remain in play, ideological hostility is absent and strong economic interdependence prevails. Intermittent cooperation could occur mixed with occasional clashes at sea. Still, the instability found in the center of the conflict over regional hegemony suggests that the center will absorb most of the superpower attention and so there will be less need for proxy combat in the periphery.[15] The renewal of globalized cold war is thus not likely.

Beginning with the premise that all bipolar structures are not alike and that regional geography can trump the influence of structure are two clever innovations to structural realism. The application to the East Asian region in comparison to the earlier European confrontation seems descriptively accurate and quite persuasive. There is a problem, though, and it is recognized by Tunsjø though not followed up on. In Alagappa's terminology, Tunsjø is describing two rivalry stalemates that are due to different circumstances. In the European case,

---

[15] It is not clear how much the axiom that a stable center leads to an unstable periphery and an unstable center means a stable periphery assumes of symmetry in center-periphery relations. In the nineteenth and early twentieth centuries, Italy chose to move into Abyssinia and Libya because French capabilities were too strong in Western Europe to compete with them there or in Tunisia. However, center relations could hardly be described as stable. On the other hand, Tunsjø might point out that they were not bipolar either.

the stalemate was achieved eventually by increasing the costs of major power warfare. In the Asian case, the stalemate is attributed to geography and the respective advantages and disadvantages of continental land power and sea power confrontations. But stalemates, like rules, are made to be broken. Tunsjø describes the Soviet Union as status-quo-oriented in Europe, but that was hardly the case elsewhere. The question is whether peripheral clashes have the same potential to escalate as central ones. The European-centric Cold War managed to avoid blowing up over Berlin, but the Cuban Missile Crisis and later crises/misperceptions/accidents (the Yom Kippur War in 1973, Able Archer 83—although that was European—or the some thirty-two broken arrow episodes involving nuclear weapons) suggest at least that a fair amount of luck was also involved.[16]

Tunsjø does not describe China as status-quo-oriented in East Asia, as evidenced by its activities in the South and East China Seas, its commitment to re-integrating Taiwan with the mainland, and the expanding interest in the first and second island chains as security targets. The construction and launching of many new submarines and aircraft carriers suggests that Chinese decision makers do not fully believe in the "stopping power of water" any more than the US Navy does. The opportunities for a limited war to break out are reinforced by the many clashes and near misses that have already occurred. Whether Tunsjø is right to argue that the sinking of a few ships would not necessarily lead to escalation to something greater than a limited engagement remains to be seen. His position is logical and hopefully correct but sometimes things do not work out the way we expect.

A second problem with stalemated rivalries is that their interactions evolve as their relative capabilities and ambitions change. As Tunsjø acknowledges, the United States had a nuclear monopoly briefly at the outset of the Cold War. The Soviet Union broke the monopoly in 1949 but still took some time to develop a capability to project nuclear weapons over distance and before the United States was willing to recognize its equality in inflicting sufficient nuclear damage sometime in the late 1960s or early 1970s. Even so, that did not stop the arms racing and the development of warhead overkill. Similarly, Soviet ambitions outside Europe took time to expand. They also hinged on a slowly developing capability of projecting force outside of the European theater.

Some of the same situation is going on in East Asia in respect to improvements in Chinese naval technology. The question is whether Chinese gains are outpacing US and allied capability improvements. The US pivot to East Asia has been

---

[16] For the Able Archer near miss, see Birch (2013). Hansen (2000) is one of many possible sources on nuclear accidents.

halting and distracted by ongoing problems elsewhere and US relative decline.[17] US naval construction continues, but the emphasis (through 2050) is more on replacement of aging vessels as opposed to fleet expansion. Chinese naval expansion, starting from a very small initial point, works in the opposite direction. Then, too, China can choose to concentrate its entire naval effort in home waters while the United States is unlikely to ever fully escape commitments around the globe in the next several decades. In other words, China's naval capability does not have to match US naval capability to achieve superiority in waters close to the East Asian littoral.

Put another way, stalemates describe circumstances at one point in time. They need not be accurate at time t + 1 if the actors in question strive to upset them. Water stops land armies only until they become effective sea powers. Granted that land powers do not have a good track record at becoming sea powers, sometimes they figure out how to get the job done. The oldest example is Sparta eventually defeating Athens at sea with the help of Persian financing—something Thucydides probably did not live to witness.

Putting aside the putative naval stalemate in waters around East Asia, there are two other, and related problems.[18] One is that East Asia does not appear to be a fixed region like Europe. There are multiple Asian sub-regions—northwest, east, southeast, central, and south—and they seem to be amalgamating into one greater Asia. As they do so, the parameters of the region in question may shift. For instance, one of the hallmarks of East Asia as Tunsjø notes is that the Chinese have come to believe that their Eurasian interior borders are now secure, thereby providing more incentive to pay attention to their maritime security problems. But that earlier concern was largely oriented toward the north and the former Soviet Union. The Russian Federation is now quite friendly with China, but there remain various reservations on both sides about how friendly those relations should become. More to the south, India has always seemed a secondary consideration to Chinese decision makers, but that could change as well. For that matter, even the nature of the water's stopping power shifts as China builds artificial islands in the South China Sea or extends its access to the Indian Ocean via its emerging string of port pearls in Cambodia, Sri Lanka, and Pakistan.

At the same time, the other and related problem is that China is aggressively seeking to build infrastructure and trade activity throughout Eurasia in its Belt

---

[17] Tunsjø seems to assume that the United States will concentrate on East Asian problems at the expense of attention to other areas. That may or may not prove to be true in the future, but it has not been the historical pattern. Global system leaders have problems concentrating on one region even when that region is becoming the political-economic center of the world economy.

[18] I am also skeptical that China is already a superpower, but I would agree that it is on a trajectory toward achieving that status in some respects, especially in terms of technological innovation, which I think may prove to be the most important element for creating a bipolar structure, either regionally or elsewhere.

and Road Initiative. No one expects these efforts to be realized fully any time soon, but what happens if Eurasian integration proceeds and the central region of focus becomes Eurasia or at least something even larger than Asia? Whatever the likelihood of that occurring in the twenty-first century, should it happen, the importance of the geography of East Asia is apt to greatly diminish.

Of course, in the long run we are all dead, as Keynes once helpfully pointed out. It may be unfair to criticize a theory for not fully taking into consideration what might happen in the unknowable future. Suffice it to say that Tunsjø has captured well the present stalemated security situation as a combination of geography and power distribution.[19] Whether the present security situation remains constant as Chinese capability improves, and US capability erodes relatively is another matter. As, or to the extent that, the rivalry between China and the United States morphs into something larger than "simply" regional hegemony in East Asia, the theoretical focus on East Asian bipolarity may have to change as well. Still, bipolarity is rarely perfect or symmetrical. Perhaps a bipolarity initially tilted in the US favor will gradually move toward a bipolarity tilted in the Chinese favor without losing its claim to bipolar categorical status. Geography tends to remain the same (although the Chinese are even working on that in the South China Sea), but its significance is not immutable. If geography can trump polarity, technology can trump geography and polarity.

Conclusion

Asian ripeness for rivalry does not appear to be the right question. The primary Asian rivalry question is how the ongoing Sino-American rivalry will play out.[20] The Thucydides Trap is based on a debatable research design. Power transition arguments may apply someday, but no real transition is yet in sight. It hinges on the distribution of technological innovation, not GDP bulk. US retrenchment may come into play, but its ultimate impact is unclear, and it is not yet the number 2 power, which is a critical assumption of the retrenchment model. The Risk Assessment theory tells us that the United States will oppose China's bid for regional hegemony. That outcome does not seem to be in doubt. Variable Time Horizons are an interesting idea, but it is hard to discern many statesmen with long-term perspectives and even if more examples of this rare species could be

[19] Truth in advertising stipulates that my appreciation for the Tunsjø argument is predicated in part on my own interest in geopolitical arguments. See, for instance, the emphasis on contrasting sea and land powers for assessing balance of power behavior in Levy and Thompson (2010).

[20] Chan and Hu (2015), incidentally, argue that it is not the endogenous characteristics of Asia that will most influence rivalry ripeness in Asia but rather exogenous characteristics that could certainly include the Sino-American rivalry. However, if Tunsjø is right, it is the interaction between endogenous and exogenous characteristics that counts most.

found, it is not clear which variables in the Time Horizon theory really do most of the heavy lifting. The Declining-Rising State Interaction Theory suggests that China is likely to play a waiting game and let its opponent weaken over time. That could very well be. An alternative dynamic is that frustrated hard-liners refuse to wait for time to do its things and choose to play hardball to improve their status in the system. These last two possibilities cannot be rejected out of hand. But we do not have good reasons to adopt them too early in the game either. We must wait and see. Much probably depends on the extent to which China and the United States are successful in decoupling their intertwined economies (see Farrell and Newman, 2020).

Only Tunsjø's geostructural realism theory predicts a rivalry stalemate that holds if geography divides the east Asian region into two parts and the power distribution remains roughly bipolar. Presumably, decision makers on both sides must also appreciate the primary grounds for stalemate and play their roles accordingly. That appears to provide the best fit to what we observe shaping up onshore and offshore in eastern Asia. Whether that proves to be an overly optimistic observation remains to be seen.

Putting aside what happens in East Asia, a less optimistic observation seems appropriate for world order in general. To the extent that two powerful states compete for systemic leadership, the likelihood is that the current order that stems from decisions made in 1944–1945 will continue to decay. It will not necessarily disappear, but its scope and heft will diminish as its main patron's scope and heft declines. It will have to share legitimacy with an expanding order associated with the main challenger that will be centered on but not necessarily restricted to Eurasia. Chapter 10 elaborates on this prediction.

10

The Future of World Order

The future world order is a popular topic. Orders reduce transaction costs in the world economy and constrain interstate behavior through a network of norms, rules, and expectations. What should we expect given fundamental changes in the distribution of power? Collapse? Continuing decay? The construction of a new order? One of the problems in answering this question is that it is hard to tell. As economists like to say, it depends. But depends on what? That is a second problem. We do not agree all that much on when orders have existed in the past, when they have disappeared, or what drives them. Without answers to these questions, projections into the future are handicapped.

As an illustration of the lack of consensus, take three recent contributions to the study of world orders. Haass (2019) argues that the current order is disintegrating much as the Concert of Europe fell apart in the years leading up to the Crimean War. A new order will need to be developed. Yet the Concert was regional in scope and not centered on any single predominant power (other than the consensus that French expansion must be contained). One thing the current order does share with the Concert is that they both emerged from global wars. How then might we develop a new global order in the absence of global war?

Braumoeller (2019) argues that periods characterized by a single order work better to constrain interstate conflict than do periods characterized by multiple coexisting orders. He tests this plausible hypothesis by correlating the amount of interstate violence associated with varying orders going back to 1816. The advantage of this approach is that he must identify how many orders have existed. He finds quite a few. The 1816 to World War I era is divided into four sub-periods: the Concert of Europe, the mid-nineteenth century, Bismarck, and Kaiser Wilhelm. He also finds four in the interwar era leading up to World War II: the postwar League of Nations and separate orders organized around Germany, the Soviet Union, and Japan. After World War II, there is a Western liberal and a Soviet-centric Communist order through the Cold War era. But the way the memberships of these orders are measured, most of the world's states are lumped in an "Other" category which sets up three more areas to examine for conflict levels: Western-Other, Communist-Other, and Other.[1] The Communist

[1] Membership in the Western liberal order tends to be restricted to affluent/developed states.

American Global Pre-eminence. William R. Thompson, Oxford University Press. © Oxford University Press 2022.
DOI: 10.1093/oso/9780197534663.003.0010

order dissolves at the end of the Cold War leaving three more periods: Western Liberal, Western-Liberal versus Other, and Other.

It is not clear whether all these periods represent orders per se. In some cases, it would seem easier to label them periods of the relative absence of order. In what sense are the "mid-nineteenth century" or the Wilhelmian periods world orders? Could Bismarck create a world order by cleverly arranging and manipulating European alliances for two decades before he was dismissed? The interwar years constitute one period with four prevailing orders, but even so, the short period is divided into a League group and a League vs. Germany, the Soviet Union, and Japan cluster. What should we make of the five observed periods/clusters identified between 1945 and the end of the Cold War? Presumably, it is a period with two competing orders, but that does not correspond to the correlations that are examined. Do non-members of the Western or Communist groups possess their own "Other" order?

Sometimes it is more prudent to evade operationalization decisions without a clear sense of what constitutes a world order. Braumoeller has identified a record number of orders but it is not clear that all of them can stand up to scrutiny. His basic hypothesis may prove to be supportable—singular orders constrain more conflict than competing orders—but the question needs to be left open to a more defensible analysis.

In contrast, Mearsheimer (2019) focuses primarily on the post–World War II period and comes up with two of the orders identified by Braumoeller (and Haass), the Western liberal and Communist ones, and a third one not found in Braumoeller (or Haass)—an order encompassing US-Soviet negotiations. Moreover, he argues that orders depend on polarity and that they work differently given different polar distributions. Unipolar orders take on the ideology of the leading state and bi-/multipolar distributions are realist (and non-ideological?). So that means the three Cold War orders were realist and the surviving Western order became liberal. We end up with four post–World War II orders—three postwar orders and one post–Cold War order.

Who knew evaluating world order performance could be so difficult? It does not need to be. If we start with three premises, the identification of historical orders becomes a bit easier. The first premise is that orders require a predominant power or at least the explicit acceptance of a new order by the major powers involved. The second is that new orders tend to appear after a period of major power warfare in which one side emerges triumphant and the other side is clearly defeated. The warfare is not sufficient, but it does seem to be necessary—at least to date.[2] It provides the war winners with an opportunity to develop new rules

---

[2] The necessary caveat is that warfare in the past has been viewed as less costly than it is now. If warfare is removed as a reasonable option, might the reliance on warfare to set up conditions for establishing new orders decline as well?

and reduces some of the opposition by weakening the losing side. There is some literature that states can construct orders without the violence or the concentrated power but acceptance of these premises suggest that it is more likely that states can only agree to continue with rules already constructed (and, of course, open to some revision) as opposed to negotiating a new order with a new set of rules.[3]

The third premise is that we need to be careful about mixing regional and global orders. The Concert of Europe was very specifically a regional order focused on Europe that lasted into the 1840s. There were some non-European territorial transfers associated with the post-Napoleonic warfare negotiations, but they were minor in comparison to the great power agreement on suppressing the re-emergence of a French regional hegemon. The post–World War II Communist order was also primarily regional with the core resident in the Soviet Union and Eastern Europe. At the end of its civil war, China was initially a member of this order, but it had begun to rebel over its status within a decade or so. Cuba violated the Eurasian nature of the Communist order but hardly in a significant way other than in 1962.

The Western order that emerged after World War II was not restricted to Western Europe. That region may have enjoyed a privileged position within the order, but the order encompassed the so-called Free World, which translates into non-Communist states. To be sure, that does not mean that the order influenced behavior equally within its core (Western Europe, North America, and Japan) and its periphery. But the order's rules and institutions did apply to non-affluent and non-democratic states. A reasonable indicator is GATT/WTO membership. Table 10.1 lists the members and when they joined or met the conditions that had to be met to be accepted as members of the club. Note that more than half of the 1948 members were not located in Western Europe. This ratio only expanded over time.

A second hint provided by the table is that the extension of the Western order after the demise of the Cold War did not change the nature of the order all that much. When the Soviet challenge collapsed, it appeared as if 1945 had taken place all over again. The threat to the incumbent systemic leadership had been defeated. The old system leader was somehow reinvigorated. A new world order was about to be established. Instead, the incumbent system leader relatively quickly became bogged down in further delegitimizing activity (delegitimizing for system leadership purposes) in Afghanistan and Iraq. The system leader retained its monopoly on global reach capabilities (much of which it had

---

[3] For the literature that is agnostic about the need for a hegemon to construct orders, see Keohane (1984), Snidal (1985), Gowa (1989), and Lake (1991). Ikenberry (2018a, 2018b) alternatively argues that the liberal order once constructed can outlive its hegemonic founder.

Table 10.1 GATT and WTO Membership

Year	GATT/WTO membership
1948	Australia, Belgium, Brazil, Canada, Cuba, France, India, Luxembourg, Myanmar, Netherlands, New Zealand, Norway, Pakistan, South Africa, Sri Lanka, United Kingdom, United States
1949	Chile
1950	Denmark, Dominican Republic, Finland, Greece, Haiti, Indonesia, Italy, Nicaragua, Sweden
1951	Austria, Germany, Peru, Turkey
1953	Uruguay
1955	Japan
1957	Ghana, Malaysia
1960	Nigeria
1961	Sierra Leone, Tanzania
1962	Israel, Portugal, Trinidad and Tobago, Uganda
1963	Benin, Burkina Faso, Cameroon, Central African Republic, Chad, Cyprus, Gabon, Ivory Coast, Jamaica, Madagascar, Mauritania, Niger, Senegal, Spain
1964	Kenya, Malawi, Malta, Togo
1965	Burundi, Gambia
1966	Guyana, Rwanda, Switzerland, Yugoslavia
1967	Argentina, Barbados, Ireland, Kuwait, Poland, South Korea
1968	Iceland
1970	Egypt, Mauritius
1971	Romania, Democratic Republic of Congo
1972	Bangladesh
1973	Hungary, Singapore
1978	Surinam
1979	Philippines
1981	Colombia
1982	Thailand, Zambia
1983	Belize, Maldives
1986	Hong Kong, Mexico
1987	Antigua, Botswana, Morocco
1988	Lesotho

Table 10.1 *Continued*

Year	GATT/WTO membership
1990	Bolivia, Costa Rico, Tunisia, Venezuela
1991	El Salvador, Guatemala, Macao
1992	Mozambique, Namibia
1993	Bahrain, Brunei, Czech Republic, Dominica, Fiji, Mali, Slovak Republic, St. Lucia, St. Vincent, Swaziland
1994	Angola, Djibouti, Greece, Guinea, Guinea Bissau, Honduras, Lichtenstein, Papua New Guinea, Qatar, Slovenia, Solomon Islands, St. Kitts and Nevis, UAE
WTO	
1996	Bulgaria, Ecuador
1997	Mongolia, Panama
1998	Kyrgyzstan
1999	Estonia, Latvia
2000	Albania, Croatia, Georgia, Jordan, Oman
2001	China, Lithuania, Moldova
2002	Taiwan
2003	Armenia
2004	Cambodia, Nepal, North Macedonia
2005	Saudi Arabia
2007	Tonga
2008	Cape Verde, Ukraine
2012	Montenegro, Russia, Samoa, Vanuatu
2013	Laos, Tajikistan
2014	Yemen
2015	Seychelles, Kazakhstan
2016	Liberia, Afghanistan
2017	
2018	
2019	

Note: Some of the states listed have changed their names. Most GATT members became WTO members quickly.

Source: based on World Trade Organization (n.d., 2019)

maintained throughout the Cold War), but it had not regained the kind of technological lead it had possessed in the 1940s. The Cold War was not a global war,
and the post–Cold War system leader no longer had the foundation for systemic
leadership it once had had.[4] By 2010, it had become more apparent that US relative decline had not been interrupted by the end of the Cold War. It had only
fooled some observers into thinking otherwise.

The former Soviet Union and Warsaw Pact states had joined the GATT and
WTO, of course, but some had joined much earlier, and most of the joiners after
the early 1990s were somewhat inconsequential additions to the membership.
Speculation about the liberal world order failing because it had been extended
after the end of the Cold War seems as dubious as the idea that a new global order
emerged in the aftermath of the Cold War. As Sargent (2015: 7) says about the US
presidential attempts to create a new world order during and after the 1970s, we
may have gotten new eras but not new orders.

With these three premises in mind, there have been fewer orders in the past
two centuries than is sometimes thought to be the case. Globally, we can talk
about a Pax Britannica that began to emerge after 1815 and a Pax Americana or
liberal world order after 1945. When the term "global" is used, it is assumed that
these orders have always been incomplete, in the sense that global orders have
never extended fully to all parts of the world. For instance, Britain had to coerce
China to embrace its global order through several wars in the mid-nineteenth
century. Its attempts to suppress slavery during that period, not surprisingly,
worked better in some parts of the world than it did in other parts. The US-centric order did not encompass much of Eurasia initially. There are still parts of the
world where its presence is weak, thin, or nonexistent, just as there are still piracy
hotspots and the movement of human trafficking.

Thus, there have not been two Western orders after World War II—only one
of varying applicability, strength, and decay. Whether it became more liberal
after the demise of the Soviet Union can be left to others to decide.[5] Similarly,
there was only a weak but single League order established after World War
I that operated extra-regionally only on the margins.[6] The Germans and
Japanese proceeded to impose orders on conquered territory but that precludes

[4] The foundations for systemic leadership are high growth rates in leading sectors, high shares in
the production of leading sectors, and a monopolistic lead in the possession of global reach capabilities. The United States possessed only the third leg of the foundation after the Cold War ended. It
possessed a great deal of economic wealth, but affluence is not the same thing as pioneering radical
new technologies that revolutionize industrial/commercial practices.

[5] There probably was more rhetoric about democracy, but the question is whether the world
order's support for that form of government moved much beyond the rhetoric.

[6] Mandates to legitimize holding on to colonial territory or new territory occupied during World
War I was one extra-regional activity, although the main beneficiaries were European in location.

explaining the conquests on their subsequent orders. Moreover, the short-lived German and Japanese orders were clearly regional in scope. Napoleon III, Bismarck, and Wilhelm were never able to create world or regional orders in the nineteenth century. The absence of a qualifying major power war ensured that lack of outcome. So, too, did the absence of concentration in economic capability. The Concert of Europe, as hinted at by its name, was a regional order that was operative during the first half of the nineteenth century. Regional and world orders can be compared, but we should be cognizant that they are not the same thing. Most important, regional orders apparently can be constructed in the absence of a regional hegemon, as illustrated by the Concert.[7] We have no evidence yet that global orders can be established in the absence of a global system leader and one that has emerged from a global war in a stronger position than it was in prior to the war.

The Persistence of the Post-1945 World Order?

World orders are finite in duration. Global orders have required bouts of intensive combat and the concentration of economic power at the end of warfare—or, at least, have done so to date. The effects of warfare wear off and states recover. Concentrations of economic power, not coincidentally, are also finite in duration. Thus, world orders decay over time. They can be modified and reinvigorated, but full transformation awaits a return to conditions that are facilitative for constructing new orders.

In the formulation developed here, world orders (really global orders) are dependent on the emergence of a lead economy that leads a coalition that is victorious in global war. At the conclusion of the global war (the macro decision phase), conditions are ripe for constructing a new regime in the world power implementation phase. But circumstances around the time of the global war are unlikely to remain constant. Reality outgrows the feasibility of adhering rigidly to rules and institutions developed for a different era. As Fu Ying (2016), a senior Chinese diplomat, put it, the framework of the prevailing world order becomes like "an old suit that no longer fits." Delegitimization sets in and continued deconcentration of power leads to coalition shopping as states align themselves with and against affiliations with the status quo.

Attina (2019) captures some of the dynamic in contemporary order decay in table 10.2. Five issue areas are delineated. In global finance, fixed exchange rates and dollar/gold convertibility have given way to floating currencies. The many

---

[7] Similarly, the Warsaw Pact suggests that regional hegemons can impose regional orders.

Table 10.2 Phases of Systemic Leadership

	Implementation	Delegitimization	Coalition building
	1945–1973	1973–2015	2015–2050
Monetary and financial institutions	Fixed exchange rate; Dollar/gold convertibility	Flexible exchange rates	Floating currencies; Digital finance and markets
Trade policy	GATT and tariff cuts	Longer rounds of GATT negotiation	Regional blocs Protectionism
Military pacts	Several initiated	Decreasing in number and size	Loose and increasing in number
Nuclear proliferation	Low proliferation	Increasing proliferation	Spreading proliferation
Peacekeeping	Low in number; UN centralized	Increasing number but still centralized	Stable in number; Decreasing centralization

Source: based on Attina (2019: 6) with some modification.

rounds of negotiations over tariff cuts, initially successful, have become more protracted and less successful as global Southern states balk at opportunities to protect their rising economies in the same way global Northern states once did. A number of military defense pacts were created in the early Cold War era. Not all have survived, and decision makers are having serious doubts about remaining in the longer-standing ones that have. New pacts are emerging. On proliferation, nuclear weaponry capabilities were restricted initially to a very small number of great powers. Gradually, the number of states with nuclear weapons has expanded with some likelihood of greater expansion in the offing. As noted earlier, initial hopes for collective security gave way to blue helmet peacekeeping between states that worked reasonably well until the program expanded into peacemaking after internal warfare far outpaced the frequency of interstate war. Interventions once centralized under United Nations oversight seems to be giving way to less centralized behavior.

There probably is no need to point out that the current world order is operating under considerable stress. No one seems to argue that there is nothing wrong with the prevailing order. Rather, the debate is more likely to form around whether the current system is on life support or already doomed or even dead. Other indicators of order decay (some of which are also found in table 10.2) are not hard to find. Haass provides thirteen that are not meant to be rank-ordered

Table 10.3 Haass's Signs of Contemporary Order Decay

---

1. Western efforts to integrate Russia into liberal world order achieved little.

2. Saddam Hussein's invasion of Kuwait would probably have been prevented by the USSR as an overly risky maneuver.

3. Arms control agreements buttressing nuclear deterrence have been broken or are fraying.

4. Russia has shown growing willingness to disrupt the status quo (Georgia, Ukraine, Syria, cyberwarfare).

5. From Russian perspective, NATO enlargement and Iraqi and Libyan interventions were acts of Western bad faith.

6. Authoritarianism is on the rise.

7. Recent rounds of WTO trade talks have ended without agreement.

8. WTO stymied by nontariff barriers and the theft of intellectual property.

9. Growing resentment over exploitation of the dollar to impose sanctions.

10. UN Security Council of little relevance to the regulation of most conflicts; the composition of the Security Council is decreasing its resemblance to the distribution of power.

11. Rhetoric against genocide R2P has not been translated into action.

12. The Nuclear Non-Proliferation Treaty has not prevented the number of nuclear powers from almost doubling.

13. Increasing resistance to US primacy.

Source: Haass (2019: 27–28).

in importance or to be exhaustive.[8] They are simply selected descriptors of a deteriorating order. Interestingly, Haass's list emphasizes Russian activities over Chinese, but that may be simply a matter of when the list of indicators starts counting. It might have started earlier, say, in 1971 with the US decision to end dollar convertibility into gold, in 1973 with Arab petroleum producers coalescing to raise the price of oil in support of Arab-Israeli relations, or in 1979 with the long-running occupation of the US embassy in Tehran. The decay did not begin around the turn of the century; it had been ongoing slowly for some time.

Even defenders of the notion that the current system is likely to live on acknowledge some misgivings. Joseph Nye (1990, 2015) has long been adamant

---

[8] Nor are they presented as a list of indicators. Instead, they have simply been extracted from Haass's discussion of symptoms of decay.

about his belief that the United States is not in decline and that the American Century will persist well into the future. However, he also notes:

> In conclusion, the American century is not over, if by that we mean the extraordinary period of American pre-eminence in military, economic, and soft power resources that have made the United States central to the workings of the global balance of power, and to the provision of global public goods. . . . But the continuation of the American century will not look like it did in the twentieth century. The American share of the world economy will be less than it was in the middle of the last century, and the complexity represented by the rise of other countries as well as the increased role of non-state actors will make it more difficult for anyone to wield influence and organize action. . . .
>
> Now, with slightly less preponderance and a much more complex world, the United States will need to make smart strategic choices both at home and abroad if it wishes to maintain its position. (Nye, 2015: 215–217)

We can quibble about how slight the preponderance has diminished but accept the notion of both less preponderance and more complexity due to the changes in the capabilities of other actors. Nye is saying that the United States will have to try harder given a less favorable structural situation if it hopes to remain central to global politics. Since he wrote that, though, we have seen neither US foreign policy trying harder in respect to organizing coalitions as opposed to going it alone or a large number of particularly smart choices emanating from Washington, DC.[9] If anything, on average the exact opposite has occurred. It has not been clear that clever diplomacy, presuming that it is forthcoming, will or can salvage a losing hand.[10]

In contrast, Cooley and Nexon (2020a) give us a useful if incomplete theory about why we should expect change in the prevailing order. They argue that orders consist of two interacting spheres: architecture and infrastructure. Architecture encompasses the norms, rules, and values on which the order is officially premised even if not always adhered to in practice. Infrastructure refers to practices, relationships, flows, and routine interactions that maintain the order. One might have thought a third component might have been a hegemon, but Cooley and Nexon seem ambivalent about the role of an order patron. It

---

[9] One exception is the decision to abandon the Afghanistan intervention and to actually carry it out. The alternative to escalate the commitment had already been proven not to work. Some minimal presence probably could not have been sustained either.

[10] Ikenberry (2018b), long associated with the argument that the liberal world order can, will, and should survive the decline of the order founder (2001, 2011, 2018a), also notes that the foundations of the postwar order are weakening and that it is possible that something new will emerge that is more consonant with prevailing global power configurations and coalitions.

may be that they wish to identify orders generically, in which some have hegemonic patrons and some do not. They believe that hegemons are not necessary to order construction endeavors. However, their argument about how orders work seems to rely very much on the existence of a hegemon that operates in the infrastructure to provide public, club, and private goods to maintain order functioning.[11] One might have thought that this approach would lead to a central theoretical generalization on hegemonic decline straining the ability of the hegemon to continue providing goods. But, oddly, they take a different approach in which they depict orders being transformed by the emergence of three types of challenges: (1) great power rivals who can provide an alternative source of good provision; (2) weaker states that seek alternative sources of good provision; and (3) transnational and subnational movements that contest the legitimacy of the prevailing order. Figure 10.1 summarizes how these three sorts of challenges lead to order transformation.

The theory is clearly pegged to power transition, which means that great power rivals are catching up to a declining hegemon or system leader. Relative decline is left implicit because all the heavy lifting of the theory is left to the agency of rivals, defectors, and counter-movements. There is nothing wrong with bestowing greater credit for order transformation on these sources if there is a reason. It seems an error, however, to leave that part of the argument implicit. Equally implicit or curiously absent is the likelihood that a declining order leader will be less likely to provide goods in the first place because it has fewer surplus resources to utilize. What is needed in Figure 10.1 is a third arrow emanating from Power Transition to the undermining of the hegemon's monopoly on good provision.

Nonetheless, power transition is very much evident in the theory. Perhaps we should just overlook the omission and add it as an elaboration of the model that they provide. After all, it is certainly worth emphasizing that orders are resisted and opposed. The greater the opposition, and the more effective it is, other things being equal, the greater is the probability of order transformation. It may be that greater external resistance and opposition can encourage the hegemon to try harder to maintain the order. But there is probably some inverse correlation between the hegemon's capability strength and the level of resistance/opposition it encounters. Greater resistance/opposition seems more likely when the hegemon's position is weakening.[12]

---

[11] Public goods can be enjoyed by everyone. Club goods benefit a smaller group like NATO. Private goods are transactions involving a smaller number than a club.

[12] There is also the question of how powerful order opponents are. Ongoing research suggests that a large number of states resist US preferences in UN voting but these opponents tend to be relatively weak states. If UN voting is weighted by capability, there is more support for US positions than opposition (Thompson et al. (2022)).

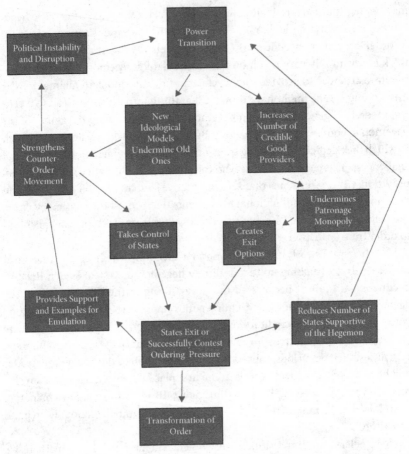

Figure 10.1 Cooley and Nexon's Order Transformation Theory

Another variable missing from figure 10.1 is resistance and opposition that is internal to the order patron. J. A. Thompson (2015: 282–283) emphasizes the interaction between relative wealth and power and the concomitants of a sense of power:

> the greatest efforts to reform, support, and police the world order was made when America's relative wealth and power was at its apogee. . . . In 1950 the United States possessed half the world's monetary gold, reserve currencies, and IMF reserves. But the proportion decline to 33 percent in 1960, 22 percent in 1965, and 16 percent in 1970. As the margin of America's economic superiority declined, so did the extent to which resources were devoted to wider foreign policy goals.

Thompson goes on to argue that a US-centric world order is a luxury good if it is not clear to supporters that prosperity and security are tied to its maintenance.[13] Luxury goods, moreover, are only desirable when it is thought that they are affordable. Should the domestic consensus emerge that the perceived costs exceed the benefits, it will not matter how much US capabilities exceed those held by rivals (as manifested in power transitions). Support for sustaining the world order is likely to disintegrate. The processes emphasized in chapter 6 suggest that there is some sizeable disgruntlement over the costs/benefits exchange process associated with hegemonic order maintenance. America First does not yet appear to be a majority position, and it is conceivable that greater domestic support for maintaining systemic leadership could be generated with more elite effort. But it is also conceivable that the benefits are diminishing while the costs have continued to rise—even though the need for systemic leadership has hardly receded.

Offhand, it is unclear whether the fourth source of order transformation, that is, the relative decline of the hegemon, is necessarily inferior to Cooley and Nexon's preferred three in contributing to order transformation. Imagine if there were no great power rivals or counter-movements but instead of power transition there was hegemonic relative decline. Would we not anticipate some likelihood of order transformation, if only decay? Since the original theory does not suggest differential weights for the three explicit sources of transformation, perhaps it is best to leave this question open-ended. Presumably, the important core of the theory is the decline in the provision of public, club, and private goods on the part of the hegemon even though other actors may be generating alternative goods. But even so, just how the order will be transformed is also left open-ended. The order could disappear entirely or remain in weakened form. The only thing that we should not anticipate, given three to four sources of transformation in play, is that the order will survive unaltered.

If the consensus is that the current world order is deteriorating, what should we expect in years to come—more of the same, something radically different, or something in between? Resistance to the prevailing order seems likely to increase given Chinese gains in its economic standing. That alone suggests that more of the same is not likely for long if we assume that power distributions are important foundations for order construction and maintenance and that decision makers find it difficult to adjust orders to accommodate shifts in the material foundation for the order. At the same time, something radically different seems unlikely because major power warfare and/or a very high level of concentration

---

[13] J. A. Thompson insists that US prosperity and security are less closely linked to world order maintenance than most people think. His argument on these scores seems a bit stretched but the emphasis on the subjective perceptions that predominate in domestic politics is well taken.

in technological innovation and the power that comes with it appear to be low probability developments for decades to come.

That leaves something in between. In this regard, Macaes (2019) offers four scenarios for the future. In all four China's economy continues to expand and standards of living approach Western levels. In the first two scenarios, China's political and economic systems converge on Western models. In scenario 1, China becomes one of the two most powerful states in the world economy with a G2 approach predominating on the most important issues. In scenario 2, China replaces the United States as the leading power but retains most of the features of the liberal world order. Scenario 3 also has China becoming the center of the world economy and world system but in this future Chinese preferences reconfigure values and structures as the new hegemon. Scenario 4 portrays division in the world economy and world system with the United States retaining some centrality in the West and China becoming the center of a separate sphere of influence. While some economic interdependence may persist, the rival spheres tend to operate autonomously in terms of rules and institutions. Conflict between the coexisting spheres is also persistent.

For Macaes, there is no evidence of convergence in Chinese and Western domestic political and economic models. That lacuna rules out scenarios 1 and 2. Scenario 3 is seen as unlikely to come about at least in the first half of the twenty-first century. China is likely to become increasingly central to the world economy but not so central by 2050 that the rest of the world will be forced to accept subordination to Beijing's preferences. Scenario 4 would seem to win by default.

But we do not have to come to it as a default option. It also seems the most probable outcome given US relative decline, Chinese gains, and the difficulties of adjusting formulas for sharing power and privilege in world politics. How might these rival spheres of influence evolve? They are already evolving with shifts in trade orientations. Table 10.4 offers a bird's-eye view of these shifts.

Focusing on an aggregated index of trade "exposure" or an indicator of how much an actor depends on interactions with another actor and a proxy for world orientation (composed of indicators for the seven largest national economies), the economic significance of China to the rest of the world has tripled in seventeen years, while the United States' significance has declined by some 22 percent. US exposure or significance to the rest of the world remains ahead of China's but their positions are converging. Note also that both of the big 2's own exposure to the rest of the world remains less than the world's dependency on either of the big 2. Yet China's exposure to the rest of the world is declining while the exposure of the United States is increasing (compare columns 3 and 5).

Table 10.4 China, United States, and World Exposures to One Another

Year	World exposure to China	China exposure to world	World exposure to US	US exposure to world
2000	.4	.8	1.8	.8
2007	.7	.9	1.6	.7
2012	1.1	.7	1.4	.9
2017	1.2	.6	1.4	.9

Source: based on information reported in Woetzel et al. (2019: 46–47).

Of course, this process is highly uneven. Woetzal et al. (2019) make the case (table 10.5) that trade dependency on China is increasing among states that are regionally proximate, export sizeable natural resources, or need external capital. Developed economies tend to be less dependent.[14] Thus, China's sphere of influence based on trade and FDI should be strongest by and large near its Eurasian borders with scattered connections to selected other states. These tendencies underline the importance of China's Belt and Road Initiative to improve connective infrastructure throughout Afro-Eurasia and Latin America. The project may be plagued by ambiguity and bad debts, but it is likely to expand and reinforce China's influence sphere, especially in Southeast and Central Asia where the project seems most active. Just how successful China's version of the earlier US Marshall Plan will be remains to be seen but, at the very least, the strong implication is that the East Asian home region for China is being expanded to incorporate adjacent regions.

The US trade profile in table 10.6 looks rather similar in some respects even though the denominators are different in the two tables. The two adjacent states, Canada and Mexico, rank high in trading share. Two resource-related states (Venezuela and Saudi Arabia) show up at the bottom of the 2010 list but, reflecting the possibly short-lived successes of fracking, not in the 2019 list. Yet the United States has closer ties with more developed economies than China does so far. It also has close links with states on Eurasia's eastern and maritime fringe such as South Korea, Japan, Taiwan, Vietnam, India, and Singapore.

Nonetheless, there are states and economies that are important to both the United States and China. They have some importance to one another. Chinese imports to the United States, US firms that utilize Chinese labor in China to

[14] Since the world proxy constructed in the previous table (table 10.3) is based primarily on developed economies, Woetzal et al.'s data suggest that the exposure calculations may be understating the rest of the world's exposure to China.

Table 10.5 Increasing Dependency on Chinese Trade

	Exports to China		Imports to China		FDI from China	
	2003–07	2013–17	2003–07	2013–17	2003–07	2013–17
Regional Proximity						
South Korea	8	11	4	6		
Malaysia	8	11	5	11		6
Philippines	12	8	6	14	6	
Singapore	10	11	12	18	2	5
Vietnam	3	11	6	13	3	
Resource-related						
Australia	4	16	3	7		3
Chile	5	13	3	10		
Costa Rica	9	9	2	5	3	
Ghana		8	5	18		4
South Africa	2	15	2	6		3
Capital Exposure						
Egypt			3	5	1	13
Pakistan			3	7	2	8
Peru	4	7		5	2	6
Portugal		2		3		
Developed Economies						
United States		2	3	6		
Germany	2	4	2	3		
Japan	4	5	3	5		
United Kingdom		2	2	5		2

Source: based on Woetzel et al. (2019: 53).
Note: Entries are % shares of domestic production (columns 2 and 3), domestic consumption (columns 4 and 5), and share of domestic investment (columns 6 and 7). Entries equal to or less than 1 percent have been deleted to simplify reading the table.

make products, and Chinese support for US public debt are three facets of the economic linkages between the two rivals. Another linkage that is more complex is that both economies participate heavily in the same global supply chains. In addition, however, the maritime fringe of East Asia is linked to both China and the United States in terms of trade and investment.

Table 10.6 Fifteen Top Trading Partners of the United States

Rank	2010		2019	
	State	% Share	State	% Share
1	Canada	16.5	Mexico	14.8
2	China	14.3	Canada	14.8
3	Mexico	12.3	China	13.5
4	Japan	5.7	Japan	5.3
5	Germany	4.1	Germany	4.5
6	United Kingdom	3.1	South Korea	3.2
7	South Korea	2.7	United Kingdom	3.2
8	France	2.1	France	2.3
9	Taiwan	1.9	India	2.2
10	Brazil	1.9	Taiwan	2.1
11	Netherlands	1.7	Netherlands	2.0
12	India	1.5	Italy	2.0
13	Singapore	1.5	Vietnam	1.9
14	Venezuela	1.4	Brazil	1.8
15	Saudi Arabia	1.3	Ireland	1.7

Data Source: US Census Bureau (2020).

Assuming limited decoupling of the Chinese and US economies in coming years, the trade patterns suggest the unlikelihood of completely autonomous spheres of influence for the two rivals.[15] There should be substantial overlap in parts of the world that implies some probability of retaining the existing order, or at least most of its parts. But orders can be thick or thin, as several observers have noted, and always less than universal. The old prewar, US-centric order should be thickest in North America and Western Europe, just as it has been in the past, and thinnest in Chinese spheres of influence in Eurasia. New rules and institutions, like the Shanghai Cooperation Organization, should emerge thickest within the Chinese influence zone.[16] In between these two structural

[15] Both the United States and China give the appearance of decoupling from their former supply chains, but it remains unclear just how far decoupling can go without paralyzing the world economy.

[16] Three types of states are members of this organization ostensibly focused on regional security but also regional development. Full members include China, India, Kazakhstan, Kyrgyzstan, Russia, Pakistan, Tajikistan, and Uzbekistan. Official Observers and presumably potential joiners are

andirons, some mixture of old and new (but more old than new) elements of order might be expected. This process could go on for several decades as long as the two potential order patrons, the incumbent and the challenger, are unable to drive the other out of business—and assuming, further, that both rivals remain relatively competitive as patrons of order.

This pattern will not resemble an amalgam of the best of both worlds. The old order is showing its age and needs reform. Yet reform, as in the construction of new orders, takes leadership. That leadership will be less evident in the future than it has been in the past. Whether the G2 or other elite states can step forward to help co-ordinate needed reforms is a conceivable but largely untested notion at the global level. There will be obvious cross-order, international problems to manage—climate change and disease control, for instance, will not respect spheres of influence. Maybe if these problems become severe enough, cross-order set of governance rules and institutions can be negotiated. They will be needed for sure. Whether they can be agreed upon in time to do any good is another question entirely.

What seems most likely is that the prevailing order will linger on in large but diminishing parts of the world. Perhaps it is more appropriate to suggest that parts of the prevailing order will linger on if one takes the position that the order encompasses a number of different issue areas.[17] Each of the issue areas may have a separate decay function or work in some places better than in others. That has been the case all along but now more decay is evident on a wider variety of topics.

We can give Joseph Nye (2019) almost the last word on the world order:

The terms "liberal international order" or "Pax Americana" have become obsolete as descriptions of the US place in the world, but the need for the largest countries to provide public goods remains. . . . It remains to be seen . . . what will remain as the 1945 package is unpacked. . . . Throughout the seven decades of American pre-eminence after 1945, there have always been degrees of leadership and degrees of influence. Now, with less preponderance and in a more complex world, American exceptionalism should focus on sharing the provision of global public goods.

Afghanistan, Belarus, Iran, and Mongolia. Dialogue Partners are Armenia, Azerbaijan, Cambodia, Nepal, Sri Lanka, and Turkey. Not too surprisingly, many of these same states have been closely linked to elements of the Chinese Belt and Road Initiative.

[17] Iain Johnston (2019) argues for there being multiple order in different domains to which states respond differentially. Some are contested, while others are tolerated as useful and fitting. But rather than try to juggle a large number of narrow orders, it seems more efficient to portray one order with a number of different issue areas of varying strength. Johnston's basic point that states do not necessarily reject orders in their entirety but, rather, they dispute specific parts, can be retained as a pertinent observation.

As noted earlier in this chapter, Nye has always been reluctant to acknowledge that US relative decline translates to a reduced probability of systemic leadership and order maintenance. The years of Trump appear to have lessened his resistance to the notion of relative decline. Even so, for him the United States remains the largest state and therefore retains the best position for leadership and order production. Yet why would a lead point to the necessity of sharing the provision of public goods? The truth is that it is not enough to just be the largest state. Over time, predominance gives way to something less imposing. "Less preponderance and [more complexity]" means that leadership and public goods will depend even more than in the past on coordinating the cooperation of multiple actors. Would-be US leaders will have to work harder to obtain results that would have been much easier to achieve in long-gone, more preponderant days. No doubt, US decision makers will return to attempts at leadership once the America First focus fades from the scene (assuming that it does soon and quickly before more damage is done to the US alliance network). Yet Nye is right that the 1945 order package has become increasingly obsolete. While the need for public goods is not going away, that does not mean that their supply will match the demand—a demand that is likely to expand in a world beset by global pandemics, global warming, and energy transitions. If anything, the gap between the supply of, and demand for, order is apt to grow larger as time goes by and the setting for systemic leadership erodes further.

There is still time and room for the exercise of selective US systemic leadership. The future for this exercise is less than infinite. Nor will it resemble the systemic leadership of the Cold War era, or even the "unipolar" post–Cold War era. Those days are gone, and the 1950s cannot be resurrected unless there is also a way to resurrect the systemic context of that time. The post-1945 international order remains a suit that no longer fits as well as it once did. It will need repair and perhaps revision—not of the wholesale variety because the context precludes the emergence of a new order, but something more piecemeal is possible. The system leader linked to this tattered order will need to relearn old tricks of coordinating partners and allies in a world that many scholars have observed has become more complex and where power is less concentrated. Neither retrenchment nor restoration (Burns, 2020; Cooley and Nexon, 2020b) will bring back the old style of American primacy. Only a new style of genuine coalition building will suffice to keep the old order afloat. It may be true that "no other country has the resources, networks, and history to support cooperation" on a global scale (Suri, 2020). But that is simply no longer enough in a world in which the leading state's lead over other states has eroded significantly. US statesmen and those of its allies, as well as its rivals, will need to exert more agency in the face of an altered systemic context of less evident power concentration and hierarchy if they wish to achieve some minimal level of coordination and cooperation on global problems. They are likely to fall short of doing what needs to be done, but the seriousness of global problems will continue to compel efforts to coordinate. Ultimately, but not all that soon, a different and more sophisticated approach to global governance other than relying so much on the leading state will need to be developed. Until then, we will need to make do with patchwork solutions put together by ad hoc coalitions of states organized for that purpose. That is why we will also continue to rely on some form of systemic leadership, however diminished, to facilitate the construction and maintenance of those international coalitions.

References

Abramowitz, A. I. 2018. *The Great Realignment: Race, Party Transformation and the Rise of Donald Trump*. New Haven, CT: Yale University Press.

Acharya, A. 2003–2004. "Will Asia's Past Be Its Future?" *International Security* 28,3: 149–164.

Acharya, A. 2014. *The End of American World Order*. New York: Polity.

Adshead, S. A. M. 1993. *Central Asia in World History*. New York: St. Martin's..

Aistrup, J. A. 1996. *The Southern Strategy Revisited: Republican Top-Down Advancement in the South*. Lexington: University Press of Kentucky.

Alagappa, M. 2014. "International Peace in Asia: Will It Endure?" *The Asian Forum, December 19*. Theasianforum.org/international-peace-in-asia-will-it-endure.

Alba, R. 2016. "The Likely Persistence of a White Majority." *The American Prospect*, January 11. Prospect.org/civil-rights/likely-persistence-white-majority/.

Alberta, T. 2019. "When Impeachment Meets a Broken Congress." *Politico*, September 27. https://www.politico.com/magazine/story/2019/09/27/impeachment-trump-congress-house-228346.

Alden, E. 2017. *Failure to Adjust: How Americans Got Left Behind in the Global Economy*. Lanham, MD: Rowman & Littlefield.

Alden, E., and Strauss, R. 2016. *How America Stacks Up: Economic Competitiveness and U.S. Policy*. New York: Council on Foreign Relations.

Alderson, A. S., Beckfield, J., and Sprague-Jones, J. 2010. "Intercity Relations and Globalisation: The Evolution of the Global Urban Hierarchy, 1981–2007." *Urban Studies* 47,9: 1899–1923.

Alexseev, M. A. 1997. *Without Warning: Threat Assessment, Intelligence and Global Struggle*. New York: Palgrave Macmillan.

Allison, G. 2017. *Destined for War: America, China and Thucydides' Trap*. Boston: Houghton Mifflin Harcourt.

AlMukhtar, S., and Nordland, R. 2019. "What Did the U.S. Get for $2 Trillion in Afghanistan?" *New York Times*, December 9. www.nytimes.com/interactive/2019/12/09/world/middleeast/Afghanistan-war-cost.html.

Ambrose, S. 1988. *America's Rise to Globalism: American Foreign Policy since 1938*. New York: Penguin.

Ambrosius, L. E. 2002. *Wilsonianism: Woodrow Wilson and His Legacy in American Foreign Relations*. New York: Palgrave Macmillan.

Anderson, F., and Cayton, A. 2005. *The Dominion of War: Empire and Liberty in North America, 1500–2000*. New York: Viking.

Atack, J., Bateman, F. and Margo, R. 2008. "Steam Power, Establishment Size, and Labor Productivity Growth in Nineteenth Century American Manufacturing." *Explorations in Economic History* 45: 185–197.

Atkinson, R. D. 2004. *The Past and Future of America's Economy: Long Waves of Innovation That Power Cycles of Growth*. Cheltenham, UK: Edward Elgar.

Atkinson, R. D., and Ezell, S. J. 2012. *Innovation Economics: The Race for Global Advantage*. New York: Oxford University Press.

Atkinson, R. D., and Foote, C. 2019. "Is China Catching Up to the United States in Innovation." Information Technology and Innovation Foundation. http://www2.itif.org/2019-china-catching-up-innovation.pdf.

Attina, F. 2019. "The Life Cycle of World Order and China's Coalition Power in the Global South." Paper delivered at the International Studies Conference, Accra, Ghana, August 1–3.

Axe, D. 2020. "Superpower or Not? Is America in Decline? Here's What an Expert Told Us." *National Interest*, January 20. Nationalinterest.org/blog/buzz/superpower-or-not-america-decline-heres-what-expert-told-us-115451.

Bacevich, A. J. 2008. *The Limits of Power: The End of American Exceptionalism*. New York: Holt McDougal.

Bacevich, A. J. 2016. *America's War for the Greater Middle East: A Military History*. New York: Random House.

Bailey, M. N., and Bosworth, B. P. 2014. "US Manufacturing: Understanding Its Past and Its Potential Future." *Journal of Economic Perspectives* 28,1: 3–26.

Bairoch, P. 1982. "International Industrialization Levels for 1750 to 1980." *Journal of European Economic History* 11,1–2: 269–333.

Balmer, R. 2014. "The Real Origins of the Religious Right." *Politico*, May 27. https://www.politico.com/magazine/story/2014/05/religious-right-real-origins-107133.

Barbier, E. B. 2011. *Scarcity and Frontiers: How Economies Have Developed through Natural Resource Exploitation*. Cambridge: Cambridge University Press.

Barnett, T. P. M. 2009. *Great Powers: America and the World after Bush*. New York: G. P. Putnam's Sons.

Beardson, T. 2013. *Stumbling Giant: The Threats to China's Future*. New Haven, CT: Yale University Press.

Beckley, M. 2011/12. "China's Century? Why America's Edge Will Endure." *International Security* 36,3: 41–78.

Beckley, M. 2018. *Unrivaled: Why America Will Remain the World's Sole Superpower*. Ithaca, NY: Cornell University Press.

Behm, A. 2019. "The Decline of US Global Leadership: Power without Authority." *The Interpreter*, October 7. Lowry Institute. Lowryinstitute.org/the-interpreter/decline-us-global-leadership-power-without-authority..

Berger, T. 2000. "Set for Stability? Prospects for Conflict and Cooperation in East Asia." *Review of International Studies* 26: 405–428.

Berman, M. 2011. *Why America Failed: The Roots of American Decline*. New York: John Wiley.

Binder, S. 2015. "The Dysfunctional Congress." *Annual Review of Political Science* 18: 85–101.

Birch, D. 2013. "The USSR and US Came Closer to Nuclear War Than We Thought." *The Atlantic*, May 28. Theatlantic.com/international/archive/2013/05/the-ussr-and-us-came-closer-to-nuclear war-than-we-thought/276290/.

Biswas, R. 2013. *Future Asia: The New Gold Rush in the East*. New York: Palgrave Macmillan.

Black, B. C. 2012. *Crude Reality: Petroleum in World History*. Lanham, MD: Rowman & Littlefield.

Black, C. 2003. *Franklin Delano Roosevelt*. New York: Public Affairs.

Boseley, S. 2020. "US Secures World Stock of Key Covid-19 Drug Remdesivir," *The Guardian*, June 30. Theguardian.com/us-news/2020/us-buys-up-world-stake-of-key-covid-19-drug.

Boyd, J. 1970. "Nixon's Southern Strategy." *New York Times*, May 17. https://www.nytimes.com/1970/05/17/archives/nixons-southern-strategy-its-all-in-the-charts.html.

Brady, D. W., and Han, H. C. 2006. "Polarization Then and Now." *America's Polarized Politics*, edited by Pietro S. Nivola and David W. Brady. Washington, DC: Brookings Institution Press.

Brands, H. W. 2003. *Woodrow Wilson*. New York: Henry Holt.

Braumoeller, B. F. 2012. *The Great Powers and the International System: Systemic Theory in Empirical Perspective*. Cambridge: Cambridge University Press.

Braumoeller, B. F. 2019. *Only the Dead: The Persistence of War in the Modern Age*. New York: Oxford University Press.

Brooks, S. G., Ikenberry, G. J., and Wohlforth, W. C. 2013. "Don't Come Home, America: The Case Against Retrenchment." *International Security* 37,3: 7–51.

Brooks, S. G., and Wohlforth, W. C. 2008. *World Out of Balance: International Relations and the Challenge of American Primacy*. Princeton, NJ: Princeton University Press.

Brooks, S. G., and Wohlforth, W. C. 2015. "The Rise and Fall of the Great Powers in the Twenty-first Century: China's Rise and the Fate of America's Global Position." *International Security* 40,3: 7–53.

Brooks, S. G., and Wohlforth, W. C. 2016a. "The Once and Future Superpower: Why China Won't Overtake the United States." *Foreign Affairs* 95,3: 91–104.

Brown, S. S. 2013. *The Future of U.S. Global Power: Delusions of Decline*. New York: Palgrave Macmillan.

Brzezinski, Z. 2012. *Strategic Vision: America and the Crisis of Global Power*. New York: Basic Books.

Buck, R. 2015. *The Oregon Trail: A New American Journey*. New York: Simon & Schuster.

Bueno de Mesquita, B. 1975. "Measuring Systemic Polarity." *Journal of Conflict Resolution*, 19: 187–216.

Bulmer-Thomas, V. 2018. *Empire in Retreat: The Past, Present, and Future of the United States*. New Haven, CT: Yale University Press.

Burns, W. J. 2020. "The United States Needs a New Foreign Policy." *The Atlantic*, July 14. The atlantic.com/ideas/archive/2020/07/united-states-nees-new-foreign-policy/614110/

Busby, J. W., and Monten, J. 2008. "Without Heirs? Assessing the Decline of Establishment Internationalism in U.S. Foreign Policy." *Perspectives on Politics* 6: 451–472.

Buzan, B. 2004. *The United States and the Great Powers: World Politics in the Twenty-first Century*. Cambridge: Polity.

Buzan, B. 2011. "A World Order without Superpowers: Decentralized Globalization." *International Relations* 25,1: 3–25.

Buzan, B., and Lawson, G. 2015. *The Global Transformation: History, Modernity, and the Making of International Relations*. Cambridge: Cambridge University Press.

Campbell, J. E. 2006. "Polarization Runs Deep, Even by Yesterday's Standards." In *America's Polarized Politics*, edited by Pietro S. Nivola and David W. Brady. Washington, DC: Brookings Institution Press.

Campbell, J. L. 2018. *American Discontent: The Rise of Donald Trump and Decline of the Golden Age*. New York: Oxford University Press.

Case, A., and Deaton, A. 2017. "Mortality and Morbidity in the 21st Century." Brookings.edu/wp-content/uploads/2017/08/casetextsp17bpea.pdf.

Case, A., and Deaton, A. 2020. *Deaths of Despair and the Future of Capitalism*. Princeton, NJ: Princeton University Press.

Cassis, Y. 2006. *Capitals of Capital: A History of International Financial Centres, 1780–2005*. Cambridge: Cambridge University Press.

Cedarman, L.-E. 2001. "Back to Kant: Reinterpreting the Democratic Peace as a Macrohistorical Learning Process." *American Political Science Review* 95,1: 15–31.

Cha, V. D. 2012. "Ripe for Rivalry." *Foreign Policy*, December 13. https://foreignpolicy.com/2012/12/13/ripe-for-rivalry/.

Chan, S. 2013. *Enduring Rivalries in the Asia-Pacific*. Cambridge: Cambridge University Press.

Chan, S. 2020. *Thucydides' Trap: Historical Interpretation, Logic of Inquiry, and the Future of Sino-American Relations*. Ann Arbor: University of Michigan Press.

Chan, S., and Hu, R. W. 2015. "East Asia's Enduring Rivalries: Ripe for Abatement?" *Journal of Asian Security and International Affairs* 2,2: 133–153.

Chase-Dunn, C., Kwon, K., Lawrence, K., and Inoue, H. 2011. "Last of the Hegemons: U.S. Decline and Global Governance." *International Review of Modern Sociology* 37,1: 1–29.

lark, S., and Hogue, S., eds. 2012. *Debating a Post-American World: What Lies Ahead*. London: Routledge.

Clements, K. A. 1999. *Woodrow Wilson: World Statesman*. Chicago: Ivan R. Dee.

Coaston, J. 2018. "In 2018, The Tea Party Is All In for Trump." *Vox*, May 16. https://www.vox.com/2018/5/15/17263774/tea-party-trump-2018.

Cohen, E. A. 1994. "The Strategy of Innocence? The United States, 1920–1945." In *The Making of Strategy: Rulers, States, and War*, edited by Williamson Murray, MacGregor Knox, and Alvin Bernstein. Cambridge: Cambridge University Press.

Colaresi, M. P. 2001. "Shocks to the System: Great Power Rivalry and Leadership Long-cycle." *Journal of Conflict Resolution* 45,5: 569–593.

Cooley, A., and Nexon, D. 2020a. *Exit from Hegemony: The Unraveling of the American Global Order*. New York: Oxford University Press.

Cooley, A., and Nexon, D. 2020b. "How Hegemony Ends: The Unraveling of American Power." *Foreign Affairs*, July/August. https://www.foreignaffairs.com/articles/united-states/2020-06-09/how-hegemony-ends.

Cooper, J. M. 2001. *Breaking the Heart of the World: Woodrow Wilson and the Fight for the League of Nations*. Cambridge: Cambridge University Press.

Council of Economic Advisors. 2019. "The Full Cost of the Opioid Crisis: $2.5 Trillion over Four Years." October 28. trumpwhitehouse.archives/articles/full-cost-opioid-crisis-2-5-trillion-four-years/.

Cowen, T. 2016. "Is Innovation Over?" *Foreign Affairs* 95,2: 42–46.

Craig, M. A., and Richeson, J. A. 2014. "On the Precipice of a 'Majority-Minority' America: Perceived Status Threat from the Perceived Demographic Shift Affects White Americans' Political ideology." *Psychological Science* 25,6: 1189–1197.

Cramer, K. J. J. 2016. *The Politics of Resentment: Rural Consciousness in Wisconsin and the Rise of Scott Walker*. Chicago: University of Chicago Press.

Crawford, N. C. 2019. "United States Budgetary Costs and Obligations of Post-9/11 Wars through FY2020: $6.4 Trillion." Costs of War Project, Watson Institute, Brown University. Watson.brown.edu/costsofwar/files/cow/imce/papers/2019/US%20Budgetary%20Costs%20of%20Wars%20November%202019.pdf.

Daggett, Stephen. 2010. "Costs of Major U.S. Wars." Congressional Research Service. Sgp.fas.org/crs/natsec/RS22926.pdf.

Dallek, Robert. 1979. *Franklin D. Roosevelt and American Foreign Policy, 1932–1945.* Oxford: Oxford University Press.

Dasgupta, Nabarun, Beletsky, Leo, and Ciccarone, Daniel. 2018. "Opioid Crisis: No Easy Fix to Its Social and Economic Determinants." *American Journal of Public Health* 108,2: 182–186.

Davis, Jeff. 2016. "The 70-Year Trend in Federal Infrastructure Spending." *ENO Transportation Weekly,* May 12. https://www.enotrans.org/article/70-year-trend-fede ral-infrastructure-spending/.

DeBruyne, N. F. 2017. "American War and Military Operations Casualties: Lists and Statistics." Congressional Research Service Report 7-5700. At sgp.fas.org/crs/natsec/RS22926pdf.

Dehio, L. 1962. *The Precarious Balance: Four Centuries of the European Power Struggle,* translated by Charles Fullman. New York: Alfred A. Knopf.

Deutsch, K. W., and Singer, J. D. 1964. "Multipolar Power Systems and International Stability." *World Politics* 16: 390–406.

De Weerdt, S. 2019. "Tracing the US Opioid Crisis to Its Roots." *Nature,* September 11. https://www.nature.com/articles/d41586-019-02686-2.

DiCicco, J. M., and Levy, J. S. 1999. "Power Shifts and Problem Shifts: The Evolution of the Power Transition Research Program." *Journal of Conflict Resolution* 43,6: 675–704.

Douthat, R. 2020. *The Decadent Society: How We Became the Victims of Our Own Success.* New York: Simon & Schuster.

Dowland, S. 2015. *Family Values and the Rise of the Christian Right.* Philadelphia: University of Pennsylvania Press.

Dueck, C. 2006. *Reluctant Crusaders: Power, Culture and Change in American Grand Strategy.* Princeton, NJ: Princeton University Press.

Dutta, S., Lanvin, B., and Wunsch-Vincent, S., eds. 2019. "Global Innovation Index 2019." Geneva: World Intellectual Property Organization. Wipo.int/publications/en/details.jsp?=4434.

Eckes, A. E., Jr., and Zeiler, T. W. 2003. *Globalization and the American Century.* Cambridge: Cambridge University Press.

Edelman, E. S. 2010. "The Broken Consensus: America's Contested Primacy." *World Affairs* 173,4: 51–60.

Edelstein, D. M. 2017. *Over the Horizon: Time, Uncertainty, and the Rise of Great Powers.* Ithaca, NY: Cornell University Press.

Ellis, J. 1990. *Brute Force: Allied Strategy and Tactics in the Second World War.* New York: Viking.

Engelhardt, T. 2018. "What Caused the United States' Decline?" *The Nation,* June 14. https://www.thenation.com/article/archive/caused-united-states-decline/.

Erlanger, S. 2020. "Another Virus Victim: The U.S. as a Global Leader in a Time of Crisis." *New York Times,* March 22. https://www.nytimes.com/2020/03/20/world/europe/trump-leadership-coronavirus-united -states.html.

Ewart, S. 2015. "US Population Trends: 2000 to 2060." Washington DC: US Census. US Department of Commerce. Ncsl.org/Portals/1/Documents/nalfo/USDemographics.pdf.

Fair, R. C. 2021. "U.S. Infrastructure, 1929–2019." Unpublished paper at fairmodel.econ.yale.edu/ray/fair/pdf/2019D.PDF.

Fallows, J. 2010. "How America Can Rise Again." *The Atlantic,* January/February. https://www.theatlantic.com/magazine/archive/2010/01/how-america-can-rise-again/307839/.

Fallows, J. 2013. "The 50 Greatest Breakthroughs since the Wheel." *The Atlantic*, November. https://www.theatlantic.com/magazine/archive/2013/11/innovation-list/309536/.

Farina, Cynthia R. 2015. "Congressional Polarization: Terminal Constitutional Dysfunction?" *Columbia Law Review* 115,7: 1689–1738. https://columbialawreview.org/content/congressional-polarization-terminal-constitutional-dysfunction/.

Farrell, H., and Newman, A. L. 2020. "Chained to Globalization: Why It's Too Late to Decouple." *Foreign Affairs* 99,1: 70–80.

Farrow, R. 2018. *War on Peace: The End of Diplomacy and the Decline of American Influence*. New York: W. W. Norton.

Fearon, P. 1987. *War, Prosperity and Depression: The US Economy, 1917–45*. Lawrence: University Press of Kansas.

Federal Reserve Bank of St. Louis. 2020. "All Employees, Manufacturing." St. Louis, Mo. https://fred.stlouisfed.org/series/MANEMP.

Ferguson, T. 1989. "Industrial Conflict and the Coming of the New Deal: The Triumph of Multinational Liberalism in America." In *The Rise and Fall of the New Deal Order, 1930–1980*, edited by Steve Fraser and Gary Gerstle. Princeton, NJ: Princeton University Press.

Fettweis, C. J. 2017. "Unipolarity, Hegemony, and the New Peace." *Security Studies* 26,3: 423–451.

Flaaen, A., and Pierce, J. 2019. "Disentangling the Effects of the 2018–2019 Tariffs on a Globally Connected U.S. Manufacturing Sector." Finance and Economics Discussion Series, 2019-086. Washington, DC: Board of Governors of the Federal Reserve System. https://doi.org/10.17016/FEDS.2019.086.

Fordham, B. O. 2007. "Revisionism Revisited: Exports and American Intervention in World War I." *International Organization* 61: 277–310.

Fountain, B. 2016. "American Crossroads: Reagan, Trump and the Devil Down South: How the Republican Party's Dog Whistle Appeal to Racism, Refined by Richard Nixon and Perfected by Ronald Reagan Led Inexorably to Donald Trump." *The Guardian*, March 5. https://www.theguardian.com/us-news/2016/mar/05/trump-reagan-nixon-republican-party-racism.

Freeman, C., and Perez, C. 1988. "Structural Crises of Adjustment, Business Cycles and Investment Behavior." In *Technical Change and Economic Theory*, edited by Giovanni Dosi, Christopher Freeman, Richard Nelson, Gerald Silverberg, and Luc Soete. London: Pinter.

Friedberg, A. L. 1993–1994. "Ripe for Rivalry: Prospects for Peace in a Multipolar Asia." *International Security* 18,3: 5–33.

Friedberg, A. L. 2011. *A Contest for Supremacy: China, America, and the Struggle for Mastery in Asia*. New York: W. W. Norton.

Frieden, J. A. 1988. "Sectoral Conflict and U.S Foreign Economic Policy, 1914–1940." *International Organization* 42: 59–90.

Friedman, T. 2005. *The World Is Flat: Hot, Flat, and Crowded*. New York: Farrar, Straus & Giroux.

Friedman, T., and Mandelbaum, M. 2011. *That Used to Be Us: How America Fell Behind in the World It Invented and How We Can Come Back*. New York: Farrar, Straus & Giroux.

Fry, R., and Stepler, R. 2017. "Women May Never Make Up Half of the US Workforce." Pew Research Center, January 3. https://www.pewresearch.org/fact-tank/2017/01/31/women-may-never-make-up-half-of-the-u-s-workforce/.

lb, L. 2009. *Power Rules: How Common Sense Can Rescue American Foreign Policy.* New York: HarperCollins.

Genovese, M. A., and Belt, T. A. 2016. *The Post-Heroic Presidency: Leveraged Leadership in the Age of Limits.* 2nd ed. Santa Barbara, CA: ABC-CLIO.

Gilberstadt, H., and Daniller, A. 2020. "Liberals Make Up the Largest Share of Democratic Voters, but Their Growth Has Slowed in Recent Years." Pew Research Center, January 17. https://www.pewresearch.org/fact-tank/2020/01/17/liberals-make-up-largest-share-of-democratic-voters/.

Glanz, J., and Robertson, C. 2020. "Lockdown Delays Cost at Least 36,000 Lives, Data Show." *New York Times,* May 20. https:/www.nytimes.com/2020/05/20/us/coronavirus-distancing-deaths.html.

Go, J. 2011. *Patterns of Empire: The British and American Empires, 1688 to Present.* New York: Cambridge University Press.

Goddard, S. E. 2018. *When Right Makes Might: Rising Powers and World Order.* Ithaca, NY: Cornell University Press.

Gordon, R. J. 2016. *The Rise and Fall of American Growth: The US Standard of Living since the Civil War.* Princeton, NJ: Princeton University Press.

Gourevitch, P. 1978. "The Second Image Reversed: The International Sources of Domestic Politics." *International Organization* 32,4: 881–912.

Gourevitch, P. 1986. *Politics in Hard Times: Comparative Responses to International Economic Crises.* Ithaca, NY: Cornell University Press.

Gowa, J. 1989. "Rational Hegemons, Excludable Goods, and Small Groups: An Epitaph for Hegemonic Stability Theory." *World Politics* 41,3: 307–324.

Gowa, J., and Ramsay, K. W. 2017. "Gulliver Untied: Entry Deterrence Uunder Unipolarity." *International Organization* 71, 3: 459–490.

Gray, R., and Peterson, J. M. 1974. *Economic Development of the United States.* Homewood, IL: Richard D. Irwin.

Grinin, L., and Korotayev, A. 2014. "Globalization Shuffles Cards of the World Pack: In Which Direction Is the Global Economic-Political Balance Shifting?" *World Futures* 70,8: 515–545.

Gross, D. 2012. *Better, Stronger, Faster: The Myth of American Decline and the Rise of a New Economy.* New York: Free Press.

Gruber, J., and Johnson, S. 2019. *Jump-starting America: How Breakthrough Science Can Revive Economic Growth and the American Dream.* New York: Public Affairs Press.

Guillory, F. 2019. "Southern Strategy: From Nixon to Trump." *Southern Cultures* 253 https://www.southerncultures.org/article/southern-strategy-from-nixon-to-trump/.

Haberman, C. 2018. "Religion and Right-Wing Politics: How Evangelicals Reshaped Elections." *New York Times,* October 28. https://www.nytimes.com/2018/10/28/us/religion-politics-evangelicals.html.

Hachigian, N., and Sutphen, M. 2008. *The Next American Century: How the US Can Thrive as Others Rise.* New York: Simon & Schuster.

Hacker, L. M. 1970. *The Course of American Economic Growth and Development.* New York: John Wiley.

Hannah, L. 1998. "Marshal's 'Trees' and the Global 'Forest': Were 'Giant Redwoods' Different?" In *Learning by Doing in Markets, Firms, and Countries,* edited by N. R. Lamereux, D. M. G. Raff, and P. Temin. Chicago: University of Chicago Press.

Hannah, L. 1999. "The World's Largest Industrial Firms, 1912, 1937, 1962, and 1987." Unpublished paper.

Hansen, B. 2012. *Unipolarity and World Politics: A Theory and Its Implications.* London: Routledge.

Hansen, C. 2000. "The Oops List." *Bulletin of the Atomic Scientists* 56,6: 64–67.

Harrison, M. 2016. "World War II: Won by American Planes and Ships, or by the Poor Bloody Russian Infantry." *Journal of Strategic Studies* 39,4: 592–598.

Hawkings, D. 2018. "The 5 M's for Describing Why Congress Is Broken." *Roll Call*, July 26. Rollcall.com/2018/07/26/the-5-ms-for-describing-why-congress-is-broken/.

He, Y. 2008. "Ripe for Cooperation or Rivalry? Commerce, Realpolitik, and War Memory in Contemporary Sino-Japanese Relations." *Asian Security* 4: 162–197.

Heath, T. R., and Thompson, W. R. 2017. "US-China Tensions Are Unlikely to Lead to War." *National Interest*, April 30. https://nationalinterest.org/feature/us-china-tensi ons-are-unlikely-lead-war-20411.

Heer, J. 2016. "How the Southern Strategy Made Donald Trump Possible." *The New Republic*, February 18. https://newrepublic.com/article/130039/southern-strategy- made-donald-trump-possible.

Heginbotham, E., Nixon, M., Morgan, F. G., Hein, J. L., Hagen, J., Sheng, L., Engstrom, J., Libicki, M. C., DeLuca, P., Shlapak, D. A., Frelinger, D. R., Laird, B., Brady, K., and Morris, L. J. 2015. *The U.S.-China Military Scorecard: Forces, Geography, and the Evolving Balance of Power, 1996–2017.* Santa Monica, CA: Rand.

Hermann, C. F. 1990. "Changing Course: When Governments Choose to Redirect Foreign Policy." *International Studies Quarterly* 34,1: 3–21.

Higgs, R. 1987. *Crisis and Leviathan: Critical Episodes in the Growth of American Government.* New York: Oxford University Press.

Hopf, T. 1991. "Polarity, the Offense Defense Balance, and War." *American Political Science Review*, 85: 475–493.

Hubbard, G. R., and Navarro, P. 2011. *Seeds of Destruction: Why the Path to Economic Ruin Runs through Washington and How to Reclaim American Prosperity.* Upper Saddle River, NJ: FT Press.

Huntington, S. P. 1988/89. "The US—Decline or Renewal?" *Foreign Affairs* 67,2: 76–96.

Ikenberry, G. J. 2001. *After Victory: Institutions, Strategic Restraint, and the Rebuilding of Order after Major Wars.* Princeton, NJ: Princeton University Press.

Ikenberry, G. J. 2011. *Liberal Leviathan: The Origins, Crisis, and Transformation of the American World Order.* Princeton, NJ: Princeton University Press.

Ikenberry, G. J. 2018a. "The End of Liberal International Order?" *International Affairs* 94,1: 7–23.

Ikenberry, G. J. 2018b. "Why the Liberal World Order Will Survive." *Ethics and International Affairs* 32,1: 17–29.

Ikenberry, G. J., Mastanduno, M., and Wohlforth, W. C., eds. 2011. *International Relations Theory and the Consequences of Unipolarity.* Cambridge: Cambridge University Press.

Inglehart, R. F. 2018. *Cultural Evolution: People's Motivations Are Changing, and Reshaping the World.* Cambridge: Cambridge University Press.

Itzkowitz Shifrinson, J. R. 2018. *Rising Titans, Falling Giants: How Great Powers Exploit Power Shifts.* Ithaca, NY: Cornell University Press.

Itzkowitz Shrifrinson, J. R., and Beckley, M. 2012/2113. "Correspondence: Debating Decline." *International Security* 37,3: 172–177.

Iyengar, S., Lelkes, Y., Levendesky, M., Malhotra, N., and Westwood, S. J. 2019. "The Origins and Consequences of Affective Polarization in the United States." *Annual Review of Political Science* 22: 129–146.

Jackson, J. K. 2017. "US Direct Investment Abroad: Trends and Current Issues." Congressional Research Service, RS 21118, June 29. https://sgp.fas.org/crs/misc/RS21 118.pdf.

Jacques, M. 2009. *When China Rules the World*. London: Penguin.

Jardina, A. 2019. *White Identity Politics*. Cambridge: Cambridge University Press.

Jewell, B. L., and Jewell, N. P. 2020. "The Huge Cost of Waiting to Contain the Pandemic." *New York Times*, April 14. https://www.nytimes.com/2020/04/14/opinion/covid-soc ial-distancing.html.

Joffe, J. 2009. "The Default Power: The False Prophecy of America's Decline." *Foreign Affairs* 88,5: 21–35.

Joffe, J. 2014. *The Myth of America's Decline: Politics, Economics, and a Half Century of False Prophecies*. New York: W. W. Norton.

Johnston, A. I. 2019. "China in a World of Orders: Rethinking Compliance and Challenge in Beijing's International Relations." *International Security* 44,2: 9–60.

Jones, C. F. 2014. *Routes of Power: Energy and Modern America*. Cambridge, MA: Harvard University Press.

Jurkowitz, M., Mitchell, A., Shearer, E., and Walker, M. 2020. "US Media Polarization and the 2020 Election: A Nation Divided." Pew Research Center, January 4. https://www. pewresearch.org/journalism/2020/01/24/u-s-media-polarization-and-the-2020-elect ion-a-nation-divided/.

Kagan, R. 2012. "Not Fade Away: Against the Myth of American Decline." The Brookings Institution, January 17. https://www.Brookings.edu/opinion/not-fade-away-against-the-myth-of-american-decline/.

Kai He. 2012. "Undermining Adversaries: Unipolarity, Threat Perception, and Negative Bandwagoning Strategies Aafter the Cold War." *Security Studies* 21,2: 154–191.

Kander, A. 2013. "The Second and Third Industrial Revolutions." In *Power to the People: Energy in Europe over the Past Five Centuries*, edited by Astrid Kander, Paola Malanima, and Paul Warde. Princeton, NJ: Princeton University Press.

Kang, D. 2003. "Getting Asia Wrong: The Need for New Analytical Frameworks." *International Security* 27,4: 57–85.

Katznelson I. 2002. "Rewriting the Epic of America," in Ira Katznelson and Martin Shefter, eds., *Shaped by War and Trade: International Influences on American Political Development*. Princeton, NJ: Princeton University Press.

Kaufmann, E. 2019. *Whiteshift: Populism, Immigration and the Future of White Majorities*. New York: Harry N. Abrams.

Kegley, C. W., Jr., and Raymond. G. A. 1994. *A Multi-Polar Peace? Great Power Politics in the Twenty-First Century*. New York: St. Martin's.

Kennedy, D. M. 1980. *Over Here: The First World War and American Society*. New York: Oxford University Press.

Kennedy, D. M. 1999. *Freedom from Fear: The American People in Depression and War*. New York: Oxford University Press.

Kennedy, D. M. 2004. *The First World War and American Society*. New York: Oxford University Press.

Kennedy, P. 1980. *The Rise of the Anglo-German Antagonism, 1860–1914*.

Kennedy, P. 1987. *The Rise and Fall of the Great Powers: Economic Change and Military Conflict from 1500 to 2000*. New York: Random House.

Keohane, R. 1984. *After Hegemony: Cooperation and Discord in the World Political Economy*. Princeton, NJ: Princeton University Press.

Keohane, R. 2012. "Hegemony and After: Knowns and Unknowns in the Debate over Decline." *Foreign Affairs* 91,4.

Kessler, G., Rizzo, S., and Kelly, M. 2020. "President Trump Made 16,241 False or Misleading Claims in His First Three Years." *Washington Post*, January 20. Washingtonpost.com/political/2020/01/20/president-trump-made16241-false-or-misleading-claims-his-first-three-years/.

Khanna, P. 2008. *The Second World: Empires and Influence in the New Global Order.* New York: Random House.

Khazan, O. 2020. "The True Cause of the Opioid Epidemic." *The Atlantic*, January 2. https:/www.theatlantic.com/health/archive/2020/01/what-caused-opioid-epidemic/604330/.

Khong, Y. F. 2013. "The American Tributary System." *Chinese Journal of International Politics* 6: 1–47.

Kingdon, J. W. 1995. *Agendas, Alternatives, and Public Policies.* 2nd ed. New York: HarperCollins.

Kinsella, W. E., Jr. 1978. *Leadership in Isolation: FDR and the Origins of the Second World War.* Cambridge, MA: Schenkman.

Kirshner, J. 2015. "The Economic Sins of Modern IR Theory and the Classical Realist Alternative." *World Politics* 67(1): 155–183.

Klein, M. 2007. *The Genesis of Industrial America, 1870–1920.* Cambridge: Cambridge University Press.

Kliman, D. M. 2014. *Fateful Transitions: How Democracies Manage Rising Powers, from the Eve of World War I to China's Ascendancy.* Philadelphia: University of Pennsylvania Press.

Knock, T. J. 1992. *To End All Wars: Woodrow Wilson and the Quest for a New World Order.* Princeton, NJ: Princeton University Press.

Koistenen, P. A. C. 1997. *Mobilizing for Modern War: The Political Economy of American Warfare, 1865–1919.* Lawrence: University Press of Kansas.

Koistenen, P. A. C. 1998. *Planning War, Pursuing Peace: The Political Economy of American Warfare, 1920–1939.* Lawrence: University Press of Kansas.

Koistenen, P. A. C. 2004. *Arsenal of the World: The Political Economy of American Warfare, 1940–1945.* Lawrence: University Press of Kansas.

Koistenen, P. A. C. 2012. *State of War: The Political Economy of American Warfare, 1945–2011.* Lawrence: University Press of Kansas.

Krasner, S. D. 1978 *Defending the National Interest: Raw Materials Investments and U.S. Foreign Policy.* Princeton, NJ: Princeton University Press.

Krauthammer, C. 1990/91. "The Unipolar Moment." *Foreign Affairs* 70: 23–33.

Kroenig, M. 2020. *The Return of Great Power Rivalry: Democracy versus Autocracy from the Ancient World to the United States and China.* New York: Oxford University Press.

Krogstad, J. M., Passel, J. S., and Cohn, D. 2019. "5 Facts about Illegal Immigration in the United States." June 12. Pew Research Center. https://www.pewresearch.org/fact-tank/2019/06/12/5-facts-about-illegal-immigration-in-the-u-s/.

Krueger, A. B. 2017. "Where Have All the Workers Gone? An Inquiry into the Decline of the US Labor Force Participation Rate." *Brookings Papers Economic Activities.* https://www.brookings.edu/wp-content/uploads/2017/09/1_krueger.pdf.

Krugman, P. 2020. *Arguing with Zombies: Economics, Politics, and the Fight for a Better Future.* New York: W. W. Norton.

Kupchan, C. A. 2011. *No One's World: The West, the Rising Rest, and the Coming Global Turn.* New York: Oxford University Press.

Kurtzleben, D. 2016. "Rural Voters Played a Big Part in Helping Trump Defeat Clinton." *NPR,* November 14. https://www.npr.org/2016/11/14/501737150/rural-voters-played-a-big-part-in-helping-trump-defeat-clinton.

Lake, D. A. 1991. "Leadership, Hegemony, and the International Economy: Naked Emperor or Tattered Monarch?" *International Studies Quarterly* 39,4: 459–489.

Lake, D. A. 1999. *Entangling Relations: American Foreign Policy in its Century.* Princeton, NJ: Princeton University Press.

Lake, D. A. 2009. *Hierarchy in International Relations* Ithaca, NY: Cornell University Press.

Layne, C. 1993. "The Unipolar Illusion: Why New Great Powers Will Rise." *International Security* 17,4: 5–51.

Layne, C. 2006. "The Unipolar Illusion Revisited: The Long End of the United States' Unipolar Moment." *International Security* 31,2: 7–41.

Layne, C. 2009. "The Waning of U.S. Hegemony: Myth or Reality?" *International Security* 34,1: 147–172.

Layne, C. 2012. "This Time It's Real: The End of Unipolarity and the Pax Americana." *International Studies Quarterly* 56,1: 203–213.

Layne, C. 2018. "The US-Chinese Power Shift and the End of the Pax Americana." *International Affairs* 94,1: 89–111.

Lebovic, J. H. 2018. "Unipolarity: The Shaky Foundation of a Fashionable Concept." In *Oxford Research Encyclopedia on Empirical Theories of International Relations,* edited by William R. Thompson. New York: Oxford University Press.

Lee, M. J., and Thompson, W. R. 2018. "Major Powers vs. Global Powers: A New Measure of Global Reach and Power Projection Capacity." In *Oxford Encyclopedia of Empirical International Relations Theory,* edited by William R. Thompson. New York: Oxford University Press.

Legro, J. W. 2005. *Rethinking the World: Great Power Strategies and International Order.* Ithaca, NY: Cornell University Press.

Levinson, M. 2016. *An Extraordinary Time: The End of the Postwar Boom and the Return of the Ordinary Economy.* New York: Basic Books.

Lieber, R. J. 2012. *Power and Willpower in the American Future: Why the United States Is Not Destined to Decline.* Cambridge: Cambridge University Press.

Levy, J. S. 1994. "Learning and Foreign Policy: Sweeping a Complex Minefield." *International Organization* 48,2: 279–312.

Levy, J. S., and Thompson, W. R. 2005. "Hegemonic Threats and Great Power Balancing in Europe, 1495–1999." *Security Studies* 14,1: 1–33.

Levy, J. S., and Thompson, W. R. 2010. "Balancing on Land and Sea: Do States Ally against the Leading Global Power." *International Security* 35,1: 7–43.

Levy, J. S., and Thompson, W. R. 2011. *The Arc of War: Origins, Escalation and Transformation.* Chicago: University of Chicago Press.

Licht, W. 1995. *Industrializing America: The Nineteenth Century.* Baltimore: Johns Hopkins University Press.

Lieber, R. J. 2012. *Power and Willpower in the American Future: Why the United States Is Not Destined to Decline.* Cambridge: Cambridge University Press.

Lind, J., and Press, D. G. 2020. "Reality Check: American Power in an Age of Constraints." *Foreign Affairs* 99,2: 41–48.

Luce, E. 2012. *Time to Start Thinking: America in the Age of Descent*. New York: Atlantic Monthly Press.

Lundestad, G. 2012. *The Rise and Decline of the American "Empire": Power and Its Limits in Comparative Perspective*. Oxford: Oxford University Press.

Macaes, B. 2019. *Belt and Road*. New York: Oxford University Press.

MacDonald, P. K., and Parent, J. M. 2011. "Graceful Decline? The Surprising Success of Great Power Retrenchment." *International Security* 35,4: 7–44.

MacDonald, P. K., and Parent, J. M. 2018. *Twilight of the Titans: Great Power Declines and Retrenchment*. Ithaca, NY: Cornell University Press.

Maddison, Angus. 2003. *The World Economy: Historical Statistics*. Paris: OECD Development Centre.

Maddox, R. J.1992. *The United States and World War II*. Boulder, CO: Westview.

Mahbubani, K. 2008. *The New Asian Hemisphere: The Irresistible Shift of Global Power to the East*. New York: Public Affairs.

Malici, A. 2008. *When Leaders Learn and When They Don't: Mikhail Gorbachev and Kim Il Sung at the End of the Cold War*. Albany: SUNY Press.

Malkasian, C. 2020. "How the Good War Went Bad: America's Slow-Motion Failure in Afghanistan." *Foreign Affairs* 99,2: 77–91.

Mandelbaum, M. 2010. *The Frugal Superpower: America's Global Leadership in a Cash-Strapped Era*. New York: Public Affairs.

Mansfield, Edward D. 1993. "Concentration, Polarity, and the Distribution of Power." *International Studies Quarterly* 37: 105–128.

Marichal, I. 2018. "The Opioid Crisis: A Consequence of US Economic Decline?" Washington, DC: Washington Center for Equitable Growth. https://equitablegrowth.org/the-opioid-crisis-a-consequence-of-u-s-economic-decline/.

Mason, L. 2018. *Uncivil Agreement: How Politics Become Our Identity*. Chicago: University of Chicago Press.

Massie, J., and Paquin, J., eds. 2019. *America's Allies and the Decline of US Hegemony*. London: Routledge..

Maxwell, A., and Shields, T. 2019. *The Long Southern Strategy: How Chasing White Voters in the South Changed American Politics*. New York: Oxford University Press.

Mayhew, David R. 2005. "War and American Politics." *Perspectives on Politics* 3: 473–493.

McCoy, A. W. 2017. *In the Shadows of the American Century: The Rise and Decline of US Global Power*. Chicago: Haymarket Books.

McDonald, F. 1968. *The Torch Is Passed: The United States in the 20th Century*. Reading, MA: Addison-Wesley.

Mearsheimer, J. J. 2019. "Bound to Fail: The Rise and Fall of the Liberal Trade Order." *International Security* 43,4: 7–50.

Meinig, D. W. 1993. *The Shaping of America: A Geographical Perspective on 500 Years of History, Vol. 2: Continental America, 1800–1867*. New Haven, CT: Yale University Press.

Migration Policy Institute. 2019. "U.S. Immigration Population and Share over Time, 1850–Present." https://www.migrationpolicy.org/programs/data-hub/charts/immigrant-population-over-time.

Milward, A. S. 1977. *Economy and Society, 1939-1945*. Berkeley: University of California Press.

Miscamble, W. D. 2009. "Roosevelt, Truman and the Development of Postwar Grand Strategy." *Orbis* 53,4: 553–570.

Mitchell, A. W., and Grygiel, J. 2011. "The Vulnerability of Peripheries." *The American Interest*. 6,4: 5–16.

Mitchell, B. R. 2003a. *International Historical Statistics, Europe: 1750–2000*. New York: Palgrave Macmillan.

Mitchell, B. R. 2003b. *International Historical Statistics, The Americas: 1750–-2000*. New York: Palgrave Macmillan.

Mitchell, B. R. 2003c. *International Historical Statistics, Africa, Asia & Oceania: 1750–2000*. New York: Palgrave Macmillan.

Modelski, G. 1974. *World Power Concentrations: Typology, Data, Explanatory Framework*. Morristown, NJ: General Learning Press.

Modelski, G. 1987. *Long Cycles in World Politics*. London: Macmillan.

Modelski, G., and Gardner, P., III. 1991. "Democratization in Long Perspective." *Technological Forecasting and Social Change* 39: 23–34.

Modelski, G., and Gardner, P., III. 2002. "'Democratization in Long Perspective' Revisited." *Technological Forecasting and Social Change* 69: 359–376.

Modelski, G., and Thompson, W. R. 1988. *Sea Power in Global Politics, 1494–1993*. London: Macmillan.

Modelski, G., and Thompson, W. R. 1996. *Leading Sectors and World Powers: The Coevolution of Global Economics and Politics*. Columbia: University of South Carolina Press.

Mokyr, J. 2009. *The Enlightened Economy: An Economic History of Britain, 1700–1850*. New Haven, CT: Yale University Press.

Monteiro, N. P. 2011/2012. "Unrest Assured: Why Unipolarity Is Not Peaceful." *International Security* 36,3: 9–40.

Monteiro, N. P. 2014. *Theory of Unipolar Politics*. Cambridge: Cambridge University Press.

Montgomery, E. B. 2016. *In the Hegemon's Shadow: Leading States and the Rise of Regional Powers*. Ithaca, NY: Cornell University Press.

Moretti, E. 2013. *The New Geography of Jobs*. Boston: Mariner Books.

Mousseau, M., Hegre, H., and Oneal, J. R. 2003. "How the Wealth of Nations Conditions the Liberal Peace." *European Journal of International Relations* 9,2: 277–314.

Mowle, T. S., and Sacko, D. H. 2007. *The Unipolar World: An Unbalanced Future*. New York: Palgrave.

Myers, Dowell, and Morris Levy. 2018. "Racial Population Projections and Reactions to Alternative News Accounts of Growing Diversity." *Annals of the American Academy of Political and Social Sciences* 677,1: 215–228.

Narizny, K. 2007. *The Political Economy of Grand Strategy*. Ithaca, NY: Cornell University Press.

National Academies of Sciences, Engineering and Medicine. 2017. *The Economic and Fiscal Consequences of Immigration*. Washington, DC: National Academies Press.

National Science Foundation. 2020a. *Science and Engineering Indicators: Production of Trade of Knowledge and Technology-Intensive Industries*. https://ncses.nsf.gov/pubs/nsb20205/production-patterns-and-trends-of-knowledge-and-technology-intensive-industries.

Nau, H. 1990. *The Myth of America's Decline: Leading the World Economy into the 1990s*. New York: Oxford University Press.

Nelson, R. R., and Wright, G. 1992. "The Rise and Fall of American Technological Leadership: The Postwar Era in Historical Perspective." *Journal of Economic Literature* 30,4: 1931–1964.

Norris, P., and Inglehart, R. 2019. *Cultural Backlash: Trump, Brexit, and Authoritarian Populism*. Cambridge: Cambridge University Press.

Norrlof, C. 2010. *America's Global Advantage: US Hegemony and International Cooperation*. Cambridge: Cambridge University Press.

Norrlof, C. 2018. "Hegemony and Inequality: Trump and the Liberal Playbook." *International Affairs* 94,1: 63–88.

Nye, J. 1990. *Bound to Lead: The Changing Nature of American Power*. New York: Basic Books.

Nye, J. 2011. *The Future of Power*. New York: Public Affairs.

Nye, J. S. 2015. *Is the American Century Over?* Cambridge: Polity.

Nye, J. S., Jr. 2019. "The Rise and Fall of American Hegemony from Wilson to Trump." *International Affairs* 95,1: 63–80.

O'Brien, P. P. 2015. *How the War Was Won: Air-Sea Power and Allied Victory in World War II*. Cambridge: Cambridge University Press.

Obstfeld, M., and Taylor, A. M. 2004. *Global Capital Markets: Integration, Crisis and Growth*. Cambridge: Cambridge University Press.

Organski, A. F. K. 1958. *World Politics*. New York: Alfred A. Knopf.

Organski, A. F. K., and Kugler, J. 1980. *The War Ledger*. Chicago: University of Chicago Press.

O'Rourke, R. 2020. "China Naval Modernization: Implications for US Navy Capabilities: Background and Issues for Congress." May 21. Congressional Research Service. Fas. org/sgp/crs/row/RL35153.pdf.

Overy, R. 1995. *Why the Allies Won*. New York: W. W. Norton.

Owen, J. M. 2003. "Why American Hegemony Is Here to Stay." *International Politics and Society* 1: 1–14.

Packer, G. 2013. *The Unwinding: Thirty Years of American Decline*. New York: Random House.

Page, B. I., and Shapiro, R. Y. 1992. *The Rational Public: Fifty Years of Trends in Americans' Policy Preferences*. Chicago: University of Chicago Press.

Parker, K., Morin, R., and Menasce Horowitz, J. 2019. "Looking to the Future, Public Sees an America in Decline on Many Fronts." Pew Research Center, March 21. https://www.pewresearch.org/social-trends/2019/03/21/public-sees-an-america-in-decline-on-many-fronts/.

Patrick, S. 2009. *The Best Laid Plans: The Origins of American Multilateralism and the Dawn of the Cold War*. Lanham, MD: Rowman and Littlefield.

Perlstein, R. 2012. "Lee Atwater's Infamous 1981 Interview on the Southern Strategy." *The Nation*, November 13. https://www.thenation.com/article/exclusive-lee-atwaters-infamous-1981-interview-southern-strategy.

Peters, J. W. 2019. "The Tea Party Didn't Get What It Wanted, but It Did Unleash the Politics of Anger." *New York Times*, August 28. https://www.nytimes.com/2019/08/28/us/politics/tea-party-trump.html.

Pew Research Center. 2019. "Public Trust in Government, 1958–2019," April 11. People-press.org/2019/04/11/public-trust-in-government-1958-2019/.

Pollack, S. 2011. *War Revenue and State-Building: Financing the Development of the American State*. Ithaca, NY: Cornell University Press.

Porter, B. D. 1994. *War and the Rise of the State: The Military Foundations of Modern Politics*. New York: Free Press.

Posen, B. 2003. "Command of the Commons: The Military Foundation of U.S. Hegemony." *International Security* 28: 5–46.

Posen, B. R. 2014. *Restraint: A New Foundation for US Grand Strategy*. Ithaca, NY: Cornell University Press.

Prestowitz, C. 2011. "New Wind Blowing: American Decline Becomes the Conventional Wisdom." *Foreign Policy*, June 15. https://foreignpolicy.com/2011/06/15/new-wind-blowing-american-decline-becomes-the-new-conventional-wisdom..

Radford, J. 2019. "Key Findings about US Immigrants." Pew Research Center, June 17. https://www.pewresearch.org/fact-tank/2019/06/17/key-findings-about-u-s-immigrants/.

Rakich, N. 2020. "How Urban and Rural Is Your State? And What Does That Mean for the 2020 Election." *FiveThirtyEight*, April 14. https://fivethirtyeight.com/features/how-urban-or-rural-is-your-state-and-what-does-that-mean-for-the-2020-election/.

Rapkin, D. P., Thompson, W. R., and Christopherson, J. A. 1979. "Bipolarity and Bipolarization in the Cold War Era: Conceptualization, Measurement and Validation." *Journal of Conflict Resolution* 23,2: 261–295.

Rapkin, D. P., and Thompson, W. R. 2013. *Transition Scenarios: China and the United States in the Twenty-First Century*. Chicago: University of Chicago Press.

Rasler, K., and Thompson, W. R. 1989. *War and State Making: The Shaping of the Global Powers*. Boston: Unwin Hyman.

Rasler, K., and Thompson, W. R. 1994. *Threat Powers and Global Struggle, 1490–1990*. Lexington: University Press of Kentucky.

Rasler, K., and Thompson, W. R. 2001. "Malign Autocracies and Major Power Warfare: Evil, Tragedy and International Relations Theory." *Security Studies* 10: 46–79.

Rasler, K., and Thompson, W. R. 2005a. *Puzzles of the Democratic Peace: Theory, Geopolitics and the Transformation of World Politics*. New York: Palgrave-Macmillan.

Rasler, K., and Thompson, W. R. 2005b. "War, Trade and the Mediation of Systemic Leadership." *Journal of Peace Research* 42,3: 251–69.

Reality Check Team. 2020. "Afghanistan War: What Has the Conflict Cost the US?" BBC News, February 28. https://www.bbc.com/news/world-47391821.

Reich, S. and Lebow, R. N. 2014. *Goodbye Hegemony! Power and Influence in the Global System*. Princeton, NJ: Princeton University Press.

Rennstich, J. 2008. *The Evolution of the Digital Global System*. New York: Palgrave-Macmillan.

Reuveny, R., and Thompson, W. R. 2004. *Growth, Trade and Systemic Leadership*. Ann Arbor: University of Michigan Press.

Reynolds, D. 1992. "Power and Superpower: The Impact of Two World Wars on America's Institutional Role." In *America Unbound: World War II and the Making of a Superpower*, edited by Warren F. Kimball. New York: St. Martin's Press.

Rockoff, H. 1998. "The United States: From Ploughshares to Swords." In *The Economic Impact of World War II: Six Great Powers in International Comparison*, edited by Mark Harrison. Cambridge: Cambridge University Press.

Rodden, J. 2019. *Why Cities Lose: The Deep Roots of the Urban-Rural Political Divide*. New York: Basic Books.

Rosecrance, R. 1986. *The Rise of the Trading State: Commerce and Conquest in the Modern World*. New York: Basic Books.

Saad, L. 2019. "US Still Leans Conservative, but Liberals Keep Recent Gains." Gallup, January 8. https://news.gallup.com/poll/245813/leans-conservative-liberals-keep-gains.aspx.

Sabrosky, A. N., ed. 1985. *Polarity and War: The Changing Structure of International Conflict*. Boulder, CO: Westview Press.

Saldin, R. P. 2010. *War, the American State, and Politics since 1898*. Cambridge: Cambridge University Press.

Saldin, R. P., and Teles, S. M. 2020. "The Never Trumpers' Next Move." *The Atlantic*, May.

Sargent, D. 2015. *A Superpower Transformed: The Remaking of American Foreign Relations in the 1970s*. New York: Oxford University Press.

Sassen, S. 2001. *The Global City: New York, London, Tokyo*. Princeton, NJ: Princeton University Press.

Scavette, A. 2019. "Exploring the Economic Effects of the Opioid Epidemic." https://www.philadelphiafed.org/the-economy/regional-economics/exploring-the-economic-effects-of-the-opioid-epidemic.

Schake, K. 2018. "Managing American Decline." *The Atlantic*, November 24. https://www.theatlantic.com/ideas/archive/2018/11/how-bad-americas-decline-relative-china/576319.

Schikler, E. 2016. *Racial Realignment: The Transformation of American Liberalism, 1932–1965*. Princeton, NJ: Princeton University Press.

Schlesinger, A. M., Jr. 1989. *The Imperial Presidency*. Boston: Houghton Mifflin.

Schlesinger, A. M., Jr. 2004. *War and the American Presidency*. New York: W. W. Norton.

Schmitz, C. J. 1995. *The Growth of Big Business in the United States and Western Europe, 1850–1939*. Cambridge: Cambridge University Press.

Schneider, S. A. 1983. *The Oil Price Revolution*. Baltimore: Johns Hopkins University Press.

Schur, S. H., and Netschert, B. C. 1960. *Energy in the American Economy, 1850–1975*. Baltimore: Johns Hopkins University Press.

Schweller, R. L. 1998. *Deadly Imbalances: Tripolarity and Hitler's Strategy of World Conquest*. New York: Columbia University Press.

Schweller, R. L. 2014. *Maxwell's Demon and the Golden Apple: Global Discord in the New Millennium*. Baltimore: Johns Hopkins University Press.

Scobell, A., Burke, E. J., Cooper, C. A., III, Lilly, S., Ohlandt, C. J. R., Warner, E., and Williams, J. D. 2020. *China's Grand Strategy: Trends, Trajectories and Long-Term Competition*. Santa Monica, CA: Rand.

Scott, J. 2019. *How the Old World Ended: The Anglo-Dutch-American Revolution, 1500–1800*. New Haven, CT: Yale University Press.

Shaffer, E. 1983. *The United States and the Control of World Oil*. New York: St. Martin's Press.

Shaffer, R. 1991. *America in the Great War: The Rise of the War Welfare State*. New York: Oxford University Press.

Sharma, R. 2020. "The Comeback Nation: U.S. Economic Supremacy Has Repeatedly Proved Declinists Wrong." *Foreign Affairs* 99: 70–81.

Shear, Michael D., Goodnough, A., Kaplan, S., Fink, S., Thomas, K., and Wedland, N. 2020. "The Lost Month: How a Failure to Test Blinded the U.S. to Covid-19." *New York Times*, March 28. https://www.nytimes.com/2020/03/28/us/testing-coronavirus-pandemic.html.

Shefter, M. 2002. "International Influences on American Political Development." In *Shaped by War and Trade: International Influences on American Political Development*, edited by Ira Katznelson and Martin Shefter. Princeton, NJ: Princeton University Press.

Sherry, M. 1997. *In the Shadow of War: The United States since the 1930s*. New Haven, CT: Yale University Press.

Sides, John, Tesler, M., and Varveck, L. 2018. *Identity Crisis: The 2016 Presidential Campaign and the Battle for the Meaning of America*. Princeton, NJ: Princeton University Press.

Singer, J. D., Bremer, S., and Stuckey, J. 1972. "Capability Distribution, Uncertainty, and Major Power War, 1820–1965." In *Peace, War, and Numbers*, edited by B. Russett. Beverly Hills, CA: Sage.

Siverson, R. M., and Sullivan, M. P. 1983. "The Distribution of Power and the Onset of War." *Journal of Conflict Resolution* 27: 473–494.

Smil, V. 2005. *Creating the Twentieth Century: Technological Innovation of 1867–1914 and Their Lasting Impact*. Oxford: Oxford University Press.

Smil, V. 2013. *Made in the USA: The Rise and Retreat of American Manufacturing*. Cambridge, MA: MIT Press.

Snidal, D. 1985. "The Limits of Hegemonic Stability Theory." *International Organization* 39,4: 579–614.

Spiezio, K. E. 1990. "British Hegemony and Major Power War, 1815–1935: An Empirical Test of Gilpin's Model of Hegemonic Governance." *International Studies Quarterly* 34: 165–181.

Sprague, S. 2017. "Below Trend: The U.S. Productivity Slowdown since the Great Recession." U.S. Bureau of Labor Statistics. https://www.bls.gov/opub/btn/volume-6/pdf/below-trend-the-us-productivity-slowdown-since-the-great-recession.pdf.

Starrs, S. 2013. "American Economic Power Hasn't Declined—It Globalized! Summoning the Data and Taking Globalization Seriously." *International Studies Quarterly* 57,4: 817–830.

Startup Genome. 2019. Global Startup Ecosystem Report 2019. https://startupgenome.com/reports/global-startup-ecosystem-report-2019.

Stein, A. A. 1978. *The Nation at War*. Baltimore: Johns Hopkins University Press.

Stone, C., Trisi, D., Sherman, A., and Beltran, J. 2020. "A Guide to Statistics on Historical Trends in Income Inequality." Center on Budget and Policy Priorities, January 13. https://www.cbpp.org/research/poverty-and-inequality/a-guide-to-statistics-on-historical-trends-in-income-inequality.

Suri, J. 2020. "What 'American Century'?" *Foreign Policy*, July 17. https://foreignpolicy.com/2020/07/17/no-american-century-demise/.

Tainter, J. 1988. *Collapse of Complex Societies*. Cambridge: Cambridge University Press.

Tammen, R. L., Kugler, J., Lemke, D., Stam, A., III, Alsharabati, C., Abdollahian, M. A., Efird, B., and Organski, A. F. K., eds. 2000. *Power Transitions: Strategies for the 21st Century*. New York: Chatham House Publishers.

Tavernise, S. 2018. "Why the Announcement of a Looming White Minority Makes Demographers Nervous." *New York Times*, November 22. https://www.nytimes.com/2018/11/22/us/white-americans-minority-population.html.

Taylor, M. Z. 2016. *The Politics of Innovation: Why Some Countries Are Better than Others at Science and Technology*. New York: Oxford University Press.

Taylor, P. J., Hoyler, M., and Smith, D. 2012. "Cities in the Making of World Hegemonies." In *International Handbook of Globalization and World Cities*, edited by Ben Derudder, Michael Hoyler, Peter J. Taylor, and Frank Witlox. Cheltenham, UK: Edward Elgar.

Tetlock, P. E. 1991. "Learning in U.S. and Soviet Foreign Policy: Search of an Elusive Concept." In *Learning in U.S. and Soviet Foreign Policy*, edited by George W. Breslauer and Philip E. Tetlock. Boulder, CO: Westview Press.

Thompson, J. A. 2015. *A Sense of Power: The Roots of America's Global Role*. Ithaca, NY: Cornell University Press.

Thompson, W. R. 1986. "Polarity, the Long Cycle and Global Power Warfare." *Journal of Conflict Resolution* 30: 587–615.

Thompson, W. R. 1988. *On Global War: Historical-Structural Approaches to World Politics.* Columbia: University of South Carolina Press.

Thompson, W. R. 1992. "Dehio, Long Cycles, and the Geohistorical Context of Structural Transitions." *World Politics* 45: 127–152.

Thompson, W. R. 1997. "The Evolution of Political-Commercial Challenges in the Active Zone." *Review of International Political Economy* 4,2: 285–317.

Thompson, W. R., ed. 1999. *Great Power Rivalries.* Columbia: University of South Carolina Press.

Thompson, W. R. 2000. *The Emergence of the Global Political Economy.* London: University College London Press/Routledge.

Thompson, W. R. 2001. "Evolving toward an Evolutionary Perspective on World Politics and International Political Economy." In *Evolutionary Interpretations of World Politics,* edited by William R. Thompson. New York: Routledge.

Thompson, W. R. 2003. "A Streetcar Named Sarajevo: Catalysts, Multiple Causation Chains and Rivalry Structures." *International Studies Quarterly* 47: 453–474.

Thompson, W. R. 2006. "A Test of a Theory of Co-evolution in War: Lengthening the Western Eurasian Military Trajectory." *International History Review* 28: 473–503.

Thompson, W. R., ed. 2008. *Systemic Transitions: Past, Present and Future.* New York: Palgrave-Macmillan.

Thompson, W. R., and Dreyer, D. R. 2011. *Handbook of International Rivalries, 1494–2010.* Washington, DC: Congressional Quarterly Press.

Thompson, W. R., and Reuveny, R. 2010. *Limits to Globalization and North-South Divergence.* London: Routledge.

Thompson, W. R., Volgy, T. J., Bezerra, P., Cramer, J., Gordell, K. M., Pardesi, M., Rasler, K., Rhaemy, J. P. Jr., Sakuwa, K., Van Nostrand, R. D., and Zakhirova, L. 2022. *Regions, Power, and Conflict: Constrained Capabilities, Hierarchy, and Rivalry.* Singapore: Springer.

Thompson, W. R., and Zakhirova, L. 2018. "Revising Leadership Long Cycle Theory." In *Oxford Encyclopedia of Empirical International Relations Theory,* edited by William R. Thompson. New York: Oxford University Press.

Thompson, W. R., and Zakhirova, L. 2019. *Racing to the Top: How Energy Fuels Systemic Leadership in World Politics.* New York: Oxford University Press.

Thompson, W. R., and Zuk, G. 1986. "World Power and the Strategic Trap of Territorial Commitments." *International Studies Quarterly* 33: 249–267.

Tocqueville, A. de. 1969. *Democracy in America.* Edited by J. P. Mayer. Garden City, NY: Anchor.

Torreon, B. S., and Plagakis, S. 2020. "Instance of Uses of United States Armed Forces Abroad, 1798–2020." Congressional Research Service, R42738. https://crsreports.congress.gov.

Trubowitz, P. 1998. *Defining the National Interest: Conflict and Change in American Foreign Policy.* Chicago: University of Chicago Press.

Tunsjø, Ø. 2018. *The Return of Bipolarity in World Politics: China, the United States, and Geostructural Realism.* New York: Columbia University Press.

U.S. Census Bureau. 2020. "Foreign Trade, Top Trading Partners." https://www.Census.gov/foreign-trade/Statistics/highlights/top/top/912yr.html.

U.S. Department of Commerce. 1975. *Historical Statistics of the United States: Colonial Times to 1970.* Washington, DC: U.S. Department of Commerce.

US National Intelligence Council. 2012. *Global Trends 2030: Alternative Worlds*. www.dni. gov/nic/globaltrends.

Vedder, R. K. 1976. *The American Economy in Historical Perspective*. Belmont, MA: Wadsworth.

Ventatarmani, A. S., Bair, E. F., O'Brien, R. J., and Tsai, A. C. 2020. "Association between Automatic Assembly Plant Closures and Opioid Overdose Mortality in the United States: A Difference-in Differences Analysis." *JAMA Internal Medicine* 180,2: 254–262.

Wallach, P., and Wallner, J. 2018. "Congress Is Broken, but Don't Blame Polarization." *R Street*, June 15. https://www.rstreet.org/2018/06/15/congress-is-broken-but-dont-blame-polarization/.

Wallerstein, I. 2011. *The Decline of American Power: The US in a Chaotic World*. New York: New Press.

Walt, S. M. 2011. "The End of the American Era." *The National Interest*, October 25. https://nationalinterest.org/article/the-end-the-american-era-6037.

Walt, S. M. 2018. *The Hell of Good Intentions: America's Foreign Policy Elite and the Decline of US Primacy*. New York: Farrar, Straus & Giroux.

Waltz, K. 1964. "The Stability of a Bipolar World." *Daedalus* 43: 881–909.

Waltz, K. 1979. *Theory of International Politics*. Reading, MA: Addison-Wesley.

Ward, S. 2017. *Status and the Challenge of Rising Powers*. Cambridge: Cambridge University Press.

Wasserman, D. 2020. "To Beat Trump, Democrats May Need to Break Out of the 'Whole Foods' Bubble." *New York Times*, February 27. https://www.nytimes.com/interactive/2020/02/27/upshot/democrats-may-need-to-break-out-of-the-whole-foods-bubble.html.

Watt, D. C. 1992. "US Globalism: The End of the Concert of Europe." In *America Unbound: World War II and the Making of a Superpower*, edited by Warren F. Kimball. New York: St. Martin's Press.

Wayman, F. W. 1984. "Bipolarity and War: The Role of Capability Concentration and Alliance Patterns among Major Powers, 1816–1965." *Journal of Peace Research* 21: 25–42.

Weigley, R. F. 1992. "The Legacy of World War II for American Conventional Military Strategy: Should We Escape It?" In *America Unbound: World War II and the Making of a Superpower*, edited by Warren F. Kimball. New York: St. Martin's Press.

Wells, S. F., Jr., Ferrell, R. H., and Trask, D. F. 1975. *The Ordeal of World Power: American Diplomacy since 1900*. Boston: Little, Brown.

Wilkins, M. 1970. *The Emergence of Multinational Enterprise: American Business Abroad from the Colonial Era to 1914*. Cambridge, MA: Harvard University Press.

Wilkins, M. 1974. *The Maturing of Multinational Enterprise: American Business Abroad from 1914 to 1972*. Cambridge, MA: Harvard University Press.

Williams, D. K. 2010. *God's Own Party: The Making of the Christian Right*. New York: Oxford University Press.

Willis, D., and Kane, P. 2018. "How Congress Stopped Working." *Propublica*, November. https://www.propublica.org/article/how-congress-stopped-working.

Woetzel, J., Seong, J., Leung, N., Ngai, J., Manyika, J., Madjavker, A., Lund, S., and Mironenka, A. 2019. *China and the World: Inside the Dynamics of a Changing Relationship*. Shanghai: McKinsey Global Institute, July. https://www.mckinsey.com/featured-insights/china/china-and-the-world-inside-the-dynamics-of-a-changing-relationship.

Wohlforth, W. 2012. "How Not to Evaluate Theories." *International Studies Quarterly* 56: 219–227.

Womack, J. P., Jones, D. T., and Roos, D. 1990. *The Machine That Changed the World.* New York: Macmillan.

Wright, G. 1990. "The Origins of American Industrial Success, 1879–1940." *American Economic Review* 80: 651–688.

Wright, G. 1997. "Towards a More Historical Approach to Technological Change." *Economic Journal* 107,444: 1560–1566.

Wright, T. 2020. "The Folly of Retrenchment: Why America Can't Withdraw from the World." *Foreign Affairs* 99,2: 10–18.

Wyne, A. 2018. "Is America Choosing Decline?" *New Republic*, June 21. https://newrepublic.com/article/149008/America-choosing-decline.

Yglesias, M. 2007. "It's the Structure, Stupid." *The Atlantic*, August 20. https://www.theatlantic.com/politics/archive/2007/08/its-the-structure-stupid/45893/.

Ying, Fu. 2016. "The U.S. World Order Is a Suit That No Longer Fits." *Financial Times*, January 6. https://www.ft.com/content/c09cbcb6-b3cb-11e5-b147-e5e5bba42e51.

Zakaria, F. 1999. *From Wealth to Power: The Unusual Origins of America's World Role.* Princeton, NJ: Princeton University Press.

Zakaria, F. 2008. *The Post-American World.* New York: W. W. Norton.

Zakaria, F. 2011. *The Post-American World: Release 2.0.* New York: W. W. Norton.

Ziblatt, D. 2017. *Conservative Parties and the Birth of Democracy.* Cambridge: Cambridge University Press.

Zieger, R. H. 2001. *America's Great War: World War I and the American Experience.* Lanham, MD: Rowman and Littlefield.

Index